BREAD FOR THE DAY

DAILY BIBLE READINGS AND PRAYERS

2019

AUGSBURG FORTRESS

Minneapolis

BREAD FOR THE DAY 2019
Daily Bible Readings and Prayers

Editors: Dennis Bushkofsky, Suzanne Burke
Cover design: Laurie Ingram
Interior design: Becky Lowe-Weyand
Cover art: Christina Saj
Interior art: Gertrud Mueller Nelson

Contributors to the weekday prayers: Amy White, Grand Rapids, Michigan (January); Elle Dowd, Chicago, Illinois (February); Rebecca Eve Schweitzer, Sterling Heights, Michigan (March); Matthew Fleming, Eden Prairie, Minnesota (April); James Rowe, Denton, Texas (May); Rebecca Ajer Frantz, Hanover, Pennsylvania (June); Jennifer Chrien, Simi Valley, California (July); Meghan Johnston Aelabouni, Fort Collins, Colorado (August); Sarah Carson, Flushing, Michigan (September); Jennifer M. Manis, Raleigh, North Carolina (October); Melissa Bills, Decorah, Iowa (November); Will Storm, Houston, Texas (December)

ACKNOWLEDGMENTS
Scripture quotations are from the New Revised Standard Version Bible © 1989 Division of Christian Education of the National Council of the Churches of Christ in the United States of America. Used by permission.

Hymn suggestions and prayers of the day for Sundays and festivals are from *Evangelical Lutheran Worship,* copyright © 2006 Evangelical Lutheran Church in America.

Materials prepared by the Consultation on Common Texts (CCT), published in *Revised Common Lectionary* © 1992 and *Revised Common Lectionary Daily Readings* © 2005. Used by permission.

"Table prayer for the season of Lent," "Table prayer for Summer," "A prayer to begin the work day," "A prayer to begin the school day," "Morning blessing," and "Evening blessing" are from *Reformation 500 Sourcebook: Anniversary Resources for Congregations,* © 2016 Augsburg Fortress.

Materials prepared by the English Language Liturgical Consultation (ELLC), published in *Praying Together* © 1988: "Blessed are you, Lord" and "My soul proclaims the greatness of the Lord." Used by permission.

ISBN 978-1-4514-9619-2
Manufactured in the U.S.A.

Contents

Foreword

Beloved of God,

For generations, the living word has sustained God's people. In times of prosperity and turmoil, joy and sorrow, the church has found hope and consolation in scripture.

The Evangelical Lutheran Church in America has embraced the initiative called Book of Faith. In it we have committed ourselves to deepening our fluency in the first language of faith, holy scripture. Bread for the Day is a wonderful resource for your daily encounter with the word. You will be nourished, encouraged, and sustained, as have the saints before you.

As the Conference of Bishops, we invite you to join us and this whole church in persistent attentiveness to the word. Your faith will be deepened, your witness empowered, and your church enriched. God bless your journey in faith.

Conference of Bishops
Evangelical Lutheran Church in America

For more about Book of Faith, visit www.bookoffaith.org.

Introduction

Daily prayer is an essential practice for those who seek to hear God's voice and cultivate an inner life. Whether you pray alone or with others, with brevity or sustained meditation, the rhythm of daily prayer reveals the life-sustaining communion to which God invites all human beings. Such prayer is a serene power silently at work, drawing us into the ancient yet vital sources of faith, hope, and love.

The guiding principle of the selection of daily readings in *Bread for the Day* is their relationship to the Sunday readings as presented in the Revised Common Lectionary (a system of readings in widespread use across denominations). The readings are chosen so that the days leading up to Sunday (Thursday through Saturday) prepare for the Sunday readings. The days flowing out from Sunday (Monday through Wednesday) reflect on the Sunday readings.

How this book is organized

- Each day's page is dated and named in relationship to the church's year. Lesser festivals are listed along with the date as part of the day heading. Commemorations are listed just below in smaller type. Notes on those commemorated can be found on pages 407–415.

- Several verses of one of the appointed scripture texts are printed. The full text citation is provided for those who would like to reflect on the entire text. In addition, two or three additional reading citations with short descriptions are provided.

- Two psalms are appointed for each week; one psalm for Monday through Wednesday and a second psalm for Thursday through Saturday. In this way the days leading up to Sunday or flowing out from Sunday have a distinct relationship with one another in addition to their relationship with the Sunday readings.

- Following the printed scripture text is a hymn suggestion from *Evangelical Lutheran Worship* and a prayer that incorporates a theme present in one or more of the readings.
- Household prayers and blessings appropriate to the changing seasons are placed throughout the book. Simplified forms of morning and evening prayer, morning and evening blessings, and prayers with children can be found on pages 424–430.

How to use this book

- Use the weekday readings to prepare for and reflect on the Sunday readings.
- Use the questions printed on page 431 to guide your reflection on the scripture texts.
- Use the resources for household prayer placed throughout the book. See the Contents on pages 3–4 for a complete list.
- Use the page at the beginning of each month to record prayer requests.
- In addition to being used to guide individual prayer, this book may also be used to guide family prayer, prayer in congregational or other settings during the week, prayer with those who are sick or homebound, or with other groups.

Even though Christians gather on the Lord's day, Sunday, for public worship, much of our time is spent in the home. We first learn the words, gestures, and songs of faith in the home. We discover our essential identity as a community of faith and mark significant transitions of life in the home. To surround and infuse the daily rhythm of sleeping and waking, working, resting, and eating with the words and gestures of Christian prayer is to discover the ancient truth of the gospel: the ordinary and the human can reveal the mystery of God and divine grace. Like planets around the sun, our daily prayer draws us to the Sunday assembly where we gather for the word and the breaking of the bread in the changing seasons of the year. From the Sunday assembly, our daily prayer flows into the week.

Prayer List for January

- Pray that Leah gets better
- Pray to help me with studying and doing my midterms
- Pray to remember my family members that have passed
- Pray to help those less fortunate

Tuesday, January 1, 2019
Name of Jesus

Luke 2:15-21
The child is named Jesus

When the angels had left them and gone into heaven, the shepherds said to one another, "Let us go now to Bethlehem and see this thing that has taken place, which the Lord has made known to us." So they went with haste and found Mary and Joseph, and the child lying in the manger. When they saw this, they made known what had been told them about this child; and all who heard it were amazed at what the shepherds told them. But Mary treasured all these words and pondered them in her heart. The shepherds returned, glorifying and praising God for all they had heard and seen, as it had been told them.

After eight days had passed, it was time to circumcise the child; and he was called Jesus, the name given by the angel before he was conceived in the womb. (Luke 2:15-21)

Psalm

Psalm 8
How exalted is your name

Additional Readings

Numbers 6:22-27
The Aaronic blessing

Galatians 4:4-7
We are no longer slaves

Hymn: All Hail the Power of Jesus' Name! ELW 634

Eternal Father, you gave your incarnate Son the holy name of Jesus to be a sign of our salvation. Plant in every heart the love of the Savior of the world, Jesus Christ our Lord, who lives and reigns with you and the Holy Spirit, one God, now and forever.

Wednesday, January 2, 2019
Week of Christmas 1

Johann Konrad Wilhelm Loehe, renewer of the church, died 1872

Proverbs 1:1-7
Grow in wisdom and knowledge

Let the wise also hear and gain in learning,
    and the discerning acquire skill,
to understand a proverb and a figure,
    the words of the wise and their riddles.

The fear of the LORD is the beginning of knowledge;
    fools despise wisdom and instruction. (Prov. 1:5-7)

Psalm
Psalm 147:12-20
Praising God in Zion

Additional Reading
James 3:13-18
The wisdom from above

Hymn: We Eat the Bread of Teaching, ELW 518

O Ancient of Days, all wisdom begins and ends in you. Grant us discerning hearts and minds that yearn to follow you and your ways both now and forever.

Thursday, January 3, 2019
Week of Christmas 1

Psalm 72
Prayers for the king

Give the king your justice, O God,
    and your righteousness to a king's son.
May he judge your people with righteousness,
    and your poor with justice.
May the kings of Tarshish and of the isles
    render him tribute,
may the kings of Sheba and Seba
    bring gifts.
May all kings fall down before him,
    all nations give him service. (Ps. 72:1-2, 10-11)

Additional Readings

Job 42:10-17
Job's family

Luke 8:16-21
Jesus' family

Hymn: Angels, from the Realms of Glory, ELW 275

We come before you, King of kings, grateful for your justice and mercy. We wait in eager anticipation and ask that you bring us to the day when all nations will gather around your throne and sing your praise.

Friday, January 4, 2019
Week of Christmas 1

Isaiah 6:1-5
The Lord high and lofty

In the year that King Uzziah died, I saw the Lord sitting on a throne, high and lofty; and the hem of his robe filled the temple. Seraphs were in attendance above him; each had six wings: with two they covered their faces, and with two they covered their feet, and with two they flew. And one called to another and said:

"Holy, holy, holy is the LORD of hosts;
the whole earth is full of his glory."

The pivots on the thresholds shook at the voices of those who called, and the house filled with smoke. And I said: "Woe is me! I am lost, for I am a man of unclean lips, and I live among a people of unclean lips; yet my eyes have seen the King, the LORD of hosts!" (Isa. 6:1-5)

Psalm
Psalm 72
Prayers for the king

Additional Reading
Acts 7:44-53
Solomon's temple cannot contain God

Hymn: The Bells of Christmas, ELW 298

Holy God, we admit we are unworthy of your abiding presence. Heaven and earth cannot contain your glory, and yet you chose to dwell among us. We are humbled by your majesty and ask for eyes with which to see all your gifts.

Saturday, January 5, 2019
Week of Christmas 1

Jeremiah 31:7-14
Joy as God's scattered flock gathers

Hear the word of the LORD, O nations,
    and declare it in the coastlands far away;
say, "He who scattered Israel will gather him,
    and will keep him as a shepherd a flock."
For the LORD has ransomed Jacob,
    and has redeemed him from hands too strong for him.
They shall come and sing aloud on the height of Zion,
    and they shall be radiant over the goodness of the LORD,
over the grain, the wine, and the oil,
    and over the young of the flock and the herd;
their life shall become like a watered garden,
    and they shall never languish again. (Jer. 31:10-12)

Psalm
Psalm 72
Prayers for the king

Additional Reading
John 1:[1-9] 10-18
God with us

Hymn: The First Noel, ELW 300

We are lost without you, God our shepherd. You lead us to joy and hope. Keep us close and overwhelm our desire to wander, that we may be nourished and sustained by you alone.

Blessing for a Home at Epiphany

Matthew writes that when the magi saw the shining star stop overhead, they were filled with joy. "On entering the house, they saw the child with Mary his mother" (Matt. 2:10-11). In the home, Christ is met in family and friends, in visitors and strangers. In the home, faith is shared, nurtured, and put into action. In the home, Christ is welcome.

Twelfth Night (January 5), Epiphany of Our Lord (January 6), or another day during the time after Epiphany offers an occasion for gathering with friends and family members for a blessing for the home. Someone may lead the greeting and blessing, while another person may read the scripture passage. Following an eastern European tradition, a visual blessing may be inscribed with white chalk above the main door; for example, 20 + CMB + 19. The numbers change with each new year. The three letters stand for either the ancient Latin blessing Christe mansionem benedicat, which means, "Christ, bless this house," or the legendary names of the magi (Caspar, Melchior, and Balthasar).

Greeting

Peace to this house and to all who enter here.
By wisdom a house is built,
and through understanding it is established;
through knowledge its rooms are filled
with rare and beautiful treasures. *(Prov. 24:3-4)*

Reading

As we prepare to ask God's blessing on this household,
let us listen to the words of scripture.
In the beginning was the Word,
and the Word was with God, and the Word was God.
He was in the beginning with God.
All things came into being through him,
and without him not one thing came into being.

What has come into being in him was life,

and the life was the light of all people.

The Word became flesh and lived among us, and we have seen his glory,

the glory as of a father's only son, full of grace and truth.

From his fullness we have all received, grace upon grace.

(John 1:1-4, 14, 16)

Inscription

This inscription may be made with chalk above the entrance:

20 + C M B + 19

Write the appropriate character (left) while speaking the text (right).

The magi of old, known as

C   Caspar,

M   Melchior, and

B   Balthasar

followed the star of God's Son who came to dwell among us

20   two thousand

19   and nineteen years ago.

+   Christ, bless this house,

+   and remain with us throughout the new year.

Prayer of Blessing

O God,

you revealed your Son to all people by the shining light of a star.

We pray that you bless this home and all who live here

with your gracious presence.

May your love be our inspiration, your wisdom our guide,

your truth our light, and your peace our benediction;

through Christ our Lord. Amen.

Then everyone may walk from room to room, blessing the house with incense or by sprinkling with water, perhaps using a branch from the Christmas tree.

Sunday, January 6, 2019
Epiphany of Our Lord

Matthew 2:1-12

Christ revealed to the nations

In the time of King Herod, after Jesus was born in Bethlehem of Judea, wise men from the East came to Jerusalem, asking, "Where is the child who has been born king of the Jews? For we observed his star at its rising, and have come to pay him homage." When King Herod heard this, he was frightened, and all Jerusalem with him; and calling together all the chief priests and scribes of the people, he inquired of them where the Messiah was to be born. They told him, "In Bethlehem of Judea; for so it has been written by the prophet." (Matt. 2:1-5)

Psalm
Psalm 72:1-7, 10-14
All shall bow down

Additional Readings
Isaiah 60:1-6
Nations come to the light

Ephesians 3:1-12
The gospel's promise for all

Hymn: O Morning Star, How Fair and Bright! ELW 308

Almighty and ever-living God, you revealed the incarnation of your Son by the brilliant shining of a star. Shine the light of your justice always in our hearts and over all lands, and accept our lives as the treasure we offer in your praise and for your service, through Jesus Christ, our Savior and Lord, who lives and reigns with you and the Holy Spirit, one God, now and forever.

Time after Epiphany

On the Epiphany of Our Lord (January 6), the household joins the church throughout the world in celebrating the manifestation, the "epiphany," of Christ to the world. The festival of Christmas is thus set within the context of outreach to the larger community; it possesses an outward movement. The festival of the Epiphany asks the Christian household: How might our faith in Christ the Light be shared with friends and family, with our neighbors, with the poor and needy in our land, with those who live in other nations?

Table Prayer for Epiphany and the Time after Epiphany (January 6–March 5)

Generous God,
you have made yourself known in Jesus, the light of the world.
As this food and drink give us refreshment,
so strengthen us by your Spirit,
that as your baptized sons and daughters
we may share your light with all the world.
Grant this through Christ our Lord.
Amen.

Monday, January 7, 2019
Time after Epiphany

Ephesians 4:17—5:1

Life lived in Christ

Now this I affirm and insist on in the Lord: you must no longer live as the Gentiles live, in the futility of their minds. They are darkened in their understanding, alienated from the life of God because of their ignorance and hardness of heart. They have lost all sensitivity and have abandoned themselves to licentiousness, greedy to practice every kind of impurity. That is not the way you learned Christ! For surely you have heard about him and were taught in him, as truth is in Jesus. You were taught to put away your former way of life, your old self, corrupt and deluded by its lusts, and to be renewed in the spirit of your minds, and to clothe yourselves with the new self, created according to the likeness of God in true righteousness and holiness. (Eph. 4:17-24)

Psalm

Psalm 72
Prayers for the king

Additional Reading

Daniel 2:1-19
The king searches for wisdom

Hymn: Bright and Glorious Is the Sky, ELW 301

God almighty, you have justified us in your Son, Jesus Christ. Now you continue the work, sanctifying our hearts and minds so we will look more and more like him. May we always receive your unwavering grace and hide our lives in you.

Tuesday, January 8, 2019
Time after Epiphany

Ephesians 5:15-20
Wise living in evil days

Be careful then how you live, not as unwise people but as wise, making
the most of the time, because the days are evil. So do not be foolish, but
understand what the will of the Lord is. Do not get drunk with wine,
for that is debauchery; but be filled with the Spirit, as you sing psalms
and hymns and spiritual songs among yourselves, singing and making
melody to the Lord in your hearts, giving thanks to God the Father
at all times and for everything in the name of our Lord Jesus Christ.
(Eph. 5:15-20)

Psalm
Psalm 72
Prayers for the king

Additional Reading
Daniel 2:24-49
Daniel reveals the dream's meaning

Hymn: How Marvelous God's Greatness, ELW 830

*Sovereign God, you call us to be holy like you are holy. We praise you for
your guidance and your wisdom. We ask that you help us to walk humbly
and live lives worthy of the calling we've received.*

Wednesday, January 9, 2019
Time after Epiphany

Luke 1:67-79

The Savior is seen

Then [John's] father Zechariah was filled with the Holy Spirit and spoke this prophecy:
"And you, child, will be called the prophet of the Most High;
for you will go before the Lord to prepare his ways,
to give knowledge of salvation to his people
by the forgiveness of their sins.
By the tender mercy of our God,
the dawn from on high will break upon us,
to give light to those who sit in darkness and in the shadow of death,
to guide our feet into the way of peace." (Luke 1:67, 76-79)

Psalm

Psalm 72
Prayers for the king

Additional Reading

Numbers 24:15-19
A star coming out of Jacob

Hymn: Blessed Be the God of Israel, ELW 552

Long ago, O God, prophets declared hope and light for the downcast, and filled with your mercy they prepared your people for the gift of your coming Son. In the same way, may you prepare our hearts for the reality of his righteousness as well.

Thursday, January 10, 2019
Time after Epiphany

Psalm 29
The voice of God upon the waters

Ascribe to the LORD, O heavenly beings,
　　ascribe to the LORD glory and strength.
Ascribe to the LORD the glory of his name;
　　worship the LORD in holy splendor.

The voice of the LORD is over the waters;
　　the God of glory thunders,
　　the LORD, over mighty waters.
The voice of the LORD is powerful;
　　the voice of the LORD is full of majesty. (Ps. 29:1-4)

Additional Readings
Ecclesiastes 1:1-11
There is nothing new under the sun

1 Corinthians 1:18-31
The power and wisdom of God

Hymn: My God, How Wonderful Thou Art, ELW 863

Living God, you are the creator of heaven and earth. We eagerly listen for your voice. We seek to hear your majesty echo throughout the world you made. As we grow in our understanding of your love, open our hearts to the mystery of your ways.

Friday, January 11, 2019
Time after Epiphany

1 Corinthians 2:1-10
The Spirit reveals the depths of God

But we speak God's wisdom, secret and hidden, which God decreed before the ages for our glory. None of the rulers of this age understood this; for if they had, they would not have crucified the Lord of glory. But, as it is written,

> "What no eye has seen, nor ear heard,
>> nor the human heart conceived,
> what God has prepared for those who love him"—

these things God has revealed to us through the Spirit; for the Spirit searches everything, even the depths of God. (1 Cor. 2:7-10)

Psalm
Psalm 29
The voice of God upon the waters

Additional Reading
Ecclesiastes 2:1-11
Toil for pleasure is ultimately vanity

Hymn: Holy Spirit, Ever Dwelling, ELW 582

Your wisdom is hidden on high, and you ordained your plan to reveal it before the world began. May your Spirit of wisdom never leave us; may it guide us always closer and closer to you, our everlasting God.

Saturday, January 12, 2019
Time after Epiphany

Ecclesiastes 3:1-15
All that is, is God's doing

What gain have the workers from their toil? I have seen the business that God has given to everyone to be busy with. He has made everything suitable for its time; moreover he has put a sense of past and future into their minds, yet they cannot find out what God has done from the beginning to the end. I know that there is nothing better for them than to be happy and enjoy themselves as long as they live; moreover, it is God's gift that all should eat and drink and take pleasure in all their toil. I know that whatever God does endures forever; nothing can be added to it, nor anything taken from it; God has done this, so that all should stand in awe before him. That which is, already has been; that which is to be, already is; and God seeks out what has gone by. (Eccles. 3:9-15)

Psalm
Psalm 29
The voice of God upon the waters

Additional Reading
1 Corinthians 2:11-16
God's wisdom taught by the Spirit

Hymn: How Small Our Span of Life, ELW 636

You are the Alpha and the Omega, the beginning and the end. No matter the number of days you set before us, we long to use them wisely, aware of your presence and living in gratitude for all you have given us.

Sunday, January 13, 2019
Baptism of Our Lord

Luke 3:15-17, 21-22
The baptism of Jesus

As the people were filled with expectation, and all were questioning in their hearts concerning John, whether he might be the Messiah, John answered all of them by saying, "I baptize you with water; but one who is more powerful than I is coming; I am not worthy to untie the thong of his sandals. He will baptize you with the Holy Spirit and fire. His winnowing fork is in his hand, to clear his threshing floor and to gather the wheat into his granary; but the chaff he will burn with unquenchable fire."

Now when all the people were baptized, and when Jesus also had been baptized and was praying, the heaven was opened, and the Holy Spirit descended upon him in bodily form like a dove. And a voice came from heaven, "You are my Son, the Beloved; with you I am well pleased." (Luke 3:15-17, 21-22)

Psalm

Psalm 29
The voice of God upon the waters

Additional Readings

Isaiah 43:1-7
Passing through the waters

Acts 8:14-17
Prayer for the Holy Spirit

Hymn: Christ, When for Us You Were Baptized, ELW 304

Almighty God, you anointed Jesus at his baptism with the Holy Spirit and revealed him as your beloved Son. Keep all who are born of water and the Spirit faithful in your service, that we may rejoice to be called children of God, through Jesus Christ, our Savior and Lord, who lives and reigns with you and the Holy Spirit, one God, now and forever.

Monday, January 14, 2019
Time after Epiphany

Psalm 106:1-12
God saves through water

Praise the LORD!
>O give thanks to the LORD, for he is good;
>>for his steadfast love endures forever.

Who can utter the mighty doings of the LORD,
>>or declare all his praise?

Happy are those who observe justice,
>>who do righteousness at all times. (Ps. 106:1-3)

Additional Readings
Judges 4:1-16   **Ephesians 6:10-17**
Israel's enemies drown   *The Christian's spiritual armor*

Hymn: Praise and Thanks and Adoration, ELW 783

We praise you, God, for your mighty works. We thank you for anointing us with your Holy Spirit and equipping us to stand firm in the faith we have received. May our praise swell to the highest heights that the whole world would know your name.

Tuesday, January 15, 2019
Time after Epiphany

Martin Luther King Jr., renewer of society, martyr, died 1968

1 John 5:13-21
The life of those born of God

We know that those who are born of God do not sin, but the one who was born of God protects them, and the evil one does not touch them. We know that we are God's children, and that the whole world lies under the power of the evil one. And we know that the Son of God has come and has given us understanding so that we may know him who is true; and we are in him who is true, in his Son Jesus Christ. He is the true God and eternal life. (1 John 5:18-20)

Psalm
Psalm 106:1-12
God saves through water

Additional Reading
Judges 5:12-21
The song of Deborah

Hymn: Songs of Thankfulness and Praise, ELW 310

Through our Lord and Savior, Jesus Christ, you baptized us into your family. Eternal God, though we turn away from you, you restore us by your love and grace. Continue to free our hearts and minds from the bondage of sin so that we may know your truth.

Wednesday, January 16, 2019
Time after Epiphany

Numbers 27:1-11
Daughters also promised inheritance

And the LORD spoke to Moses, saying: The daughters of Zelophehad are right in what they are saying; you shall indeed let them possess an inheritance among their father's brothers and pass the inheritance of their father on to them. You shall also say to the Israelites, "If a man dies, and has no son, then you shall pass his inheritance on to his daughter. If he has no daughter, then you shall give his inheritance to his brothers. If he has no brothers, then you shall give his inheritance to his father's brothers. And if his father has no brothers, then you shall give his inheritance to the nearest kinsman of his clan, and he shall possess it. It shall be for the Israelites a statute and ordinance, as the LORD commanded Moses." (Num. 27:6-11)

Psalm
Psalm 106:1-12
God saves through water

Additional Reading
Luke 11:33-36
Your body full of light

Hymn: Children of the Heavenly Father, ELW 781

Everlasting Father, you are faithful from generation to generation. Help us to pass on the knowledge of your good works to our children, teaching them to do the same. We ask that you make our lives a living testimony to your light and love.

Thursday, January 17, 2019
Time after Epiphany

Antony of Egypt, renewer of the church, died around 356
Pachomius, renewer of the church, died 346

Psalm 36:5-10
We feast on the abundance of God's house

Your steadfast love, O LORD, extends to the heavens,
> your faithfulness to the clouds.
Your righteousness is like the mighty mountains,
> your judgments are like the great deep;
> you save humans and animals alike, O LORD.

How precious is your steadfast love, O God!
> All people may take refuge in the shadow of your wings.
They feast on the abundance of your house,
> and you give them drink from the river of your delights.
For with you is the fountain of life;
> in your light we see light. (Ps. 36:5-9)

Additional Readings
Jeremiah 3:1-5
Unfaithful Israel

Acts 8:18-24
God's gifts cannot be purchased

Hymn: Hail to the Lord's Anointed, ELW 311

God most high, your love overwhelms the earth. Teach us to seek your face wherever we go, that your love may flow through us and touch all people everywhere.

Friday, January 18, 2019
Confession of Peter

Week of Prayer for Christian Unity begins

Matthew 16:13-19

Peter confesses: You are the Messiah

[Jesus] said to [his disciples], "But who do you say that I am?" Simon Peter answered, "You are the Messiah, the Son of the living God." And Jesus answered him, "Blessed are you, Simon son of Jonah! For flesh and blood has not revealed this to you, but my Father in heaven. And I tell you, you are Peter, and on this rock I will build my church, and the gates of Hades will not prevail against it. I will give you the keys of the kingdom of heaven, and whatever you bind on earth will be bound in heaven, and whatever you loose on earth will be loosed in heaven." (Matt. 16:15-19)

Psalm

Psalm 18:1-6, 16-19
My God, my rock, worthy of praise

Additional Readings

Acts 4:8-13
Salvation is in no one other than Jesus

1 Corinthians 10:1-5
Drinking from the spiritual rock of Christ

Hymn: Oh, Praise the Gracious Power, ELW 651

Almighty God, you inspired Simon Peter to confess Jesus as the Messiah and Son of the living God. Keep your church firm on the rock of this faith, so that in unity and peace it may proclaim one truth and follow one Lord, your Son, Jesus Christ our Savior, who lives and reigns with you and the Holy Spirit, one God, now and forever.

Saturday, January 19, 2019
Time after Epiphany

Henry, Bishop of Uppsala, martyr, died 1156

Jeremiah 4:1-4

A call to repentance

> If you return, O Israel,
>> says the LORD,
>> if you return to me,
> if you remove your abominations from my presence,
>> and do not waver,
> and if you swear, "As the LORD lives!"
>> in truth, in justice, and in uprightness,
> then nations shall be blessed by him,
>> and by him they shall boast.

For thus says the LORD to the people of Judah and to the inhabitants of Jerusalem:

> Break up your fallow ground,
>> and do not sow among thorns.
> Circumcise yourselves to the LORD,
>> remove the foreskin of your hearts,
>> O people of Judah and inhabitants of Jerusalem,
> or else my wrath will go forth like fire,
>> and burn with no one to quench it,
>> because of the evil of your doings. (Jer. 4:1-4)

Psalm

Psalm 36:5-10
We feast on the abundance of God's house

Additional Reading

Luke 11:14-23
Looking for signs from heaven

Hymn: Great God, Your Love Has Called Us, ELW 358

You are holy and good. You are our Father who forgives. When we choose to go our own ways and when we live in darkness instead of your light, give us hearts of repentance that turn back to you.

Sunday, January 20, 2019
Second Sunday after Epiphany

John 2:1-11
The wedding at Cana

When the steward tasted the water that had become wine, and did not know where it came from (though the servants who had drawn the water knew), the steward called the bridegroom and said to him, "Everyone serves the good wine first, and then the inferior wine after the guests have become drunk. But you have kept the good wine until now." Jesus did this, the first of his signs, in Cana of Galilee, and revealed his glory; and his disciples believed in him. (John 2:9-11)

Psalm

Psalm 36:5-10
We feast on the abundance of God's house

Additional Readings

Isaiah 62:1-5
God like the bridegroom and the bride

1 Corinthians 12:1-11
A variety of gifts but one Spirit

Hymn: Jesus, Come! For We Invite You, ELW 312

Lord God, source of every blessing, you showed forth your glory and led many to faith by the works of your Son, who brought gladness and salvation to his people. Transform us by the Spirit of his love, that we may find our life together in him, Jesus Christ, our Savior and Lord.

Monday, January 21, 2019
Time after Epiphany

Agnes, martyr, died around 304

Psalm 145
Praise God's faithfulness

I will extol you, my God and King,
>and bless your name forever and ever.
Every day I will bless you,
>and praise your name forever and ever.
Great is the LORD, and greatly to be praised;
>his greatness is unsearchable.

One generation shall laud your works to another,
>and shall declare your mighty acts.
On the glorious splendor of your majesty,
>and on your wondrous works, I will meditate. (Ps. 145:1-5)

Additional Readings
Isaiah 54:1-8
God is married to Israel

Romans 12:9-21
Live in harmony with one another

Hymn: All Creatures, Worship God Most High! ELW 835

God our rock and redeemer, you sent your Son, Jesus Christ, to save us from our sin. You alone are worthy to be praised. May our lips be forever worshipful and our lives serve as an expression of our adoration.

Tuesday, January 22, 2019
Time after Epiphany

Song of Solomon 4:1-8
The bride's beauty extolled

You are altogether beautiful, my love;
     there is no flaw in you.
Come with me from Lebanon, my bride;
     come with me from Lebanon.
Depart from the peak of Amana,
     from the peak of Senir and Hermon,
from the dens of lions,
     from the mountains of leopards. (Song of Sol. 4:7-8)

Psalm
Psalm 145
Praise God's faithfulness

Additional Reading
1 Corinthians 1:3-17
Appeal for unity

Hymn: We Are Baptized in Christ Jesus, ELW 451

Your all-consuming love is without comparison. You passionately wooed us through the life and death of our Savior, Jesus Christ. God of love, may we be receptive to your tender pursuit.

Wednesday, January 23, 2019
Time after Epiphany

Luke 5:33-39
Christ the bridegroom

Then [the Pharisees and their scribes] said to [Jesus], "John's disciples, like the disciples of the Pharisees, frequently fast and pray, but your disciples eat and drink." Jesus said to them, "You cannot make wedding guests fast while the bridegroom is with them, can you? The days will come when the bridegroom will be taken away from them, and then they will fast in those days." (Luke 5:33-35)

Psalm
Psalm 145
Praise God's faithfulness

Additional Reading
Song of Solomon 4:9—5:1
A love song

Hymn: Love Divine, All Loves Excelling, ELW 631

Glorious God, you offer us freedom in your Son; through his words and ways we see you more clearly. May we not get distracted but stay focused on your joy so that it overflows in our lives and points others to you.

Thursday, January 24, 2019
Time after Epiphany

Psalm 19
The law revives the soul

The law of the LORD is perfect,
    reviving the soul;
the decrees of the LORD are sure,
    making wise the simple;
the precepts of the LORD are right,
    rejoicing the heart;
the commandment of the LORD is clear,
    enlightening the eyes;
the fear of the LORD is pure,
    enduring forever;
the ordinances of the LORD are true
    and righteous altogether.
More to be desired are they than gold,
    even much fine gold;
sweeter also than honey,
    and drippings of the honeycomb. (Ps. 19:7-10)

Additional Readings
Isaiah 61:1-7
The spirit of God is upon me

Romans 7:1-6
The new life of the Spirit

Hymn: Let the Whole Creation Cry, ELW 876

Your laws, O God, are like a healing balm, easing burdens and offering freedom and life to all who choose to follow you. Teach us to meditate on your ways as we praise your name above all else.

Friday, January 25, 2019
Conversion of Paul

Week of Prayer for Christian Unity ends

Galatians 1:11-24

Paul receives a revelation of Christ

You have heard, no doubt, of my earlier life in Judaism. I was violently persecuting the church of God and was trying to destroy it. I advanced in Judaism beyond many among my people of the same age, for I was far more zealous for the traditions of my ancestors. But when God, who had set me apart before I was born and called me through his grace, was pleased to reveal his Son to me, so that I might proclaim him among the Gentiles, I did not confer with any human being, nor did I go up to Jerusalem to those who were already apostles before me, but I went away at once into Arabia, and afterwards I returned to Damascus. (Gal. 1:13-17)

Psalm

Psalm 67
Let all the peoples praise you, O God

Additional Readings

Acts 9:1-22
Saul is converted to Christ

Luke 21:10-19
The end times will require endurance

Hymn: For by Grace You Have Been Saved, ELW 598

O God, by the preaching of your apostle Paul you have caused the light of the gospel to shine throughout the world. Grant that we may follow his example and be witnesses to the truth of your Son, Jesus Christ, our Savior and Lord, who lives and reigns with you and the Holy Spirit, one God, now and forever.

Saturday, January 26, 2019
Time after Epiphany

Timothy, Titus, and Silas, missionaries

Luke 2:39-52

Jesus increases in wisdom

After three days [Jesus' parents] found [Jesus] in the temple, sitting among the teachers, listening to them and asking them questions. And all who heard him were amazed at his understanding and his answers. When his parents saw him they were astonished; and his mother said to him, "Child, why have you treated us like this? Look, your father and I have been searching for you in great anxiety." He said to them, "Why were you searching for me? Did you not know that I must be in my Father's house?" (Luke 2:46-49)

Psalm

Psalm 19
The law revives the soul

Additional Reading

Nehemiah 5:1-13
Nehemiah deals with oppression

Hymn: Dear Christians, One and All, Rejoice, ELW 594

Jesus Christ, our Lord and Savior, showed us by his perfect example what it means to seek you and abide in you always, our great God. We long to live in your presence every moment of every day that we may grow closer to you.

Sunday, January 27, 2019
Third Sunday after Epiphany

Lydia, Dorcas, and Phoebe, witnesses to the faith

Luke 4:14-21

Jesus reads the prophet Isaiah

When [Jesus] came to Nazareth, where he had been brought up, he went to the synagogue on the sabbath day, as was his custom. He stood up to read, and the scroll of the prophet Isaiah was given to him. He unrolled the scroll and found the place where it was written:

> "The Spirit of the Lord is upon me,
>> because he has anointed me
>>> to bring good news to the poor.
> He has sent me to proclaim release to the captives
>> and recovery of sight to the blind,
>>> to let the oppressed go free,
> to proclaim the year of the Lord's favor." (Luke 4:16-19)

Psalm

Psalm 19
The law revives the soul

Additional Readings

Nehemiah 8:1-3, 5-6, 8-10
Ezra reads the law

1 Corinthians 12:12-31a
You are the body of Christ

Hymn: O Zion, Haste, ELW 668

Blessed Lord God, you have caused the holy scriptures to be written for the nourishment of your people. Grant that we may hear them, read, mark, learn, and inwardly digest them, that, comforted by your promises, we may embrace and forever hold fast to the hope of eternal life, through your Son, Jesus Christ our Lord.

Monday, January 28, 2019
Time after Epiphany

Thomas Aquinas, teacher, died 1274

Psalm 119:89-96
The law of God gives life

The Lord exists forever;
>   your word is firmly fixed in heaven.
Your faithfulness endures to all generations;
>   you have established the earth, and it stands fast.
By your appointment they stand today,
>   for all things are your servants.
If your law had not been my delight,
>   I would have perished in my misery.
I will never forget your precepts,
>   for by them you have given me life. (Ps. 119:89-93)

Additional Readings

Jeremiah 36:1-10
The scroll is read in the temple

1 Corinthians 14:1-12
The assembly's gifts

Hymn: Oh, That the Lord Would Guide My Ways, ELW 772

God of knowledge and wisdom, your ways bring restoration and wholeness. We yearn to live in the protection of your statutes and decrees. May your laws guard our hearts and guide our steps.

Tuesday, January 29, 2019
Time after Epiphany

Jeremiah 36:11-26
Jehoiakim burns the scroll

Now the king was sitting in his winter apartment (it was the ninth month), and there was a fire burning in the brazier before him. As Jehudi read three or four columns, the king would cut them off with a penknife and throw them into the fire in the brazier, until the entire scroll was consumed in the fire that was in the brazier. Yet neither the king, nor any of his servants who heard all these words, was alarmed, nor did they tear their garments. Even when Elnathan and Delaiah and Gemariah urged the king not to burn the scroll, he would not listen to them. (Jer. 36:22-25)

Psalm
Psalm 119:89-96
The law of God gives life

Additional Reading
2 Corinthians 7:2-12
Grief leads to repentance

Hymn: Lord, Keep Us Steadfast in Your Word, ELW 517

Everlasting God, you established your righteous ways in your infinite wisdom and grace. We humbly acknowledge that the desire to go our own way can be overwhelming, and we ask for courage in each day's journey. May we set our eyes on the path you've placed before us.

Wednesday, January 30, 2019
Time after Epiphany

Jeremiah 36:27-32
Jeremiah dictates a second scroll

Now, after the king had burned the scroll with the words that Baruch wrote at Jeremiah's dictation, the word of the LORD came to Jeremiah: Take another scroll and write on it all the former words that were in the first scroll, which King Jehoiakim of Judah has burned. And concerning King Jehoiakim of Judah you shall say: Thus says the LORD, You have dared to burn this scroll, saying, Why have you written in it that the king of Babylon will certainly come and destroy this land, and will cut off from it human beings and animals? Therefore thus says the LORD concerning King Jehoiakim of Judah: He shall have no one to sit upon the throne of David, and his dead body shall be cast out to the heat by day and the frost by night. And I will punish him and his offspring and his servants for their iniquity; I will bring on them, and on the inhabitants of Jerusalem, and on the people of Judah, all the disasters with which I have threatened them—but they would not listen. (Jer. 36:27-31)

Psalm
Psalm 119:89-96
The law of God gives life

Additional Reading
Luke 4:38-44
Jesus heals and preaches in synagogues

Hymn: O God of Love, O King of Peace, ELW 749

In your graciousness you gave us your perfect law, Father. Yet we actively oppose it in our desire for control. In your love and mercy separate us from our sin, and may your generous Spirit forever lead us back to the solid foundation you have laid for us, our rock and redeemer.

Thursday, January 31, 2019
Time after Epiphany

Psalm 71:1-6
You have been my strength

In you, O LORD, I take refuge;
    let me never be put to shame.
In your righteousness deliver me and rescue me;
    incline your ear to me and save me.
Be to me a rock of refuge,
    a strong fortress, to save me,
    for you are my rock and my fortress.

Rescue me, O my God, from the hand of the wicked,
    from the grasp of the unjust and cruel.
For you, O Lord, are my hope,
    my trust, O LORD, from my youth. (Ps. 71:1-5)

Additional Readings
2 Chronicles 34:1-7
Youthful Josiah inaugurates reform

Acts 10:44-48
Gentiles receive the Holy Spirit

Hymn: How Firm a Foundation, ELW 796

You are the God who sees. You see our needs and our sorrows, our struggles and our joys. We gladly acknowledge that you are sufficient, God. Grow our trust in you that we will seek you alone for refuge.

Prayer List for February

- Pray that Grampy can stay with us for longer
- Pray for my strength
- Pray to help my relatives and I through a difficult part of our lives
- Pray for anyone experiencing loss of a loved one
- Pray for anyone in the middle of a war

Friday, February 1, 2019
Time after Epiphany

2 Chronicles 35:20-27
Jeremiah laments the death of Josiah

The archers shot King Josiah; and the king said to his servants, "Take me away, for I am badly wounded." So his servants took him out of the chariot and carried him in his second chariot and brought him to Jerusalem. There he died, and was buried in the tombs of his ancestors. All Judah and Jerusalem mourned for Josiah. Jeremiah also uttered a lament for Josiah, and all the singing men and singing women have spoken of Josiah in their laments to this day. They made these a custom in Israel; they are recorded in the Laments. Now the rest of the acts of Josiah and his faithful deeds in accordance with what is written in the law of the LORD, and his acts, first and last, are written in the Book of the Kings of Israel and Judah. (2 Chron. 35:23-27)

Psalm
Psalm 71:1-6
You have been my strength

Additional Reading
Acts 19:1-10
Believers speak in tongues

Hymn: O God, Why Are You Silent, ELW 703

O God of our ancestors, you have given us faithful leaders, martyrs, and witnesses throughout history. Strengthen us and grant us courage, that we might act as they did, in accordance with your holy law and love.

Saturday, February 2, 2019
Presentation of Our Lord

Luke 2:22-40
The child is brought to the temple

Simeon took [the child Jesus] in his arms and praised God, saying,
> "Master, now you are dismissing your servant in peace,
>> according to your word;
> for my eyes have seen your salvation,
>> which you have prepared in the presence of all peoples,
> a light for revelation to the Gentiles
>> and for glory to your people Israel." (Luke 2:28-32)

Psalm
Psalm 84
How dear to me is your dwelling, O God

Additional Readings
Malachi 3:1-4
My messenger, a refiner and purifier

Hebrews 2:14-18
Jesus shares human flesh and sufferings

Hymn: In His Temple Now Behold Him, ELW 417

Almighty and ever-living God, your only-begotten Son was presented this day in the temple. May we be presented to you with clean and pure hearts by the same Jesus Christ, our great high priest, who lives and reigns with you and the Holy Spirit, one God, now and forever.

Sunday, February 3, 2019
Fourth Sunday after Epiphany

Ansgar, Bishop of Hamburg, missionary to Denmark and Sweden, died 865

Luke 4:21-30
The prophet Jesus not accepted

Then [Jesus] began to say to [all in the synagogue], "Today this scripture has been fulfilled in your hearing." All spoke well of him and were amazed at the gracious words that came from his mouth. They said, "Is not this Joseph's son?" He said to them, "Doubtless you will quote to me this proverb, 'Doctor, cure yourself!' And you will say, 'Do here also in your hometown the things that we have heard you did at Capernaum.' " And he said, "Truly I tell you, no prophet is accepted in the prophet's hometown." (Luke 4:21-24)

Psalm

Psalm 71:1-6
You have been my strength

Additional Readings

Jeremiah 1:4-10
A prophet to the nations

1 Corinthians 13:1-13
Without love, a noisy gong

Hymn: He Comes to Us As One Unknown, ELW 737

Almighty and ever-living God, increase in us the gifts of faith, hope, and love; and that we may obtain what you promise, make us love what you command, through your Son, Jesus Christ, our Savior and Lord.

Monday, February 4, 2019
Time after Epiphany

Psalm 56
In God I trust

Be gracious to me, O God, for people trample on me;
    all day long foes oppress me;
my enemies trample on me all day long,
    for many fight against me.
O Most High, when I am afraid,
    I put my trust in you.
In God, whose word I praise,
    in God I trust; I am not afraid;
    what can flesh do to me? (Ps. 56:1-4)

Additional Readings

1 Kings 17:8-16
The widow of Zarephath fed

1 Corinthians 2:6-16
Interpreting spiritual things

Hymn: O Day of Peace, ELW 711

Gracious God, you hold dear all those who have been trampled upon and oppressed. Help us to trust you in the midst of our fears so that we may be fed by your saving word.

Tuesday, February 5, 2019
Time after Epiphany

The Martyrs of Japan, died 1597

2 Kings 5:1-14
Naaman the Syrian healed

Naaman came with his horses and chariots, and halted at the entrance of Elisha's house. Elisha sent a messenger to him, saying, "Go, wash in the Jordan seven times, and your flesh shall be restored and you shall be clean." But Naaman became angry and went away, saying, "I thought that for me he would surely come out, and stand and call on the name of the LORD his God, and would wave his hand over the spot, and cure the leprosy! Are not Abana and Pharpar, the rivers of Damascus, better than all the waters of Israel? Could I not wash in them, and be clean?" He turned and went away in a rage. But his servants approached and said to him, "Father, if the prophet had commanded you to do something difficult, would you not have done it? How much more, when all he said to you was, 'Wash, and be clean'?" (2 Kings 5:9-13)

Psalm
Psalm 56
In God I trust

Additional Reading
1 Corinthians 14:13-25
Interpreting tongues

Hymn: Healer of Our Every Ill, ELW 612

Holy Healer, you revive, restore, and replenish us into new life. Pour your cleansing waters over us. Cure our ills and soothe us in the midst of our doubts and fears, that we may be made holy and complete in you.

Wednesday, February 6, 2019
Time after Epiphany

Jeremiah 1:11-19
Jeremiah warns of disaster

Then the LORD said to me: Out of the north disaster shall break out on all the inhabitants of the land. For now I am calling all the tribes of the kingdoms of the north, says the LORD; and they shall come and all of them shall set their thrones at the entrance of the gates of Jerusalem, against all its surrounding walls and against all the cities of Judah. And I will utter my judgments against them, for all their wickedness in forsaking me; they have made offerings to other gods, and worshiped the works of their own hands. But you, gird up your loins; stand up and tell them everything that I command you. Do not break down before them, or I will break you before them. (Jer. 1:14-17)

Psalm
Psalm 56
In God I trust

Additional Reading
Luke 19:41-44
Recognizing the works of God

Hymn: How Great Thou Art, ELW 856

God of all authority, you are sovereign over all creation. You call your people forth as a witness to your power. Strengthen us for the struggle, that we might be steady in faith and firm in the truth.

Thursday, February 7, 2019
Time after Epiphany

Psalm 138
I will bow toward your holy temple

I give you thanks, O Lord, with my whole heart;
>   before the gods I sing your praise;

I bow down toward your holy temple
>   and give thanks to your name for your steadfast love and your
>   faithfulness;

>   for you have exalted your name and your word

>   above everything.

On the day I called, you answered me,
>   you increased my strength of soul.

All the kings of the earth shall praise you, O Lord,
>   for they have heard the words of your mouth.

They shall sing of the ways of the Lord,
>   for great is the glory of the Lord. (Ps. 138:1-5)

Additional Readings
Numbers 20:22-29
Eleazar succeeds Aaron

Acts 9:19b-25
Saul's call is questioned

Hymn: Great Is Thy Faithfulness, ELW 733

O God, the whole earth resounds with the songs of your glory. Your praise reverberates throughout all creation, from the echoes of mountains and valleys to the exclamation of peasants and rulers. Open our mouths to sing your praise forever.

Friday, February 8, 2019
Time after Epiphany

Acts 9:26-31

The apostles reluctantly welcome Saul

When [Saul] had come to Jerusalem, he attempted to join the disciples; and they were all afraid of him, for they did not believe that he was a disciple. But Barnabas took him, brought him to the apostles, and described for them how on the road he had seen the Lord, who had spoken to him, and how in Damascus he had spoken boldly in the name of Jesus. So he went in and out among them in Jerusalem, speaking boldly in the name of the Lord. He spoke and argued with the Hellenists; but they were attempting to kill him. When the believers learned of it, they brought him down to Caesarea and sent him off to Tarsus.

Meanwhile the church throughout Judea, Galilee, and Samaria had peace and was built up. Living in the fear of the Lord and in the comfort of the Holy Spirit, it increased in numbers. (Acts 9:26-31)

Psalm
Psalm 138
I will bow toward your holy temple

Additional Reading
Numbers 27:12-23
God's choice of Joshua

Hymn: Lord Jesus Christ, Be Present Now, ELW 527

Holy and mysterious God, your divine plan takes shape in ways we often do not understand. Help us to recognize your image among those people and places we least expect.

Saturday, February 9, 2019
Time after Epiphany

Judges 3:7-11
God's spirit rests on Othniel

Israelites did what was evil in the sight of the LORD, forgetting the LORD their God, and worshiping the Baals and the Asherahs. Therefore the anger of the LORD was kindled against Israel, and he sold them into the hand of King Cushan-rishathaim of Aram-naharaim; and the Israelites served Cushan-rishathaim eight years. But when the Israelites cried out to the LORD, the LORD raised up a deliverer for the Israelites, who delivered them, Othniel son of Kenaz, Caleb's younger brother. The spirit of the LORD came upon him, and he judged Israel; he went out to war, and the LORD gave King Cushan-rishathaim of Aram into his hand; and his hand prevailed over Cushan-rishathaim. So the land had rest forty years. Then Othniel son of Kenaz died. (Judg. 3:7-11)

Psalm
Psalm 138
I will bow toward your holy temple

Additional Reading
Luke 4:42-44
Jesus preaches

Hymn: If You But Trust in God to Guide You, ELW 769

Righteous God, you heard the cries of your people in Israel and sent your spirit to deliver them. Send your Spirit to deliver us also from violence and war, that all people might find rest in you.

Sunday, February 10, 2019
Fifth Sunday after Epiphany

Luke 5:1-11

Jesus calls the disciples to fish for people

When [the disciples had let down the nets], they caught so many fish that their nets were beginning to break. . . . But when Simon Peter saw it, he fell down at Jesus' knees, saying, "Go away from me, Lord, for I am a sinful man!" For he and all who were with him were amazed at the catch of fish that they had taken; and so also were James and John, sons of Zebedee, who were partners with Simon. Then Jesus said to Simon, "Do not be afraid; from now on you will be catching people." When they had brought their boats to shore, they left everything and followed him. (Luke 5:6, 8-11)

Psalm

Psalm 138
I will bow toward your holy temple

Additional Readings

Isaiah 6:1-8 [9-13]
Send me

1 Corinthians 15:1-11
I am the least of the apostles

Hymn: You Have Come Down to the Lakeshore, ELW 817

Most holy God, the earth is filled with your glory, and before you angels and saints stand in awe. Enlarge our vision to see your power at work in the world, and by your grace make us heralds of your Son, Jesus Christ, our Savior and Lord.

Monday, February 11, 2019
Time after Epiphany

Psalm 115
God blesses the chosen people

May the LORD give you increase,
    both you and your children.
May you be blessed by the LORD,
    who made heaven and earth.

The heavens are the LORD's heavens,
    but the earth he has given to human beings.
The dead do not praise the LORD,
    nor do any that go down into silence.
But we will bless the LORD
    from this time on and forevermore.
Praise the LORD! (Ps. 115:14-18)

Additional Readings

Judges 5:1-11
Deborah the judge sings God's praise

1 Corinthians 14:26-40
Advice about worship

Hymn: Praise to the Lord, the Almighty, ELW 858

God, you are the Lord of all creation. You have given this good earth to your people. Enable us to care for the precious gifts of this world in ways that glorify you.

Tuesday, February 12, 2019
Time after Epiphany

1 Samuel 9:15—10:1b
The call of Saul

When [Saul and Samuel] came down from the shrine into the town, a bed was spread for Saul on the roof, and he lay down to sleep. Then at the break of dawn Samuel called to Saul upon the roof, "Get up, so that I may send you on your way." Saul got up, and both he and Samuel went out into the street.

As they were going down to the outskirts of the town, Samuel said to Saul, "Tell the boy to go on before us, and when he has passed on, stop here yourself for a while, that I may make known to you the word of God." Samuel took a vial of oil and poured it on his head, and kissed him; he said, "The LORD has anointed you ruler over his people Israel. You shall reign over the people of the LORD and you will save them from the hand of their enemies all around." (1 Sam. 9:25—10:1b)

Psalm
Psalm 115
God blesses the chosen people

Additional Reading
1 Timothy 3:1-9
Qualities needed by church leaders

Hymn: Here I Am, Lord, ELW 574

God, you call and anoint leaders in every generation. We pray for our leaders, that they may serve you by ruling justly, with concern for the well-being of the poor and oppressed.

Wednesday, February 13, 2019
Time after Epiphany

Luke 5:27-32
The call of Levi

Then Levi gave a great banquet for him in his house; and there was a large crowd of tax collectors and others sitting at the table with them. The Pharisees and their scribes were complaining to his disciples, saying, "Why do you eat and drink with tax collectors and sinners?" Jesus answered, "Those who are well have no need of a physician, but those who are sick; I have come to call not the righteous but sinners to repentance." (Luke 5:29-32)

Psalm
Psalm 115
God blesses the chosen people

Additional Reading
Isaiah 8:1-15
Resisting the call

Hymn: Softly and Tenderly Jesus Is Calling, ELW 608

Subversive God, you sent your Son to be a friend to those on the margins. Empower us also to be in solidarity with those who others may disregard as sinners.

Thursday, February 14, 2019
Time after Epiphany

Cyril, monk, died 869; Methodius, bishop, died 885; missionaries to the Slavs

Psalm 1
Trees planted by streams of water

Happy are those
    who do not follow the advice of the wicked,
or take the path that sinners tread,
    or sit in the seat of scoffers;
but their delight is in the law of the LORD,
    and on his law they meditate day and night.
They are like trees
    planted by streams of water,
which yield their fruit in its season,
    and their leaves do not wither.
In all that they do, they prosper. (Ps. 1:1-3)

Additional Readings
Jeremiah 13:12-19
The threat of exile

Acts 13:26-34
God raised Jesus from the dead

Hymn: You Are the Way, ELW 758

God of love, you give us the gift of your law. Help us to meditate constantly on your holy word, that we might find delight in the guidance of your truth.

Friday, February 15, 2019
Time after Epiphany

1 Peter 1:17—2:1
Born anew

Now that you have purified your souls by your obedience to the truth so that you have genuine mutual love, love one another deeply from the heart. You have been born anew, not of perishable but of imperishable seed, through the living and enduring word of God.
For

"All flesh is like grass
and all its glory like the flower of grass.
The grass withers,
and the flower falls,
but the word of the Lord endures forever."

That word is the good news that was announced to you. (1 Peter 1:22-25)

Psalm
Psalm 1
Trees planted by streams of water

Additional Reading
Jeremiah 13:20-27
Can leopards change their spots?

Hymn: The Word of God Is Source and Seed, ELW 506

Everlasting God, you make all things new again. Cleanse us and give us new hearts, that we might radiate with love for you and our neighbors.

Saturday, February 16, 2019
Time after Epiphany

Jeremiah 17:1-4
A heritage lost

The sin of Judah is written with an iron pen; with a diamond point it is engraved on the tablet of their hearts, and on the horns of their altars, while their children remember their altars and their sacred poles, beside every green tree, and on the high hills, on the mountains in the open country. Your wealth and all your treasures I will give for spoil as the price of your sin throughout all your territory. By your own act you shall lose the heritage that I gave you, and I will make you serve your enemies in a land that you do not know, for in my anger a fire is kindled that shall burn forever. (Jer. 17:1-4)

Psalm
Psalm 1
Trees planted by streams of water

Additional Reading
Luke 11:24-28
Blessings on those who hear the word

Hymn: Jesus, Priceless Treasure, ELW 775

Generous God, we confess that we have sinned against you and against others. We have valued our wealth, our possessions, and our prestige over obedience to you and care for our neighbor. Help us, gracious God, to move into right relationship with you and with others.

Sunday, February 17, 2019
Sixth Sunday after Epiphany

Luke 6:17-26

Blessings on the poor, woes on the rich

Then [Jesus] looked up at his disciples and said:
> "Blessed are you who are poor,
>> for yours is the kingdom of God.
> "Blessed are you who are hungry now,
>> for you will be filled.
> "Blessed are you who weep now,
>> for you will laugh.

"Blessed are you when people hate you, and when they exclude you, revile you, and defame you on account of the Son of Man. Rejoice in that day and leap for joy, for surely your reward is great in heaven; for that is what their ancestors did to the prophets." (Luke 6:20-22)

Psalm

Psalm 1
Trees planted by streams of water

Additional Readings

Jeremiah 17:5-10
Those who trust the Lord are like trees

1 Corinthians 15:12-20
Christ has been raised

Hymn: Blest Are They, ELW 728

Living God, in Christ you make all things new. Transform the poverty of our nature by the riches of your grace, and in the renewal of our lives make known your glory, through Jesus Christ, our Savior and Lord.

Monday, February 18, 2019
Time after Epiphany

Martin Luther, renewer of the church, died 1546

Psalm 120

Woe to me

In my distress I cry to the LORD,
> that he may answer me:
"Deliver me, O LORD,
> from lying lips,
> from a deceitful tongue."

Woe is me, that I am an alien in Meshech,
> that I must live among the tents of Kedar.
Too long have I had my dwelling
> among those who hate peace.
I am for peace;
> but when I speak,
> they are for war. (Ps. 120:1-2, 5-7)

Additional Readings

2 Kings 24:18—25:21
Woes come upon Jerusalem

1 Corinthians 15:20-34
The end time

Hymn: How Long, O God, ELW 698

O God, you hear all who cry out to you in distress. You see all who wander as refugees without a place to call home. Comfort all who live among discord, violence, and war. Lift up and encourage those who work diligently for peace.

Tuesday, February 19, 2019
Time after Epiphany

2 Corinthians 1:12-19
The day of the Lord Jesus

Indeed, this is our boast, the testimony of our conscience: we have behaved in the world with frankness and godly sincerity, not by earthly wisdom but by the grace of God—and all the more toward you. For we write you nothing other than what you can read and also understand; I hope you will understand until the end—as you have already understood us in part—that on the day of the Lord Jesus we are your boast even as you are our boast. (2 Cor. 1:12-14)

Psalm
Psalm 120
Woe to me

Additional Reading
Ezra 1:1-11
Blessings return to Jerusalem

Hymn: O Jesus, Joy of Loving Hearts, ELW 658

Source of all goodness, through your grace you set us free to live righteously. Continue to enable us to live lives of authenticity and sincerity, for your Son's sake.

Wednesday, February 20, 2019
Time after Epiphany

Jeremiah 22:11-17
Woe to the unjust

Woe to him who builds his house by unrighteousness,
    and his upper rooms by injustice;
who makes his neighbors work for nothing,
    and does not give them their wages;
who says, "I will build myself a spacious house
    with large upper rooms,"
and who cuts out windows for it,
    paneling it with cedar,
    and painting it with vermilion.
Are you a king
    because you compete in cedar?
Did not your father eat and drink
    and do justice and righteousness?
    Then it was well with him.
He judged the cause of the poor and needy;
    then it was well.
Is not this to know me?
    says the LORD. (Jer. 22:13-16)

Psalm
Psalm 120
Woe to me

Additional Reading
Luke 11:37-52
Woe to the sinners

Hymn: All Who Love and Serve Your City, ELW 724

God of justice, you created all of humankind in your image, vested with inherent dignity and worthy of respect. Grant us the creativity and courage to work towards a society in which all people are valued as your children.

Thursday, February 21, 2019
Time after Epiphany

Psalm 37:1-11, 39-40
The lowly shall possess the land

Refrain from anger, and forsake wrath.
> Do not fret—it leads only to evil.
For the wicked shall be cut off,
> but those who wait for the Lord shall inherit the land.

Yet a little while, and the wicked will be no more;
> though you look diligently for their place, they will not be there.
But the meek shall inherit the land,
> and delight themselves in abundant prosperity. (Ps. 37:8-11)

Additional Readings
Genesis 43:16-34
Joseph welcomes his brother Benjamin

Romans 8:1-11
You are one in the Spirit

Hymn: O God of Every Nation, ELW 713

O God, we chase after worldly ideas of dominance and control. Help us to release our hunger for power in favor of a thirst for your justice.

Friday, February 22, 2019
Time after Epiphany

1 John 2:12-17

The world and its desires are passing away

Do not love the world or the things in the world. The love of the Father is not in those who love the world; for all that is in the world—the desire of the flesh, the desire of the eyes, the pride in riches—comes not from the Father but from the world. And the world and its desire are passing away, but those who do the will of God live forever. (1 John 2:15-17)

Psalm
Psalm 37:1-11, 39–40
The lowly shall possess the land

Additional Reading
Genesis 44:1-17
Joseph detains his brother Benjamin

Hymn: Let Streams of Living Justice, ELW 710

Heavenly Ruler, you give us gifts of eternal inheritance. Help us to release our tight grip on our earthly possessions and instead turn our hearts toward your never-ending promises.

Saturday, February 23, 2019
Time after Epiphany

Polycarp, Bishop of Smyrna, martyr, died 156

Luke 12:57-59

Settling with your opponent

"And why do you not judge for yourselves what is right? Thus, when you go with your accuser before a magistrate, on the way make an effort to settle the case, or you may be dragged before the judge, and the judge hand you over to the officer, and the officer throw you in prison. I tell you, you will never get out until you have paid the very last penny." (Luke 12:57-59)

Psalm
Psalm 37:1-11, 39-40
The lowly shall possess the land

Additional Reading
Genesis 44:18-34
Judah offers himself in Benjamin's place

Hymn: Forgive Our Sins As We Forgive, ELW 605

God of compassion, it is your desire that your children would live among one another in peace. Be with us in conflicts with our neighbors. Grant us patience and empathy toward those with whom we disagree.

Sunday, February 24, 2019
Seventh Sunday after Epiphany

Luke 6:27-38

Love your enemies

"But I say to you that listen, Love your enemies, do good to those who hate you, bless those who curse you, pray for those who abuse you. If anyone strikes you on the cheek, offer the other also; and from anyone who takes away your coat do not withhold even your shirt. Give to everyone who begs from you; and if anyone takes away your goods, do not ask for them again. Do to others as you would have them do to you." (Luke 6:27-31)

Psalm

Psalm 37:1-11, 39–40
The lowly shall possess the land

Additional Readings

Genesis 45:3-11, 15
Joseph forgives his brothers

1 Corinthians
15:35-38, 42–50
The mystery of the resurrection

Hymn: Lord, You Give the Great Commission, ELW 579

O Lord Jesus, make us instruments of your peace, that where there is hatred, we may sow love, where there is injury, pardon, and where there is despair, hope. Grant, O divine master, that we may seek to console, to understand, and to love in your name, for you live and reign with the Father and the Holy Spirit, one God, now and forever.

Monday, February 25, 2019
Time after Epiphany

Elizabeth Fedde, deaconess, died 1921

Psalm 38
Confession of sin

I confess my iniquity;
    I am sorry for my sin.
Those who are my foes without cause are mighty,
    and many are those who hate me wrongfully.
Those who render me evil for good
    are my adversaries because I follow after good.

Do not forsake me, O LORD;
    O my God, do not be far from me;
make haste to help me,
    O Lord, my salvation. (Ps. 38:18-22)

Additional Readings
Genesis 33:1-17
Jacob and Esau reconcile

1 Corinthians 11:2-16
Advice for church life

Hymn: Lord Jesus, Think on Me, ELW 599

Faithful God, you are not far from us in our distress. You come quickly to our aid when we are in need of your saving grace. Grant us hearts that turn eagerly toward you, that we may remain strong in the face of adversity.

Tuesday, February 26, 2019
Time after Epiphany

1 Corinthians 11:17-22, 27-33

Advice concerning the Lord's supper

Now in the following instructions I do not commend you, because when you come together it is not for the better but for the worse. For, to begin with, when you come together as a church, I hear that there are divisions among you; and to some extent I believe it. Indeed, there have to be factions among you, for only so will it become clear who among you are genuine. When you come together, it is not really to eat the Lord's supper. For when the time comes to eat, each of you goes ahead with your own supper, and one goes hungry and another becomes drunk. What! Do you not have homes to eat and drink in? Or do you show contempt for the church of God and humiliate those who have nothing? What should I say to you? Should I commend you? In this matter I do not commend you! (1 Cor. 11:17-22)

Psalm
Psalm 38
Confession of sin

Additional Reading
1 Samuel 24:1-22
David spares Saul's life

Hymn: What Is This Place, ELW 524

Gracious God, you lavish bountiful good gifts upon humanity, yet in our greed we often fail to share with those in need. Help us to trust in the faithfulness of your generosity and to give freely to all who are in need.

Time after Epiphany

Luke 17:1-4
Forgiving seven times

Jesus said to his disciples, "Occasions for stumbling are bound to come, but woe to anyone by whom they come! It would be better for you if a millstone were hung around your neck and you were thrown into the sea than for you to cause one of these little ones to stumble. Be on your guard! If another disciple sins, you must rebuke the offender, and if there is repentance, you must forgive. And if the same person sins against you seven times a day, and turns back to you seven times and says, 'I repent,' you must forgive." (Luke 17:1-4)

Psalm
Psalm 38
Confession of sin

Additional Reading
Leviticus 5:1-13
Offering for pardon

Hymn: Beloved, God's Chosen, ELW 648

Parent God, you fiercely protect the vulnerable and defenseless like a mother watching over a child. Thank you for the times you have sheltered and defended us. Empower us to guard and care for those among us who are in need of sanctuary.

Thursday, February 28, 2019
Time after Epiphany

Psalm 99
Worship upon God's holy hill

The LORD is king; let the peoples tremble!
>   He sits enthroned upon the cherubim; let the earth quake!
The LORD is great in Zion;
>   he is exalted over all the peoples.
Let them praise your great and awesome name.
>   Holy is he!
Mighty King, lover of justice,
>   you have established equity;
you have executed justice
>   and righteousness in Jacob.

Extol the LORD our God,
>   and worship at his holy mountain;
>   for the LORD our God is holy. (Ps. 99:1-4, 9)

Additional Readings
Deuteronomy 9:1-5
God's oath to Abraham, Isaac, and Jacob

Acts 3:11-16
Abraham, Isaac, and Jacob's God glorifies Jesus

Hymn: Oh, Worship the King, ELW 842

Holy and mighty God, you are great beyond our human imagining. Help us to love justice and righteousness the way that you do, that we might work for peace and equity across all the earth.

Prayer List for March

Pray for Leah

Pray for Amelia

Pray for those that
are suffering with
depression or suicidal
thoughts

Pray for Diana and Aunt
Arlene

Pray for Uncle Rocky is
happy in heaven

Friday, March 1, 2019
Time after Epiphany

George Herbert, hymnwriter, died 1633

Acts 10:1-8
The vision of Cornelius

In Caesarea there was a man named Cornelius, a centurion of the Italian Cohort, as it was called. He was a devout man who feared God with all his household; he gave alms generously to the people and prayed constantly to God. One afternoon at about three o'clock he had a vision in which he clearly saw an angel of God coming in and saying to him, "Cornelius." He stared at him in terror and said, "What is it, Lord?" He answered, "Your prayers and your alms have ascended as a memorial before God." (Acts 10:1-4)

Psalm
Psalm 99
Worship upon God's holy hill

Additional Reading
Deuteronomy 9:6-14
Remember your rebellion in the wilderness

Hymn: Lord, Teach Us How to Pray Aright, ELW 745

O God of answers, you know everything and you hear our pleas. You faithfully attend to our petitions. Guide us in our prayers so we may honor your name and open our hearts to your response.

Saturday, March 2, 2019
Time after Epiphany

John Wesley, died 1791; Charles Wesley, died 1788; renewers of the church

Deuteronomy 9:15-24
Moses on the blazing mountain

So I turned and went down from the mountain, while the mountain was ablaze; the two tablets of the covenant were in my two hands. Then I saw that you had indeed sinned against the Lord your God, by casting for yourselves an image of a calf; you had been quick to turn from the way that the Lord had commanded you. So I took hold of the two tablets and flung them from my two hands, smashing them before your eyes. Then I lay prostrate before the Lord as before, forty days and forty nights; I neither ate bread nor drank water, because of all the sin you had committed, provoking the Lord by doing what was evil in his sight. For I was afraid that the anger that the Lord bore against you was so fierce that he would destroy you. But the Lord listened to me that time also. (Deut. 9:15-19)

Psalm
Psalm 99
Worship upon God's holy hill

Additional Reading
Luke 10:21-24
Blessed are the eyes that see what you see

Hymn: Oh, Wondrous Image, Vision Fair, ELW 316

Lord of righteousness, you have given us endless grace. You hear our prayers and forgive our sins. Guide us in our worship that we may offer praise worthy of our glorious blessings.

Sunday, March 3, 2019
Transfiguration of Our Lord

Luke 9:28-36 [37-43a]

Jesus is transfigured on the mountain

Now about eight days after these sayings Jesus took with him Peter and John and James, and went up on the mountain to pray. And while he was praying, the appearance of his face changed, and his clothes became dazzling white. Suddenly they saw two men, Moses and Elijah, talking to him. They appeared in glory and were speaking of his departure, which he was about to accomplish at Jerusalem. Now Peter and his companions were weighed down with sleep; but since they had stayed awake, they saw his glory and the two men who stood with him. (Luke 9:28-32)

Psalm

Psalm 99
Worship upon God's holy hill

Additional Readings

Exodus 34:29-35
Moses' face shone

2 Corinthians 3:12—4:2
We will be transformed

Hymn: Jesus on the Mountain Peak, ELW 317

Holy God, mighty and immortal, you are beyond our knowing, yet we see your glory in the face of Jesus Christ. Transform us into the likeness of your Son, who renewed our humanity so that we may share in his divinity, Jesus Christ our Lord, who lives and reigns with you and the Holy Spirit, one God, now and forever.

Monday, March 4, 2019
Time after Epiphany

Psalm 35:11-28

Do not be far from me

You have seen, O Lord; do not be silent!
>O Lord, do not be far from me!
Wake up! Bestir yourself for my defense,
>for my cause, my God and my Lord!
Vindicate me, O Lord, my God,
>according to your righteousness,
>and do not let them rejoice over me.
Do not let them say to themselves,
>"Aha, we have our heart's desire."
Do not let them say, "We have swallowed you up."

Let all those who rejoice at my calamity
>be put to shame and confusion;
let those who exalt themselves against me
>be clothed with shame and dishonor. (Ps. 35:22-26)

Additional Readings
Exodus 35:1-29
Offerings for the tent of meeting

Acts 10:9-23a
Peter's vision of what God makes clean

Hymn: Jesus Lives, My Sure Defense, ELW 621

God of rest and protection, you guard and guide us. You set before us righteous paths. Help us to walk in your ways that we may stay close with you and never be far from your reach.

Tuesday, March 5, 2019
Time after Epiphany

Acts 10:23b-33
Cornelius and Peter

On Peter's arrival Cornelius met him, and falling at his feet, worshiped him. But Peter made him get up, saying, "Stand up; I am only a mortal." And as he talked with him, he went in and found that many had assembled; and he said to them, "You yourselves know that it is unlawful for a Jew to associate with or to visit a Gentile; but God has shown me that I should not call anyone profane or unclean." (Acts 10:25-28)

Psalm
Psalm 35:11-28
Do not be far from me

Additional Reading
Ezekiel 1:1—2:1
Ezekiel's vision of the chariot

Hymn: We Are Called, ELW 720

Holy and divine God, you direct our paths and you show us your righteous ways. Reveal to us how we should serve you. Give us your wise guidance that we may walk close to you and honor your calling in our lives.

Lent

Lent is a forty-day journey to Easter. Christians keep company with Noah and his family, who were in the ark for forty days; with the Hebrews, who journeyed through the desert for forty years; and with Moses, Elijah, and Jesus, who fasted for forty days before they embarked on the tasks God had prepared for them.

During Lent Christians journey with those who are making final preparations for baptism at Easter. Together, Christians struggle with the meaning of their baptismal promises: Do you reject evil? Do you believe in God the Father, the Son, and the Holy Spirit? Do you believe in the church, the forgiveness of sins, the resurrection of the dead?

The disciples of the Lord Jesus are called to contend against everything that leads them away from love of God and neighbor. Fasting, prayer, and works of love—the disciplines of Lent—help the household rejoice in the gifts of baptism: God's forgiveness and mercy.

Table Prayer for the Season of Lent

Blessed are you, O God, giver of all.
You adorn our tables with food
and give companionship for our journeys.
Be present with us as we are fed in body and spirit
that our sharing this meal is a sign of your life
broken and shared for the world.
In Jesus' name we pray.
Amen.

Wednesday, March 6, 2019
Ash Wednesday

Matthew 6:1-6, 16-21
The practice of faith

[Jesus said,] "And whenever you fast, do not look dismal, like the hypocrites, for they disfigure their faces so as to show others that they are fasting. Truly I tell you, they have received their reward. But when you fast, put oil on your head and wash your face, so that your fasting may be seen not by others but by your Father who is in secret; and your Father who sees in secret will reward you." (Matt. 6:16-18)

Psalm
Psalm 51:1-17
Plea for mercy

Additional Readings
Joel 2:1-2, 12-17
Return to God

2 Corinthians 5:20b—6:10
Now is the day of salvation

Hymn: Savior, When in Dust to You, ELW 601

Gracious God, out of your love and mercy you breathed into dust the breath of life, creating us to serve you and our neighbors. Call forth our prayers and acts of kindness, and strengthen us to face our mortality with confidence in the mercy of your Son, Jesus Christ, our Savior and Lord, who lives and reigns with you and the Holy Spirit, one God, now and forever.

Thursday, March 7, 2019
Week before Lent 1

Perpetua and Felicity and companions, martyrs at Carthage, died 202

Psalm 91:1-2, 9-16
God shall keep you

You who live in the shelter of the Most High,
> who abide in the shadow of the Almighty,
will say to the LORD, "My refuge and my fortress;
> my God, in whom I trust."

Because you have made the LORD your refuge,
> the Most High your dwelling place,
no evil shall befall you,
> no scourge come near your tent.

For he will command his angels concerning you
> to guard you in all your ways. (Ps. 91:1-2, 9-11)

Additional Readings

Exodus 5:10-23
Israel labors in Egypt

Acts 7:30-34
Moses, called from the burning bush to the exodus

Hymn: On Eagle's Wings, ELW 787

Omnipotent Lord of our protection, you give us refuge and keep us safe from the evils of this world. You set us free from bondage and offer us shelter. Keep us always in your light that we may serve you in all our ways.

Friday, March 8, 2019
Week before Lent 1

Exodus 6:1-13
God promises deliverance

Then the LORD spoke to Moses, "Go and tell Pharaoh king of Egypt to let the Israelites go out of his land." But Moses spoke to the LORD, "The Israelites have not listened to me; how then shall Pharaoh listen to me, poor speaker that I am?" Thus the LORD spoke to Moses and Aaron, and gave them orders regarding the Israelites and Pharaoh king of Egypt, charging them to free the Israelites from the land of Egypt. (Exod. 6:10-13)

Psalm
Psalm 91:1-2, 9-16
God shall keep you

Additional Reading
Acts 7:35-42
The people complain to Moses

Hymn: Lift Every Voice and Sing, ELW 841

All-knowing God of hope and help, you hear our pleas and you know our shortcomings. Give us confidence in your provisions. Help us share the glorious stories of your deliverance boldly.

Saturday, March 9, 2019
Week before Lent 1

Ecclesiastes 3:1-8
For everything a season

For everything there is a season, and a time for every matter under heaven:

> a time to be born, and a time to die;
> a time to plant, and a time to pluck up what is planted;
> a time to kill, and a time to heal;
> a time to break down, and a time to build up. (Eccles. 3:1-3)

Psalm
Psalm 91:1-2, 9-16
God shall keep you

Additional Reading
John 12:27-36
Jesus announces his passion

Hymn: O Christ the Same, ELW 760

We praise your name, God of light. You guide our paths that we might walk in your glory. Give us patience to wait on your perfect timing and help us to glorify you in all our ways.

Sunday, March 10, 2019
First Sunday in Lent

Harriet Tubman, died 1913; Sojourner Truth, died 1883; renewers of society

Luke 4:1-13
The temptation of Jesus

Jesus, full of the Holy Spirit, returned from the Jordan and was led by the Spirit in the wilderness, where for forty days he was tempted by the devil. He ate nothing at all during those days, and when they were over, he was famished. The devil said to him, "If you are the Son of God, command this stone to become a loaf of bread." Jesus answered him, "It is written, 'One does not live by bread alone.'" (Luke 4:1-4)

Psalm
Psalm 91:1-2, 9-16
God shall keep you

Additional Readings
Deuteronomy 26:1-11
Saved from Egypt

Romans 10:8b-13
You will be saved

Hymn: O Lord, throughout These Forty Days, ELW 319

O Lord God, you led your people through the wilderness and brought them to the promised land. Guide us now, so that, following your Son, we may walk safely through the wilderness of this world toward the life you alone can give, through Jesus Christ, our Savior and Lord, who lives and reigns with you and the Holy Spirit, one God, now and forever.

Monday, March 11, 2019
Week of Lent 1

Psalm 17
Prayer for protection from evil ones

I call upon you, for you will answer me, O God;
      incline your ear to me, hear my words.
Wondrously show your steadfast love,
      O savior of those who seek refuge
      from their adversaries at your right hand.

Guard me as the apple of the eye;
      hide me in the shadow of your wings. (Ps. 17:6-8)

Additional Readings
1 Chronicles 21:1-17
Satan tempts David

1 John 2:1-6
Obey God's commandments

Hymn: Lord, Keep Us Steadfast in Your Word, ELW 517

Lord of love and deliverance, you answer our calls and offer us refuge from those who would do us harm. Guard our hearts in you and protect us as we follow your commandments. Keep us on the right path and deliver us from temptations.

Tuesday, March 12, 2019
Week of Lent 1

Gregory the Great, Bishop of Rome, died 604

Zechariah 3:1-10
Satan tempts Joshua

Then the angel of the LORD assured Joshua, saying "Thus says the LORD of hosts: If you will walk in my ways and keep my requirements, then you shall rule my house and have charge of my courts, and I will give you the right of access among those who are standing here. Now listen, Joshua, high priest, you and your colleagues who sit before you! For they are an omen of things to come: I am going to bring my servant the Branch. For on the stone that I have set before Joshua, on a single stone with seven facets, I will engrave its inscription, says the LORD of hosts, and I will remove the guilt of this land in a single day. On that day, says the LORD of hosts, you shall invite each other to come under your vine and fig tree." (Zech. 3:6-10)

Psalm
Psalm 17
Prayer for protection from evil ones

Additional Reading
2 Peter 2:4-21
Believers who fall into sin

Hymn: Let Us Ever Walk with Jesus, ELW 802

Righteous God who cleanses us from sin, you are holy and worthy of our obedience. Guide us, that we may walk uprightly, honoring you in all we do. Protect us from sin, that we may remain steadfast in your word.

Wednesday, March 13, 2019
Week of Lent 1

Job 1:1-22
Satan tempts Job

Then Job arose, tore his robe, shaved his head, and fell on the ground and worshiped. He said, "Naked I came from my mother's womb, and naked shall I return there; the LORD gave, and the LORD has taken away; blessed be the name of the LORD."

In all this Job did not sin or charge God with wrongdoing. (Job 1:20-22)

Psalm
Psalm 17
Prayer for protection from evil ones

Additional Reading
Luke 21:34—22:6
Satan enters Judas

Hymn: By Gracious Powers, ELW 626

God of wisdom, you bless us greatly and show us your mercy when we call out to you. You know our hearts and protect us from evil. Help us bless your name in times of trouble as much as in times of ease. Keep us from sin and help us not to doubt your judgment.

Thursday, March 14, 2019
Week of Lent 1

Psalm 27
The Lord shall keep me safe

The Lord is my light and my salvation;
>   whom shall I fear?
The Lord is the stronghold of my life;
>   of whom shall I be afraid?

When evildoers assail me
>   to devour my flesh—
my adversaries and foes—
>   they shall stumble and fall.

Though an army encamp against me,
>   my heart shall not fear;
though war rise up against me,
>   yet I will be confident. (Ps. 27:1-3)

Additional Readings
Genesis 13:1-7, 14-18
Abram begins his pilgrimage

Philippians 3:2-12
Paul affirms the Abrahamic tradition

Hymn: If God My Lord Be for Me, ELW 788

Glorious God of light, you deliver us from evil and keep us safe from adversaries. No matter the trouble, you save us. Help us to trust in your strength. Set fear far from our hearts. Help us rest in your salvation.

Friday, March 15, 2019
Week of Lent 1

Philippians 3:17-20
Our citizenship is in heaven

Brothers and sisters, join in imitating me, and observe those who live according to the example you have in us. For many live as enemies of the cross of Christ; I have often told you of them, and now I tell you even with tears. Their end is destruction; their god is the belly; and their glory is in their shame; their minds are set on earthly things. But our citizenship is in heaven, and it is from there that we are expecting a Savior, the Lord Jesus Christ. (Phil. 3:17-20)

Psalm
Psalm 27
The Lord shall keep me safe

Additional Reading
Genesis 14:17-24
Abram is blessed by Melchizedek

Hymn: Come, We That Love the Lord, ELW 625

Lord of love and salvation, you are holy and worthy of all our praise. You bless us and guard us from evil. Lift our minds from earthly things and set them on your eternal promises.

Saturday, March 16, 2019
Week of Lent 1

Psalm 118:26-29

A pilgrimage song of praise

Blessed is the one who comes in the name of the LORD.
> We bless you from the house of the LORD.
The LORD is God,
> and he has given us light.
Bind the festal procession with branches,
> up to the horns of the altar.

You are my God, and I will give thanks to you;
> you are my God, I will extol you.

O give thanks to the LORD, for he is good,
> for his steadfast love endures forever. (Ps. 118:26-29)

Psalm

Psalm 27
The Lord shall keep me safe

Additional Reading

Matthew 23:37-39
Jesus laments over Jerusalem

Hymn: Immortal, Invisible, God Only Wise, ELW 834

Loving and eternal God, you are endless in your charity and generous with your blessings. Help us to be grateful for the light you shine in our lives that we may bless your name forever.

Sunday, March 17, 2019
Second Sunday in Lent

Patrick, bishop, missionary to Ireland, died 461

Luke 13:31-35
A hen gathering her brood

At that very hour some Pharisees came and said to [Jesus], "Get away from here, for Herod wants to kill you." He said to them, "Go and tell that fox for me, 'Listen, I am casting out demons and performing cures today and tomorrow, and on the third day I finish my work. Yet today, tomorrow, and the next day I must be on my way, because it is impossible for a prophet to be killed outside of Jerusalem.' Jerusalem, Jerusalem, the city that kills the prophets and stones those who are sent to it! How often have I desired to gather your children together as a hen gathers her brood under her wings, and you were not willing! See, your house is left to you. And I tell you, you will not see me until the time comes when you say, 'Blessed is the one who comes in the name of the Lord.' " (Luke 13:31-35)

Psalm
Psalm 27
The Lord shall keep me safe

Additional Readings
Genesis 15:1-12, 17-18
The covenant with Abram

Philippians 3:17—4:1
Our citizenship is in heaven

Hymn: When Twilight Comes, ELW 566

God of the covenant, in the mystery of the cross you promise everlasting life to the world. Gather all peoples into your arms, and shelter us with your mercy, that we may rejoice in the life we share in your Son, Jesus Christ, our Savior and Lord, who lives and reigns with you and the Holy Spirit, one God, now and forever.

Monday, March 18, 2019
Week of Lent 2

Psalm 105:1-15 [16-41] 42
God's covenant with Abraham

O give thanks to the LORD, call on his name,
  make known his deeds among the peoples.
Sing to him, sing praises to him;
  tell of all his wonderful works.
Glory in his holy name;
  let the hearts of those who seek the LORD rejoice.
Seek the LORD and his strength;
  seek his presence continually. (Ps. 105:1-4)

Additional Readings
Exodus 33:1-6
Abraham's descendants lament

Romans 4:1-12
The faith of Abraham

Hymn: Praise and Thanksgiving, ELW 689

O Lord, you are wonderful. Your hand stretches out across the land in mercy and love. You work wonders in our lives. Glory be to you. Guide us as we seek you. Help us to trust in your power and delight in your presence.

Tuesday, March 19, 2019
Joseph, Guardian of Jesus

Matthew 1:16, 18-21, 24a
The Lord appears to Joseph in a dream

Now the birth of Jesus the Messiah took place in this way. When his mother Mary had been engaged to Joseph, but before they lived together, she was found to be with child from the Holy Spirit. Her husband Joseph, being a righteous man and unwilling to expose her to public disgrace, planned to dismiss her quietly. But just when he had resolved to do this, an angel of the Lord appeared to him in a dream and said, "Joseph, son of David, do not be afraid to take Mary as your wife, for the child conceived in her is from the Holy Spirit. She will bear a son, and you are to name him Jesus, for he will save his people from their sins." (Matt. 1:18-21)

Psalm
Psalm 89:1-29
The Lord's steadfast love is established forever

Additional Readings
2 Samuel 7:4, 8-16
God makes a covenant with David

Romans 4:13-18
The promise to those who share Abraham's faith

Hymn: Of the Father's Love Begotten, ELW 295

O God, from the family of your servant David you raised up Joseph to be the guardian of your incarnate Son and the husband of his blessed mother. Give us grace to imitate his uprightness of life and his obedience to your commands, through Jesus Christ, our Savior and Lord, who lives and reigns with you and the Holy Spirit, one God, now and forever.

Wednesday, March 20, 2019
Week of Lent 2

2 Chronicles 20:1-22
The king prays for Jerusalem

Jehoshaphat stood in the assembly of Judah and Jerusalem, in the house of the LORD, before the new court, and said, "O LORD, God of our ancestors, are you not God in heaven? Do you not rule over all the kingdoms of the nations? In your hand are power and might, so that no one is able to withstand you. Did you not, O our God, drive out the inhabitants of this land before your people Israel, and give it forever to the descendants of your friend Abraham? They have lived in it, and in it have built you a sanctuary for your name, saying, 'If disaster comes upon us, the sword, judgment, or pestilence, or famine, we will stand before this house, and before you, for your name is in this house, and cry to you in our distress, and you will hear and save.'" (2 Chron. 20:5-9)

Psalm
Psalm 105:1-15 [16-41] 42
God's covenant with Abraham

Additional Reading
Luke 13:22-31
The narrow door

Hymn: Lead On, O King Eternal! ELW 805

O holy and powerful Lord, as you have shown mercy to the faithful who came before us, so show us your mercy and power. Strengthen us to call upon your name always.

Thursday, March 21, 2019
Week of Lent 2

Thomas Cranmer, Bishop of Canterbury, martyr, died 1556

Psalm 63:1-8
O God, eagerly I seek you

O God, you are my God, I seek you,
>   my soul thirsts for you;
my flesh faints for you,
>   as in a dry and weary land where there is no water.
So I have looked upon you in the sanctuary,
>   beholding your power and glory.
Because your steadfast love is better than life,
>   my lips will praise you.
So I will bless you as long as I live;
>   I will lift up my hands and call on your name. (Ps. 63:1-4)

Additional Readings
Daniel 3:19-30
Servants of God vindicated

Revelation 2:8-11
Warning to the church in Smyrna

Hymn: All My Hope on God Is Founded, ELW 757

O God of love, you are worthy to be praised. You are our rest in troubled times. You are our safety from harm. Give us respite in your arms. Guide us as we seek you. We will always praise your name.

Friday, March 22, 2019
Week of Lent 2

Jonathan Edwards, teacher, missionary to American Indians, died 1758

Revelation 3:1-6
Warning to the church in Sardis

"And to the angel of the church in Sardis write: These are the words of him who has the seven spirits of God and the seven stars:

"I know your works; you have a name of being alive, but you are dead. Wake up, and strengthen what remains and is on the point of death, for I have not found your works perfect in the sight of my God. Remember then what you received and heard; obey it, and repent. If you do not wake up, I will come like a thief, and you will not know at what hour I will come to you. Yet you have still a few persons in Sardis who have not soiled their clothes; they will walk with me, dressed in white, for they are worthy. If you conquer, you will be clothed like them in white robes, and I will not blot your name out of the book of life; I will confess your name before my Father and before his angels." (Rev. 3:1-5)

Psalm
Psalm 63:1-8
O God, eagerly I seek you

Additional Reading
Daniel 12:1-4
God sends Michael

Hymn: Come, My Way, My Truth, My Life, ELW 816

Lord of righteousness and light, you show us your ways and direct us in your paths. You do not turn from your faithful servants. Set our eyes on your ways that we may honor you with our lives.

Saturday, March 23, 2019
Week of Lent 2

Isaiah 5:1-7
The song of the vineyard

Let me sing for my beloved
    my love-song concerning his vineyard:
My beloved had a vineyard
    on a very fertile hill.
He dug it and cleared it of stones,
    and planted it with choice vines;
he built a watchtower in the midst of it,
    and hewed out a wine vat in it;
he expected it to yield grapes,
    but it yielded wild grapes.

And now, inhabitants of Jerusalem
    and people of Judah,
judge between me
    and my vineyard.
What more was there to do for my vineyard
    that I have not done in it?
When I expected it to yield grapes,
    why did it yield wild grapes? (Isa. 5:1-4)

Psalm
Psalm 63:1-8
O God, eagerly I seek you

Additional Reading
Luke 6:43-45
A tree and its fruits

Hymn: Lord of Glory, You Have Bought Us, ELW 707

O Lord of heaven and earth, you lavish us with your love abundantly. You fill us up that we may pour out your love for others. Help us to stay rooted in your word so we may grow and honor you with the fruit we produce.

Sunday, March 24, 2019
Third Sunday in Lent

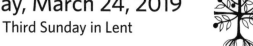

Oscar Arnulfo Romero, Bishop of El Salvador, martyr, died 1980

Luke 13:1-9
The parable of the fig tree

Then [Jesus] told this parable: "A man had a fig tree planted in his vineyard; and he came looking for fruit on it and found none. So he said to the gardener, 'See here! For three years I have come looking for fruit on this fig tree, and still I find none. Cut it down! Why should it be wasting the soil?' He replied, 'Sir, let it alone for one more year, until I dig around it and put manure on it. If it bears fruit next year, well and good; but if not, you can cut it down.'" (Luke 13:6-9)

Psalm
Psalm 63:1-8
O God, eagerly I seek you

Additional Readings
Isaiah 55:1-9
Come to the water

1 Corinthians 10:1-13
Israel, baptized in cloud and seas

Hymn: I Heard the Voice of Jesus Say, ELW 611

Eternal God, your kingdom has broken into our troubled world through the life, death, and resurrection of your Son. Help us to hear your word and obey it, and bring your saving love to fruition in our lives, through Jesus Christ, our Savior and Lord, who lives and reigns with you and the Holy Spirit, one God, now and forever.

Monday, March 25, 2019
Annunciation of Our Lord

Luke 1:26-38
The angel greets Mary

In the sixth month the angel Gabriel was sent by God to a town in Galilee called Nazareth, to a virgin engaged to a man whose name was Joseph, of the house of David. The virgin's name was Mary. And he came to her and said, "Greetings, favored one! The Lord is with you." But she was much perplexed by his words and pondered what sort of greeting this might be. The angel said to her, "Do not be afraid, Mary, for you have found favor with God. And now, you will conceive in your womb and bear a son, and you will name him Jesus." (Luke 1:26-31)

Psalm

Psalm 45
Your name will be remembered

Additional Readings

Isaiah 7:10-14
A young woman will bear a son

Hebrews 10:4-10
The offering of Jesus' body sanctifies us

Hymn: The Angel Gabriel from Heaven Came, ELW 265

Pour your grace into our hearts, O God, that we who have known the incarnation of your Son, Jesus Christ, announced by an angel, may by his cross and passion be brought to the glory of his resurrection; for he lives and reigns with you, in the unity of the Holy Spirit, one God, now and forever.

Tuesday, March 26, 2019
Week of Lent 3

Psalm 39
My hope is in God

"And now, O Lord, what do I wait for?
　　My hope is in you.
Deliver me from all my transgressions.
　　Do not make me the scorn of the fool.
I am silent; I do not open my mouth,
　　for it is you who have done it.
Remove your stroke from me;
　　I am worn down by the blows of your hand." (Ps. 39:7-10)

Additional Readings
Ezekiel 17:1-10
Allegory of the vine

Romans 2:12-16
What the law requires is written on the heart

Hymn: Salvation unto Us Has Come, ELW 590

Lord of hope, you deliver us from our sins and set us back on the path of righteousness. You correct us when we stray and guide us with your word. Help us keep your commandments in our hearts that we may follow your word.

Wednesday, March 27, 2019
Week of Lent 3

Numbers 13:17-27
The fruit of the promised land

Moses sent [men] to spy out the land of Canaan, and said to them, "Go up there into the Negeb, and go up into the hill country, and see what the land is like, and whether the people who live in it are strong or weak, whether they are few or many."

At the end of forty days they returned from spying out the land. And they came to Moses and Aaron and to all the congregation of the Israelites in the wilderness of Paran, at Kadesh; they brought back word to them and to all the congregation, and showed them the fruit of the land. And they told him, "We came to the land to which you sent us; it flows with milk and honey, and this is its fruit." (Num. 13:17-18, 25-27)

Psalm
Psalm 39
My hope is in God

Additional Reading
Luke 13:18-21
Parables of the mustard seed, yeast

Hymn: O Bread of Life from Heaven, ELW 480

Perfect God of blessings, just as you guided Israel through the wilderness, you guide us through our struggles. We praise you for your grace. Help us to keep our trust in you and set our sights on your calling.

Thursday, March 28, 2019
Week of Lent 3

Psalm 32
Be glad, you righteous

Happy are those whose transgression is forgiven,
    whose sin is covered.
Happy are those to whom the LORD imputes no iniquity,
    and in whose spirit there is no deceit.

Be glad in the LORD and rejoice, O righteous,
    and shout for joy, all you upright in heart. (Ps. 32:1-2, 11)

Additional Readings
Joshua 4:1-13
Joshua leads the people across the Jordan

2 Corinthians 4:16—5:5
Paul comforts with a promise of glory

Hymn: In All Our Grief, ELW 615

Holy Lord of heaven and earth, we rejoice in your glory and we shout with gladness for your mercy and forgiveness. Grant us joy as we follow your commands. Show us the perfect path so we may serve you with all our hearts.

Friday, March 29, 2019
Week of Lent 3

Hans Nielsen Hauge, renewer of the church, died 1824

2 Corinthians 5:6-15

Walking by faith and not by sight

So we are always confident; even though we know that while we are at home in the body we are away from the Lord—for we walk by faith, not by sight. Yes, we do have confidence, and we would rather be away from the body and at home with the Lord. So whether we are at home or away, we make it our aim to please him. For all of us must appear before the judgment seat of Christ, so that each may receive recompense for what has been done in the body, whether good or evil. (2 Cor. 5:6-10)

Psalm

Psalm 32
Be glad, you righteous

Additional Reading

Joshua 4:14-24
God's people come through the waters dry-shod

Hymn: We Walk by Faith, ELW 635

God, you are faithful in all things, and you are a fair and righteous judge. We worship you and thank you for all you have done for us. We humbly ask that you strengthen our spirits so we may stay strong in you.

Saturday, March 30, 2019
Week of Lent 3

Exodus 32:7-14

Moses begs forgiveness

Moses implored the L ORD his God, and said, "O L ORD, why does your wrath burn hot against your people, whom you brought out of the land of Egypt with great power and with a mighty hand? Why should the Egyptians say, 'It was with evil intent that he brought them out to kill them in the mountains, and to consume them from the face of the earth'? Turn from your fierce wrath; change your mind and do not bring disaster on your people. Remember Abraham, Isaac, and Israel, your servants, how you swore to them by your own self, saying to them, 'I will multiply your descendants like the stars of heaven, and all this land that I have promised I will give to your descendants, and they shall inherit it forever.' " And the L ORD changed his mind about the disaster that he planned to bring on his people. (Exod. 32:11-14)

Psalm

Psalm 32
Be glad, you righteous

Additional Reading

Luke 15:1-10
Parables of a lost sheep and a lost coin

Hymn: Come, Thou Fount of Every Blessing, ELW 807

Faithful and just Lord, you rule over all things. Just as you showed mercy to Israel, so also you show it to us. Help us never to stray from you. May we stand fast in your promises and heed your commandments.

Sunday, March 31, 2019
Fourth Sunday in Lent

John Donne, poet, died 1631

Luke 15:1-3, 11b-32
The parable of the forgiving father

[The elder son] answered his father, "Listen! For all these years I have been working like a slave for you, and I have never disobeyed your command; yet you have never given me even a young goat so that I might celebrate with my friends. But when this son of yours came back, who has devoured your property with prostitutes, you killed the fatted calf for him!" Then the father said to him, "Son, you are always with me, and all that is mine is yours. But we had to celebrate and rejoice, because this brother of yours was dead and has come to life; he was lost and has been found." (Luke 15:29-32)

Psalm
Psalm 32
Be glad, you righteous

Additional Readings
Joshua 5:9-12
Israel eats bread and grain

2 Corinthians 5:16-21
The mystery and ministry of reconciliation

Hymn: Our Father, We Have Wandered, ELW 606

God of compassion, you welcome the wayward, and you embrace us all with your mercy. By our baptism clothe us with garments of your grace, and feed us at the table of your love, through Jesus Christ, our Savior and Lord, who lives and reigns with you and the Holy Spirit, one God, now and forever.

Prayer List for April

Pray for mom that she becomes
a better Catholic

Pray for Leah and her
well-being

Pray for Angela and her
family

Pray for Amelia and her
emotional health

Pray for those going
through tough times

Monday, April 1, 2019
Week of Lent 4

Psalm 53
Restoring our fortunes

God looks down from heaven on humankind
    to see if there are any who are wise,
    who seek after God.

They have all fallen away, they are all alike perverse;
    there is no one who does good,
    no, not one.

O that deliverance for Israel would come from Zion!
    When God restores the fortunes of his people,
    Jacob will rejoice; Israel will be glad. (Ps. 53:2-3, 6)

Additional Readings
Leviticus 23:26-41
Days for confession and celebration

Revelation 19:1-8
The marriage supper of the Lamb

Hymn: Restore in Us, O God, ELW 328

Left to our own devices, O God, we pervert your wisdom, forgetting peace and refusing justice. Deliver us from our sins of action or inaction that we might celebrate with all your children the abundant fortune of life you desire for us.

Tuesday, April 2, 2019
Week of Lent 4

Revelation 19:9-10

Blessed are those invited to the marriage supper

And the angel said to me, "Write this: Blessed are those who are invited to the marriage supper of the Lamb." And he said to me, "These are true words of God." Then I fell down at his feet to worship him, but he said to me, "You must not do that! I am a fellow servant with you and your comrades who hold the testimony of Jesus. Worship God! For the testimony of Jesus is the spirit of prophecy." (Rev. 19:9-10)

Psalm

Psalm 53
Restoring our fortunes

Additional Reading

Leviticus 25:1-19
The jubilee celebration

Hymn: I Received the Living God, ELW 477

Holy God, you welcome us as guests to your feast of wholeness and life. Speak truth into our spirits and breathe life into our bones so we may worship you in our service to your kingdom.

Wednesday, April 3, 2019
Week of Lent 4

Luke 9:10-17
Jesus feeds 5000

The day was drawing to a close, and the twelve came to [Jesus] and said, "Send the crowd away, so that they may go into the surrounding villages and countryside, to lodge and get provisions; for we are here in a deserted place." But he said to them, "You give them something to eat." They said, "We have no more than five loaves and two fish—unless we are to go and buy food for all these people." For there were about five thousand men. And he said to his disciples, "Make them sit down in groups of about fifty each." They did so and made them all sit down. And taking the five loaves and the two fish, he looked up to heaven, and blessed and broke them, and gave them to the disciples to set before the crowd. And all ate and were filled. What was left over was gathered up, twelve baskets of broken pieces. (Luke 9:12-17)

Psalm
Psalm 53
Restoring our fortunes

Additional Reading
2 Kings 4:1-7
The widow saved

Hymn: You Satisfy the Hungry Heart, ELW 484

God of abundance, from five loaves and two fish you provided leftovers for all. Free us from lives of scarcity to see the resources that you grow in us, where there is enough for everyone.

Thursday, April 4, 2019
Week of Lent 4

Benedict the African, confessor, died 1589

Psalm 126
Sowing with tears, reaping with joy

Restore our fortunes, O LORD,
    like the watercourses in the Negeb.
May those who sow in tears
    reap with shouts of joy.
Those who go out weeping,
    bearing the seed for sowing,
shall come home with shouts of joy,
    carrying their sheaves. (Ps. 126:4-6)

Additional Readings
Isaiah 43:1-7
God will gather through fire and water

Philippians 2:19-24
Apostolic visits are promised

Hymn: As the Sun with Longer Journey, ELW 329

God of renewal, you till the soil of our mourning and bring forth deep rivers of joy. Give us tears to weep for the suffering, spirits overflowing with hope, and voices that shout in acts of love and service.

Friday, April 5, 2019
Week of Lent 4

Isaiah 43:8-15
God is Lord, Holy One, Creator, Ruler

I, I am the LORD,
>   and besides me there is no savior.
I declared and saved and proclaimed,
>   when there was no strange god among you;
>   and you are my witnesses, says the LORD.
I am God, and also henceforth I am He;
>   there is no one who can deliver from my hand;
>   I work and who can hinder it?

Thus says the LORD,
>   your Redeemer, the Holy One of Israel:
For your sake I will send to Babylon
>   and break down all the bars,
>   and the shouting of the Chaldeans will be turned to lamentation.
I am the LORD, your Holy One,
>   the Creator of Israel, your King. (Isa. 43:11-15)

Psalm
Psalm 126
Sowing with tears, reaping with joy

Additional Reading
Philippians 2:25—3:1
Paul praises a coworker

Hymn: Praise God, from Whom All Blessings Flow, ELW 884/885

Lord God, you alone can save us from our selfishness and ignorance. Redeem us from vain distraction and declare salvation for each of us that we might work with you for the freedom of all.

Saturday, April 6, 2019
Week of Lent 4

Albrecht Dürer, died 1528; Matthias Grünewald, died 1529; Lucas Cranach, died 1553; artists

Exodus 12:21-27
Passover instituted to celebrate the exodus

Then Moses called all the elders of Israel and said to them, "Go, select lambs for your families, and slaughter the passover lamb. Take a bunch of hyssop, dip it in the blood that is in the basin, and touch the lintel and the two doorposts with the blood in the basin. None of you shall go outside the door of your house until morning. For the LORD will pass through to strike down the Egyptians; when he sees the blood on the lintel and on the two doorposts, the LORD will pass over that door and will not allow the destroyer to enter your houses to strike you down. You shall observe this rite as a perpetual ordinance for you and your children. When you come to the land that the LORD will give you, as he has promised, you shall keep this observance." (Exod. 12:21-25)

Psalm
Psalm 126
Sowing with tears, reaping with joy

Additional Reading
John 11:45-57
Plotting against Jesus during Passover

Hymn: A Lamb Goes Uncomplaining Forth, ELW 340

God of the exodus, you freed your people from pharaoh and led them to promised land. We pray for the Jewish people, who first responded to your call of deliverance and freedom. May we all witness your shalom.

Sunday, April 7, 2019
Fifth Sunday in Lent

John 12:1-8
Mary anoints Jesus for his burial

Mary took a pound of costly perfume made of pure nard, anointed Jesus' feet, and wiped them with her hair. The house was filled with the fragrance of the perfume. But Judas Iscariot, one of his disciples (the one who was about to betray him), said, "Why was this perfume not sold for three hundred denarii and the money given to the poor?" (He said this not because he cared about the poor, but because he was a thief; he kept the common purse and used to steal what was put into it.) Jesus said, "Leave her alone. She bought it so that she might keep it for the day of my burial." (John 12:3-7)

Psalm
Psalm 126
Sowing with tears, reaping with joy

Additional Readings
Isaiah 43:16-21
The Lord gives water in the wilderness

Philippians 3:4b-14
To know Christ and his resurrection

Hymn: Take My Life, That I May Be, ELW 685

Creator God, you prepare a new way in the wilderness, and your grace waters our desert. Open our hearts to be transformed by the new thing you are doing, that our lives may proclaim the extravagance of your love given to all through your Son, Jesus Christ, our Savior and Lord, who lives and reigns with you and the Holy Spirit, one God, now and forever.

Monday, April 8, 2019
Week of Lent 5

Psalm 20
Victory for God's anointed

Now I know that the LORD will help his anointed;
    he will answer him from his holy heaven
    with mighty victories by his right hand.
Some take pride in chariots, and some in horses,
    but our pride is in the name of the LORD our God.
They will collapse and fall,
    but we shall rise and stand upright.

Give victory to the king, O LORD;
    answer us when we call. (Ps. 20:6-9)

Additional Readings
Exodus 40:1-15
Anointing the holy things

Hebrews 10:19-25
Jesus, priest for the people of God

Hymn: Jesus Is a Rock in a Weary Land, ELW 333

Dear God, pride is traded like currency in our world. Ground us in our baptismal identity that we may rise in you and find our pride in the well-being of our neighbors.

Tuesday, April 9, 2019
Week of Lent 5

Dietrich Bonhoeffer, theologian, died 1945

1 John 2:18-28
Knowing the Son

Let what you heard from the beginning abide in you. If what you heard from the beginning abides in you, then you will abide in the Son and in the Father. And this is what he has promised us, eternal life.

I write these things to you concerning those who would deceive you. As for you, the anointing that you received from him abides in you, and so you do not need anyone to teach you. But as his anointing teaches you about all things, and is true and is not a lie, and just as it has taught you, abide in him.

And now, little children, abide in him, so that when he is revealed we may have confidence and not be put to shame before him at his coming. (1 John 2:24-28)

Psalm
Psalm 20
Victory for God's anointed

Additional Reading
Judges 9:7-15
Anointing the bramble

Hymn: Now We Remain, ELW 500

Everlasting God, the gift of faith resides in our muscles and sinews through the power of your Spirit. Give us confidence in Christ so that we may embody your promise of life eternal.

Wednesday, April 10, 2019
Week of Lent 5

Mikael Agricola, Bishop of Turku, died 1557

Luke 18:31-34
Jesus foretells his death

Then [Jesus] took the twelve aside and said to them, "See, we are going up to Jerusalem, and everything that is written about the Son of Man by the prophets will be accomplished. For he will be handed over to the Gentiles; and he will be mocked and insulted and spat upon. After they have flogged him, they will kill him, and on the third day he will rise again." But they understood nothing about all these things; in fact, what he said was hidden from them, and they did not grasp what was said. (Luke 18:31-34)

Psalm
Psalm 20
Victory for God's anointed

Additional Reading
Habakkuk 3:2-15
God will save the anointed

Hymn: Jesus, I Will Ponder Now, ELW 345

Lord God, we misunderstand your promises daily by repeating the mockery and insult that you endured in Jesus Christ. Give us faith so we might trust your words and offer kindness and love to our neighbors in need.

Thursday, April 11, 2019
Week of Lent 5

Psalm 31:9-16
I commend my spirit

Be gracious to me, O Lord, for I am in distress;
      my eye wastes away from grief,
      my soul and body also.
For my life is spent with sorrow,
      and my years with sighing;
my strength fails because of my misery,
      and my bones waste away.

But I trust in you, O Lord;
      I say, "You are my God."
My times are in your hand;
      deliver me from the hand of my enemies and persecutors.
Let your face shine upon your servant;
      save me in your steadfast love. (Ps. 31:9-10, 14-16)

Additional Readings
Isaiah 53:10-12
The suffering one bears the sin of many

Hebrews 2:1-9
God's care for humankind

Hymn: Day by Day, ELW 790

You are our God who comforts us in sorrow and fortifies our bodies in distress. In our despair, grant us trust; in longing, offer hope; in oppression, deliver us. Ground us in steadfast love and comfort all whose sorrow seems endless.

Friday, April 12, 2019
Week of Lent 5

Isaiah 54:9-10

God's love is steadfast

This is like the days of Noah to me:
    Just as I swore that the waters of Noah
    would never again go over the earth,
so I have sworn that I will not be angry with you
    and will not rebuke you.
For the mountains may depart
    and the hills be removed,
but my steadfast love shall not depart from you,
    and my covenant of peace shall not be removed,
    says the LORD, who has compassion on you. (Isa. 54:9-10)

Psalm
Psalm 31:9-16
I commend my spirit

Additional Reading
Hebrews 2:10-18
Jesus' suffering binds him to humankind

Hymn: If You But Trust in God to Guide You, ELW 769

Eternal God, your promise persists, though the earth shakes and the peoples tremble. Renew your peace for us as we are ambassadors of your steadfast love for all.

Saturday, April 13, 2019
Week of Lent 5

Leviticus 23:1-8

Sabbath and passover

The Lord spoke to Moses, saying: Speak to the people of Israel and say to them: These are the appointed festivals of the Lord that you shall proclaim as holy convocations, my appointed festivals.

Six days shall work be done; but the seventh day is a sabbath of complete rest, a holy convocation; you shall do no work: it is a sabbath to the Lord throughout your settlements. (Lev. 23:1-3)

Psalm
Psalm 31:9-16
I commend my spirit

Additional Reading
Luke 22:1-13
Jesus prepares for Passover with his disciples

Hymn: O Day of Rest and Gladness, ELW 521

God of peace, you ordained the sabbath to return your people to humanity. When your work is done, breathe in us the rest of your Spirit and life abundant. Bless our labors with the dignity you desire for all your children.

Holy Week

On the Sunday of the Passion, Christians enter into Holy Week. This day opens before the Christian community the final period of preparation before the celebration of the Three Days of the Lord's passion, death, and resurrection.

In many churches, palm branches will be given to worshipers for the procession into the worship space. Following an ancient custom, many Christians bring their palms home and place them in the household prayer center, behind a cross or sacred image, or above the indoor lintel of the entryway.

At sunset on Maundy Thursday, Lent comes to an end as the church begins the celebration of the events through which Christ has become the life and the resurrection for all who believe.

Prayer for Placing Palms in the Home

Use this blessing when placing palms in the home after the Palm Sunday liturgy.

Blessed is the one who comes in the name of the Lord!
May we who place these palms receive Christ into our midst
with the joy that marked the entrance to Jerusalem.
May we hold no betrayal in our hearts,
but peacefully welcome Christ
who lives and reigns with you and the Holy Spirit,
one God, now and forever. Amen.

Sunday, April 14, 2019
Sunday of the Passion
Palm Sunday

Luke 22:14—23:56

The passion and death of Jesus

Pilate, wanting to release Jesus, addressed [the chief priests, the leaders, and the people] again; but they kept shouting, "Crucify, crucify him!" A third time he said to them, "Why, what evil has he done? I have found in him no ground for the sentence of death; I will therefore have him flogged and then release him." But they kept urgently demanding with loud shouts that he should be crucified; and their voices prevailed. So Pilate gave his verdict that their demand should be granted. He released the man they asked for, the one who had been put in prison for insurrection and murder, and he handed Jesus over as they wished. (Luke 23:20-25)

Psalm
Psalm 31:9-16
I commend my spirit

Additional Readings
Isaiah 50:4-9a
The servant submits to suffering

Philippians 2:5-11
Death on a cross

Hymn: My Song Is Love Unknown, ELW 343

Everlasting God, in your endless love for the human race you sent our Lord Jesus Christ to take on our nature and to suffer death on the cross. In your mercy enable us to share in his obedience to your will and in the glorious victory of his resurrection, who lives and reigns with you and the Holy Spirit, one God, now and forever.

Monday, April 15, 2019
Monday in Holy Week

Psalm 36:5-11
Refuge under the shadow of your wings

Your steadfast love, O LORD, extends to the heavens,
    your faithfulness to the clouds.
Your righteousness is like the mighty mountains,
    your judgments are like the great deep;
    you save humans and animals alike, O LORD.

How precious is your steadfast love, O God!
    All people may take refuge in the shadow of your wings.
They feast on the abundance of your house,
    and you give them drink from the river of your delights.
For with you is the fountain of life;
    in your light we see light. (Ps. 36:5-9)

Additional Readings

Isaiah 42:1-9
The servant brings forth justice

Hebrews 9:11-15
The blood of Christ redeems for eternal life

John 12:1-11
Mary of Bethany anoints Jesus

Hymn: Lord, Thee I Love with All My Heart, ELW 750

O God, your Son chose the path that led to pain before joy and to the cross before glory. Plant his cross in our hearts, so that in its power and love we may come at last to joy and glory, through Jesus Christ, our Savior and Lord, who lives and reigns with you and the Holy Spirit, one God, now and forever.

Tuesday, April 16, 2019
Tuesday in Holy Week

Isaiah 49:1-7
The servant brings salvation to earth's ends

And now the Lord says,
>who formed me in the womb to be his servant,
to bring Jacob back to him,
>and that Israel might be gathered to him,
for I am honored in the sight of the Lord,
>and my God has become my strength—
he says,
"It is too light a thing that you should be my servant
>to raise up the tribes of Jacob
>and to restore the survivors of Israel;
I will give you as a light to the nations,
>that my salvation may reach to the end of the earth." (Isa. 49:5-6)

Psalm

Psalm 71:1-14
From my mother's womb you have been my strength

Additional Readings

1 Corinthians 1:18-31
The cross of Christ reveals God's power and wisdom

John 12:20-36
Jesus speaks of his death

Hymn: Will You Let Me Be Your Servant, ELW 659

Lord Jesus, you have called us to follow you. Grant that our love may not grow cold in your service, and that we may not fail or deny you in the time of trial, for you live and reign with the Father and the Holy Spirit, one God, now and forever.

Wednesday, April 17, 2019
Wednesday in Holy Week

Hebrews 12:1-3

Look to Jesus, who endured the cross

Therefore, since we are surrounded by so great a cloud of witnesses, let us also lay aside every weight and the sin that clings so closely, and let us run with perseverance the race that is set before us, looking to Jesus the pioneer and perfecter of our faith, who for the sake of the joy that was set before him endured the cross, disregarding its shame, and has taken his seat at the right hand of the throne of God.

Consider him who endured such hostility against himself from sinners, so that you may not grow weary or lose heart. (Heb. 12:1-3)

Psalm

Psalm 70
Be pleased, O God, to deliver me

Additional Readings

Isaiah 50:4-9a
The servant is vindicated by God

John 13:21-32
Jesus foretells his betrayal

Hymn: Beneath the Cross of Jesus, ELW 338

Almighty God, your Son our Savior suffered at human hands and endured the shame of the cross. Grant that we may walk in the way of his cross and find it the way of life and peace, through Jesus Christ, our Savior and Lord, who lives and reigns with you and the Holy Spirit, one God, now and forever.

The Three Days

As the sun sets on Maundy Thursday, so Lent ends and the Three Days begin, ending with sunset on Easter Day. During these central days, Christians prepare to celebrate God's gift of new life given in baptism. Indeed, the readings of the Three Days move toward the baptismal font where new brothers and sisters are born of water and the Spirit, and where the baptized renew their baptismal promises.

In the home and in the church community, special attention is given to these days through prayer and keeping greater silence until the great Vigil of Easter is celebrated. Many Christians keep a fast from food, work, and entertainment on Good Friday and Holy Saturday. In the home, preparations can be made for the celebration of Easter: cleaning, coloring eggs, baking Easter breads, gathering greens or flowers to adorn crosses and sacred images. In those communities where baptisms will be celebrated, prayers may be offered for those to be received into the church.

Table Prayer for the Three Days

Blessed are you, O Lord our God.
With this food strengthen us on our journey from death to life.
We glory in the cross of Christ.
Raise us, with him, to the joy of the resurrection,
through Jesus Christ our Lord. Amen.

Thursday, April 18, 2019
Maundy Thursday

Exodus 12:1-4 [5-10] 11-14
The passover of the Lord

Tell the whole congregation of Israel that on the tenth of this month they are to take a lamb for each family, a lamb for each household.

This is how you shall eat it: your loins girded, your sandals on your feet, and your staff in your hand; and you shall eat it hurriedly. It is the passover of the LORD. For I will pass through the land of Egypt that night, and I will strike down every firstborn in the land of Egypt, both human beings and animals; on all the gods of Egypt I will execute judgments: I am the LORD. The blood shall be a sign for you on the houses where you live: when I see the blood, I will pass over you, and no plague shall destroy you when I strike the land of Egypt. (Exod. 12:3, 11-13)

Psalm
Psalm 116:1-2, 12-19
The cup of salvation

Additional Readings
1 Corinthians 11:23-26
Proclaim the Lord's death

John 13:1-17, 31b-35
The service of Christ: footwashing and meal

Hymn: Where Charity and Love Prevail, ELW 359

Eternal God, in the sharing of a meal your Son established a new covenant for all people, and in the washing of feet he showed us the dignity of service. Grant that by the power of your Holy Spirit these signs of our life in faith may speak again to our hearts, feed our spirits, and refresh our bodies, through Jesus Christ, our Savior and Lord, who lives and reigns with you and the Holy Spirit, one God, now and forever.

Friday, April 19, 2019
Good Friday

Olavus Petri, priest, died 1552; Laurentius Petri, Bishop of Uppsala, died 1573; renewers of the church

John 18:1—19:42
The passion and death of Jesus

Joseph of Arimathea, who was a disciple of Jesus, though a secret one because of his fear of the Jews, asked Pilate to let him take away the body of Jesus. Pilate gave him permission; so he came and removed his body. Nicodemus, who had at first come to Jesus by night, also came, bringing a mixture of myrrh and aloes, weighing about a hundred pounds. They took the body of Jesus and wrapped it with the spices in linen cloths, according to the burial custom of the Jews. Now there was a garden in the place where he was crucified, and in the garden there was a new tomb in which no one had ever been laid. And so, because it was the Jewish day of Preparation, and the tomb was nearby, they laid Jesus there. (John 19:38-42)

Psalm

Psalm 22
Why have you forsaken me?

Additional Readings

Isaiah 52:13—53:12
The suffering servant

Hebrews 10:16-25
The way to God is opened

Hymn: There in God's Garden, ELW 342

Merciful God, your Son was lifted up on the cross to draw all people to himself. Grant that we who have been born out of his wounded side may at all times find mercy in him, Jesus Christ, our Savior and Lord, who lives and reigns with you and the Holy Spirit, one God, now and forever.

Saturday, April 20, 2019

Resurrection of Our Lord
Vigil of Easter

Romans 6:3-11

Dying and rising with Christ

Do you not know that all of us who have been baptized into Christ Jesus were baptized into his death? Therefore we have been buried with him by baptism into death, so that, just as Christ was raised from the dead by the glory of the Father, so we too might walk in newness of life.

For if we have been united with him in a death like his, we will certainly be united with him in a resurrection like his. (Rom. 6:3-5)

Psalm

Psalm 46
The God of Jacob is our stronghold

Additional Readings

Genesis 7:1-5, 11-18; 8:6-18; 9:8-13
Flood

John 20:1-18
Seeing the risen Christ

Hymn: Come, You Faithful, Raise the Strain, ELW 363

O God, you are the creator of the world, the liberator of your people, and the wisdom of the earth. By the resurrection of your Son free us from our fears, restore us in your image, and ignite us with your light, through Jesus Christ, our Savior and Lord, who lives and reigns with you and the Holy Spirit, one God, now and forever.

Sunday, April 21, 2019
Resurrection of Our Lord
Easter Day

Anselm, Bishop of Canterbury, died 1109

Luke 24:1-12
Women proclaim the resurrection

On the first day of the week, at early dawn, the women came to the tomb, taking the spices that they had prepared. They found the stone rolled away from the tomb, but when they went in, they did not find the body. While they were perplexed about this, suddenly two men in dazzling clothes stood beside them. The women were terrified and bowed their faces to the ground, but the men said to them, "Why do you look for the living among the dead? He is not here, but has risen. Remember how he told you, while he was still in Galilee, that the Son of Man must be handed over to sinners, and be crucified, and on the third day rise again." Then they remembered his words, and returning from the tomb, they told all this to the eleven and to all the rest. (Luke 24:1-9)

Psalm
Psalm 118:1-2, 14-24
On this day God has acted

Additional Readings
Acts 10:34-43
God raised Jesus on the third day

1 Corinthians 15:19-26
Christ raised from the dead

Hymn: Now All the Vault of Heaven Resounds, ELW 367

God of mercy, we no longer look for Jesus among the dead, for he is alive and has become the Lord of life. Increase in our minds and hearts the risen life we share with Christ, and help us to grow as your people toward the fullness of eternal life with you, through Jesus Christ, our Savior and Lord, who lives and reigns with you and the Holy Spirit, one God, now and forever.

Easter

The Three Days flow into the rejoicing of the fifty days of Easter. During this "week of weeks," Christians explore the meaning of the central actions of baptism for daily life: the renouncing of evil and the professing of faith, washing in water, being marked with the cross, clothing in the white robe, receiving the light of the paschal/Easter candle, and eating and drinking the bread of life and the cup of salvation.

The fifty days were once called *Pentecost*, Greek for "fifty." On the fiftieth day of Easter, Christians celebrate the pentecostal mystery of the risen Christ breathing on the church the breath, the wind, and the fire of the Holy Spirit.

Table Prayer for the Season of Easter

O God of our risen Lord, we praise you, we bless you,
we worship you for the gifts of life you give us.
Always you offer us life, and for this we bless your holy name.
And we ask you,
give your life also to all who know only hunger and the pangs of death.
So may the whole world be raised to life,
through Jesus Christ, our Savior and Lord. Amen.

Monday, April 22, 2019
Week of Easter 1

Psalm 118:1-2, 14-24
On this day God has acted

I thank you that you have answered me
    and have become my salvation.
The stone that the builders rejected
    has become the chief cornerstone.
This is the LORD's doing;
    it is marvelous in our eyes.
This is the day that the LORD has made;
    let us rejoice and be glad in it. (Ps. 118:21-24)

Additional Readings
Joshua 10:16-27
Joshua defeats five kings

1 Corinthians 5:6b-8
Celebrating with sincerity and truth

Hymn: Christ Is Made the Sure Foundation, ELW 645

Lord God, we rejoice in this day because you made it. You answer when we call, and you build us into your people. Give us joy in our daily endeavors so we may be glad in all you provide.

Tuesday, April 23, 2019
Week of Easter 1

Toyohiko Kagawa, renewer of society, died 1960

Revelation 12:1-12

The woman, the dragon, the child

War broke out in heaven; Michael and his angels fought against the dragon. The dragon and his angels fought back, but they were defeated, and there was no longer any place for them in heaven. The great dragon was thrown down, that ancient serpent, who is called the Devil and Satan, the deceiver of the whole world—he was thrown down to the earth, and his angels were thrown down with him. (Rev. 12:7-9)

Psalm
Psalm 118:1-2, 14-24
On this day God has acted

Additional Reading
Judges 4:17-23; 5:24-31a
Jael kills Sisera

Hymn: At the Lamb's High Feast We Sing, ELW 362

Almighty God, in the resurrection of Christ you defeated the devil and all his empty promises. We renounce the deceits of this world and long to grasp your vision of a new kingdom of peace. Give us a glimpse of eternity so we may step into your promise of life everlasting.

Wednesday, April 24, 2019
Week of Easter 1

2 Samuel 6:1-15

David dances before the ark

It was told King David, "The LORD has blessed the household of Obed-edom and all that belongs to him, because of the ark of God." So David went and brought up the ark of God from the house of Obed-edom to the city of David with rejoicing; and when those who bore the ark of the LORD had gone six paces, he sacrificed an ox and a fatling. David danced before the LORD with all his might; David was girded with a linen ephod. So David and all the house of Israel brought up the ark of the LORD with shouting, and with the sound of the trumpet. (2 Sam. 6:12-15)

Psalm

Psalm 118:1-2, 14-24
On this day God has acted

Additional Reading

Luke 24:1-12
Women proclaim the resurrection

Hymn: Oh, Sing to the Lord, ELW 822

Living God, the whole earth rejoices in your presence. We dance before you because you have provided for us. May all our movements participate in your vision of hope for all creation.

Thursday, April 25, 2019
Mark, Evangelist

Mark 1:1-15

The beginning of the gospel of Jesus Christ

The beginning of the good news of Jesus Christ, the Son of God.
　　As it is written in the prophet Isaiah,
　　　　"See, I am sending my messenger ahead of you,
　　　　　　who will prepare your way;
　　　　the voice of one crying out in the wilderness:
　　　　　　'Prepare the way of the Lord,
　　　　　　make his paths straight,'"
John the baptizer appeared in the wilderness, proclaiming a baptism
of repentance for the forgiveness of sins. And people from the whole
Judean countryside and all the people of Jerusalem were going out to
him, and were baptized by him in the river Jordan, confessing their
sins. (Mark 1:1-5)

Psalm

Psalm 57
Be merciful to me, O God

Additional Readings

Isaiah 52:7-10
*The messenger announces
salvation*

2 Timothy 4:6-11, 18
The good fight of faith

Hymn: When Jesus Came to Jordan, ELW 305

*Almighty God, you have enriched your church with Mark's proclamation of
the gospel. Give us grace to believe firmly in the good news of salvation and
to walk daily in accord with it, through Jesus Christ, our Savior and Lord,
who lives and reigns with you and the Holy Spirit, one God, now and forever.*

Friday, April 26, 2019
Week of Easter 1

Psalm 150
Let everything praise the Lord

Praise the LORD!
Praise God in his sanctuary;
      praise him in his mighty firmament!
Praise him for his mighty deeds;
      praise him according to his surpassing greatness!

Praise him with trumpet sound;
      praise him with lute and harp!
Praise him with tambourine and dance;
      praise him with strings and pipe!
Praise him with clanging cymbals;
      praise him with loud clashing cymbals!
Let everything that breathes praise the LORD!
Praise the LORD! (Ps. 150:1-6)

Additional Readings
1 Samuel 17:19-32
David announces he will fight Goliath

Acts 5:17-26
The apostles freed from prison

Hymn: With High Delight Let Us Unite, ELW 368

God of new creation, you are bending the world to resurrection, and we are witnesses to your mighty acts. Surprise us in our daily labor with the simple beauty of your creation so we might sing of your goodness with every breath.

Saturday, April 27, 2019
Week of Easter 1

1 Samuel 17:32-51

David conquers Goliath

When the Philistine drew nearer to meet David, David ran quickly toward the battle line to meet the Philistine. David put his hand in his bag, took out a stone, slung it, and struck the Philistine on his forehead; the stone sank into his forehead, and he fell face down on the ground.

So David prevailed over the Philistine with a sling and a stone, striking down the Philistine and killing him; there was no sword in David's hand. Then David ran and stood over the Philistine; he grasped his sword, drew it out of its sheath, and killed him; then he cut off his head with it.

When the Philistines saw that their champion was dead, they fled. (1 Sam. 17:48-51)

Psalm

Psalm 150
Let everything praise the Lord

Additional Reading

Luke 24:36-40
Beholding the wounds of the risen Christ

Hymn: Thine Is the Glory, ELW 376

Lord God, in the resurrection of Christ you announce your defeat of the Goliaths of the world. Whether we are in places of influence or humble vocations, strengthen us so we may tell truth to power and strike down oppressors.

Sunday, April 28, 2019
Second Sunday of Easter

John 20:19-31

Beholding the wounds of the risen Christ

A week later [Jesus'] disciples were again in the house, and Thomas was with them. Although the doors were shut, Jesus came and stood among them and said, "Peace be with you." Then he said to Thomas, "Put your finger here and see my hands. Reach out your hand and put it in my side. Do not doubt but believe." Thomas answered him, "My Lord and my God!" Jesus said to him, "Have you believed because you have seen me? Blessed are those who have not seen and yet have come to believe." (John 20:26-29)

Psalm

Psalm 118:14-29
Glad songs of victory

Additional Readings

Acts 5:27-32
The God of our ancestors raised up Jesus

Revelation 1:4-8
Jesus Christ, firstborn of the dead

Hymn: The Risen Christ, ELW 390

O God of life, you reach out to us amid our fears with the wounded hands of your risen Son. By your Spirit's breath revive our faith in your mercy, and strengthen us to be the body of your Son, Jesus Christ, our Savior and Lord, who lives and reigns with you and the Holy Spirit, one God, now and forever.

Monday, April 29, 2019
Week of Easter 2

Catherine of Siena, theologian, died 1380

Psalm 122
Peace in Jerusalem

I was glad when they said to me,
>"Let us go to the house of the LORD!"
Our feet are standing
>within your gates, O Jerusalem.

Pray for the peace of Jerusalem:
>"May they prosper who love you.
Peace be within your walls,
>and security within your towers."
For the sake of my relatives and friends
>I will say, "Peace be within you." (Ps. 122:1-2, 6-8)

Additional Readings
Esther 7:1-10
Esther prevails over Haman

Revelation 1:9-20
A vision of Christ

Hymn: Grant Peace, We Pray, in Mercy, Lord, ELW 784

God of homecoming, you welcome your people into your church. In our interactions with others, give us your peace and your understanding so we might build communities of trust and reconciliation.

Tuesday, April 30, 2019
Week of Easter 2

Esther 8:1-17
Destruction of the Jews is averted

Then Mordecai went out from the presence of the king, wearing royal robes of blue and white, with a great golden crown and a mantle of fine linen and purple, while the city of Susa shouted and rejoiced. For the Jews there was light and gladness, joy and honor. In every province and in every city, wherever the king's command and his edict came, there was gladness and joy among the Jews, a festival and a holiday. Furthermore, many of the peoples of the country professed to be Jews, because the fear of the Jews had fallen upon them. (Esther 8:15-17)

Psalm
Psalm 122
Peace in Jerusalem

Additional Reading
Revelation 2:8-11
Words to the church at Smyrna

Hymn: Sing Praise to God, the Highest Good, ELW 871

Lord God, you emboldened Esther to stand for her people. Fortify us to profess your expectation of justice for all and equip us to be ambassadors of your peace.

Prayer List for May

Pray for Amelia

Pray for those who are suffering from the loss of a loved one

Pray for those who are ill

Pray for my family and friends

Pray for those who are victims of abuse or bullying

Pray for those who are lonely

Pray for those in need

Wednesday, May 1, 2019
Philip and James, Apostles

John 14:8-14
The Son and the Father are one

Philip said to [Jesus], "Lord, show us the Father, and we will be satisfied." Jesus said to him, "Have I been with you all this time, Philip, and you still do not know me? Whoever has seen me has seen the Father. How can you say, 'Show us the Father'? Do you not believe that I am in the Father and the Father is in me? The words that I say to you I do not speak on my own; but the Father who dwells in me does his works." (John 14:8-10)

Psalm
Psalm 44:1-3, 20-26
Save us for the sake of your love

Additional Readings
Isaiah 30:18-21
God's mercy and justice

2 Corinthians 4:1-6
Proclaiming Jesus Christ as Lord

Hymn: God, Whose Almighty Word, ELW 673

Almighty God, you gave to your apostles Philip and James grace and strength to bear witness to your Son. Grant that we, remembering their victory of faith, may glorify in life and death the name of our Lord Jesus Christ, who lives and reigns with you and the Holy Spirit, one God, now and forever.

Thursday, May 2, 2019
Week of Easter 2

Athanasius, Bishop of Alexandria, died 373

Psalm 30
My wailing turns to dancing

I will extol you, O LORD, for you have drawn me up,
    and did not let my foes rejoice over me.
O LORD my God, I cried to you for help,
    and you have healed me.
O LORD, you brought up my soul from Sheol,
    restored me to life from among those gone down to the Pit.
(Ps. 30:1-3)

Additional Readings
Isaiah 5:11-17
Appetites that lead to hunger

Revelation 3:14-22
Words to the church at Laodicea

Hymn: All Glory Be to God on High, ELW 410

O Lord, you know how often we call out to you in times of need and distress. Thank you for hearing our prayers of help. Give us an awareness of your saving presence always.

Friday, May 3, 2019
Week of Easter 2

Isaiah 6:1-4
Heaven's holy, holy, holy

In the year that King Uzziah died, I saw the Lord sitting on a throne, high and lofty; and the hem of his robe filled the temple. Seraphs were in attendance above him; each had six wings: with two they covered their faces, and with two they covered their feet, and with two they flew. And one called to another and said:

"Holy, holy, holy is the LORD of hosts;
the whole earth is full of his glory."

The pivots on the thresholds shook at the voices of those who called, and the house filled with smoke. (Isa. 6:1-4)

Psalm
Psalm 30
My wailing turns to dancing

Additional Reading
Revelation 4:1-11
Heaven's holy, holy, holy

Hymn: You Are Holy, ELW 525

Holy are you, Lord of hosts. Your glory is present in all places throughout the whole earth. Empower us to see your presence all around us in every person, creature, and place.

Saturday, May 4, 2019
Week of Easter 2

Monica, mother of Augustine, died 387

Genesis 18:1-8
Abraham and Sarah's hospitality to the Lord

The LORD appeared to Abraham by the oaks of Mamre, as he sat at the entrance of his tent in the heat of the day. He looked up and saw three men standing near him. When he saw them, he ran from the tent entrance to meet them, and bowed down to the ground. He said, "My lord, if I find favor with you, do not pass by your servant. Let a little water be brought, and wash your feet, and rest yourselves under the tree. Let me bring a little bread, that you may refresh yourselves, and after that you may pass on—since you have come to your servant." So they said, "Do as you have said." (Gen. 18:1-5)

Psalm
Psalm 30
My wailing turns to dancing

Additional Reading
Luke 14:12-14
Welcome those in need to your table

Hymn: Let Us Talents and Tongues Employ, ELW 674

Lord God, you come to us in unexpected ways through a rich variety of people. Help us to welcome you in the people who cross our paths every day.

Sunday, May 5, 2019
Third Sunday of Easter

John 21:1-19
Jesus appears to the disciples

When [the disciples] had finished breakfast, Jesus said to Simon Peter, "Simon son of John, do you love me more than these?" He said to him, "Yes, Lord; you know that I love you." Jesus said to him, "Feed my lambs." A second time he said to him, "Simon son of John, do you love me?" He said to him, "Yes, Lord; you know that I love you." Jesus said to him, "Tend my sheep." He said to him the third time, "Simon son of John, do you love me?" Peter felt hurt because he said to him the third time, "Do you love me?" And he said to him, "Lord, you know everything; you know that I love you." Jesus said to him, "Feed my sheep. Very truly, I tell you, when you were younger, you used to fasten your own belt and to go wherever you wished. But when you grow old, you will stretch out your hands, and someone else will fasten a belt around you and take you where you do not wish to go." (He said this to indicate the kind of death by which he would glorify God.) After this he said to him, "Follow me." (John 21:15-19)

Psalm

Psalm 30
My wailing turns to dancing

Additional Readings

Acts 9:1-6 [7-20]
Paul's conversion, baptism, and preaching

Revelation 5:11-14
The song of the living creatures to the Lamb

Hymn: God Is Here! ELW 526

Eternal and all-merciful God, with all the angels and all the saints we laud your majesty and might. By the resurrection of your Son, show yourself to us and inspire us to follow Jesus Christ, our Savior and Lord, who lives and reigns with you and the Holy Spirit, one God, now and forever.

Monday, May 6, 2019
Week of Easter 3

Psalm 121
God will preserve your life

The LORD is your keeper;
>   the LORD is your shade at your right hand.
The sun shall not strike you by day,
>   nor the moon by night.

The LORD will keep you from all evil;
>   he will keep your life.
The LORD will keep
>   your going out and your coming in
>   from this time on and forevermore. (Ps. 121:5-8)

Additional Readings
Ezekiel 1:1-25
Ezekiel's vision of four living creatures

Acts 9:19b-31
Saul joins the apostles in Jerusalem

Hymn: To You, before the Close of Day, ELW 567

Great keeper of our lives, you persist in holding on to us no matter where the changes of life take us. Be in our hearts and minds throughout this day.

Tuesday, May 7, 2019
Week of Easter 3

Ezekiel 1:26—2:1

Ezekiel's vision of God's glory

And above the dome over their heads there was something like a throne, in appearance like sapphire; and seated above the likeness of a throne was something that seemed like a human form. Upward from what appeared like the loins I saw something like gleaming amber, something that looked like fire enclosed all around; and downward from what looked like the loins I saw something that looked like fire, and there was a splendor all around. Like the bow in a cloud on a rainy day, such was the appearance of the splendor all around. This was the appearance of the likeness of the glory of the LORD.

When I saw it, I fell on my face, and I heard the voice of someone speaking.

He said to me: O mortal, stand up on your feet, and I will speak with you. (Ezek. 1:26—2:1)

Psalm

Psalm 121
God will preserve your life

Additional Reading

Acts 26:1-18
Paul preaches before Agrippa

Hymn: Let All Mortal Flesh Keep Silence, ELW 490

Gracious God, your glory is too wonderful for us to imagine, and yet you speak to us and come among us. Grant us ears to hear you, hearts to love you, and faithfulness to do your will.

Wednesday, May 8, 2019
Week of Easter 3

Julian of Norwich, renewer of the church, died around 1416

Luke 5:1-11
Simon's catch of fish

Once while Jesus was standing beside the lake of Gennesaret, and the crowd was pressing in on him to hear the word of God, he saw two boats there at the shore of the lake; the fishermen had gone out of them and were washing their nets. He got into one of the boats, the one belonging to Simon, and asked him to put out a little way from the shore. Then he sat down and taught the crowds from the boat. When he had finished speaking, he said to Simon, "Put out into the deep water and let down your nets for a catch." Simon answered, "Master, we have worked all night long but have caught nothing. Yet if you say so, I will let down the nets." When they had done this, they caught so many fish that their nets were beginning to break. (Luke 5:1-6)

Psalm
Psalm 121
God will preserve your life

Additional Reading
Isaiah 6:1-8
Isaiah in the presence of God

Hymn: Praise, Praise! You Are My Rock, ELW 862

O God, you call us to follow, but we often have excuses for not doing so. Remind us of your faith in us and give us the strength to follow you when we are reluctant.

Thursday, May 9, 2019
Week of Easter 3

Nicolaus Ludwig von Zinzendorf, renewer of the church, hymnwriter, died 1760

Psalm 23
God our shepherd

The LORD is my shepherd, I shall not want.
> He makes me lie down in green pastures;
he leads me beside still waters;
> he restores my soul.
He leads me in right paths
> for his name's sake.

Even though I walk through the darkest valley,
> I fear no evil;
for you are with me;
> your rod and your staff—
> they comfort me. (Ps. 23:1-4)

Additional Readings
Ezekiel 11:1-25
Ezekiel prophesies against the shepherds of Israel

Revelation 5:1-10
The throne and the elders

Hymn: The Lord's My Shepherd, ELW 778

Shepherding God, you are with us through every moment of our lives. You provide for us and lead us. Give us such a sense of your constant care that we trust your presence in good times and bad.

Friday, May 10, 2019
Week of Easter 3

Revelation 6:1—7:4
The servants of God are sealed

After this I saw four angels standing at the four corners of the earth, holding back the four winds of the earth so that no wind could blow on earth or sea or against any tree. I saw another angel ascending from the rising of the sun, having the seal of the living God, and he called with a loud voice to the four angels who had been given power to damage earth and sea, saying, "Do not damage the earth or the sea or the trees, until we have marked the servants of our God with a seal on their foreheads."

And I heard the number of those who were sealed, one hundred forty-four thousand, sealed out of every tribe of the people of Israel. (Rev. 7:1-4)

Psalm
Psalm 23
God our shepherd

Additional Reading
Ezekiel 20:39-44
God will gather the scattered people

Hymn: Lift High the Cross, ELW 660

Living God, the whole world is beautiful and full of your glory. Grant us wisdom to recognize the damage our actions have brought to your creation and grant us the patience and compassion to restore it.

Saturday, May 11, 2019
Week of Easter 3

Ezekiel 28:25-26

God gathers the people into safety

Thus says the Lord GOD: When I gather the house of Israel from the peoples among whom they are scattered, and manifest my holiness in them in the sight of the nations, then they shall settle on their own soil that I gave to my servant Jacob. They shall live in safety in it, and shall build houses and plant vineyards. They shall live in safety, when I execute judgments upon all their neighbors who have treated them with contempt. And they shall know that I am the LORD their God. (Ezek. 28:25-26)

Psalm

Psalm 23
God our shepherd

Additional Reading

Luke 12:29-32
Do not fear, little flock

Hymn: Have No Fear, Little Flock, ELW 764

Lord God, you desire that your people of every time and place live in safety and peace with their neighbors. We thank you for the diversity of our communities. Give relief to those who live in unsafe places.

Sunday, May 12, 2019
Fourth Sunday of Easter

John 10:22-30
Jesus promises life to his sheep

[Jesus said,] "My sheep hear my voice. I know them, and they follow me. I give them eternal life, and they will never perish. No one will snatch them out of my hand. What my Father has given me is greater than all else, and no one can snatch it out of the Father's hand. The Father and I are one." (John 10:27-30)

Psalm

Psalm 23
God our shepherd

Additional Readings

Acts 9:36-43
Peter raises Tabitha from the dead

Revelation 7:9-17
A multitude sings before the Lamb

Hymn: The King of Love My Shepherd Is, ELW 502

O God of peace, you brought again from the dead our Lord Jesus Christ, the great shepherd of the sheep. By the blood of your eternal covenant, make us complete in everything good that we may do your will, and work among us all that is well-pleasing in your sight, through Jesus Christ, our Savior and Lord, who lives and reigns with you and the Holy Spirit, one God, now and forever.

Monday, May 13, 2019
Week of Easter 4

Psalm 100
We are God's sheep

Make a joyful noise to the LORD, all the earth.
> Worship the LORD with gladness;
> come into his presence with singing.

Know that the LORD is God.
> It is he that made us, and we are his;
> we are his people, and the sheep of his pasture.

Enter his gates with thanksgiving,
> and his courts with praise.
> Give thanks to him, bless his name.

For the LORD is good;
> his steadfast love endures forever,
> and his faithfulness to all generations. (Ps. 100:1-5)

Additional Readings
Ezekiel 37:15-28
God will unite the flock

Revelation 15:1-4
The song of the Lamb

Hymn: All People That on Earth Do Dwell, ELW 883

O Lord, we praise you that your steadfast love endures forever and that we are the sheep of your pasture. Give us such an awareness of your gracious love that we see each day as an opportunity to give thanks and bless your holy name.

Tuesday, May 14, 2019
Matthias, Apostle

Luke 6:12-16
Jesus calls the Twelve

Now during those days [Jesus] went out to the mountain to pray; and he spent the night in prayer to God. And when day came, he called his disciples and chose twelve of them, whom he also named apostles: Simon, whom he named Peter, and his brother Andrew, and James, and John, and Philip, and Bartholomew, and Matthew, and Thomas, and James son of Alphaeus, and Simon, who was called the Zealot, and Judas son of James, and Judas Iscariot, who became a traitor. (Luke 6:12-16)

Psalm

Psalm 56
I am bound by the vow I made to you

Additional Readings

Isaiah 66:1-2
Heaven is God's throne, earth is God's footstool

Acts 1:15-26
The apostles cast lots for Matthias

Hymn: The Son of God, Our Christ, ELW 584

Almighty God, you chose your faithful servant Matthias to be numbered among the twelve. Grant that your church may always be taught and guided by faithful and true pastors, through Jesus Christ our shepherd, who lives and reigns with you and the Holy Spirit, one God, now and forever.

Wednesday, May 15, 2019
Week of Easter 4

Jeremiah 50:17-20
Israel will be fed

Israel is a hunted sheep driven away by lions. First the king of Assyria devoured it, and now at the end King Nebuchadrezzar of Babylon has gnawed its bones. Therefore, thus says the LORD of hosts, the God of Israel: I am going to punish the king of Babylon and his land, as I punished the king of Assyria. I will restore Israel to its pasture, and it shall feed on Carmel and in Bashan, and on the hills of Ephraim and in Gilead its hunger shall be satisfied. In those days and at that time, says the LORD, the iniquity of Israel shall be sought, and there shall be none; and the sins of Judah, and none shall be found; for I will pardon the remnant that I have spared. (Jer. 50:17-20)

Psalm
Psalm 100
We are God's sheep

Additional Reading
John 10:31-42
The Son and the Father are one

Hymn: We Come to the Hungry Feast, ELW 479

Merciful God, there are times when we feel like sheep hunted by lions. You promise us that such times do not last forever. Thank you for your faithfulness and sustain us with the hope of hunger satisfied, wrongdoings forgiven, and sins pardoned.

Thursday, May 16, 2019
Week of Easter 4

Psalm 148
God's splendor is over earth and heaven

Praise the LORD!
Praise the LORD from the heavens;
    praise him in the heights!
Praise him, all his angels;
    praise him, all his host!

Praise him, sun and moon;
    praise him, all you shining stars!
Praise him, you highest heavens,
    and you waters above the heavens!

Let them praise the name of the LORD,
    for he commanded and they were created.
He established them forever and ever;
    he fixed their bounds, which cannot be passed. (Ps. 148:1-6)

Additional Readings
Ezekiel 2:8—3:11
Eating the scroll

Revelation 10:1-11
Eating the scroll

Hymn: Let the Whole Creation Cry, ELW 876

God, we praise you for your wonderful works and the splendor of your world! Your creation constantly reminds us of your love for us. Help us to see your creative mark in every person and part of the universe that we encounter.

Friday, May 17, 2019
Week of Easter 4

Daniel 7:13-14

An everlasting dominion is given

As I watched in the night visions,
>I saw one like a human being
>>coming with the clouds of heaven.
>And he came to the Ancient One
>>and was presented before him.
>To him was given dominion
>>and glory and kingship,
>that all peoples, nations, and languages
>>should serve him.
>His dominion is an everlasting dominion
>>that shall not pass away,
>and his kingship is one
>>that shall never be destroyed. (Dan. 7:13-14)

Psalm

Psalm 148
God's splendor is over earth and heaven

Additional Reading

Revelation 11:15
God's reign at the end of time

Hymn: Immortal, Invisible, God Only Wise, ELW 834

Ancient One, in your boundless compassion you created a world rich in a variety of peoples, nations, and languages. Grant us caring hearts that see beauty in the rich diversity of your people and that are willing to serve you always.

Saturday, May 18, 2019
Week of Easter 4

Erik, King of Sweden, martyr, died 1160

Revelation 11:16-19
God's reign at the end of time

Then the twenty-four elders who sit on their thrones before God fell on their faces and worshiped God, singing,

"We give you thanks, Lord God Almighty,
who are and who were,
for you have taken your great power
and begun to reign.
The nations raged,
but your wrath has come,
and the time for judging the dead,
for rewarding your servants, the prophets
and saints and all who fear your name,
both small and great,
and for destroying those who destroy the earth." (Rev. 11:16-18)

Psalm
Psalm 148
God's splendor is over earth and heaven

Additional Reading
Daniel 7:27
A dominion for the holy ones of the Most High

Hymn: Blessing and Honor, ELW 854

Lord God Almighty, we give you thanks that you judge all with mercy. Give us your grace when we come before you. Empower us to be your saintly servants in times of comfort and hardship.

Sunday, May 19, 2019
Fifth Sunday of Easter

John 13:31-35
Love one another

When [Judas] had gone out, Jesus said, "Now the Son of Man has been glorified, and God has been glorified in him. If God has been glorified in him, God will also glorify him in himself and will glorify him at once. Little children, I am with you only a little longer. You will look for me; and as I said to the Jews so now I say to you, 'Where I am going, you cannot come.' I give you a new commandment, that you love one another. Just as I have loved you, you also should love one another. By this everyone will know that you are my disciples, if you have love for one another." (John 13:31-35)

Psalm

Psalm 148
God's splendor is over earth and heaven

Additional Readings

Acts 11:1-18
God saves the Gentiles

Revelation 21:1-6
New heaven, new earth

Hymn: Ubi caritas et amor, ELW 642

O Lord God, you teach us that without love, our actions gain nothing. Pour into our hearts your most excellent gift of love, that, made alive by your Spirit, we may know goodness and peace, through your Son, Jesus Christ, our Savior and Lord, who lives and reigns with you and the Holy Spirit, one God, now and forever.

Monday, May 20, 2019
Week of Easter 5

Psalm 133
How good it is to live in unity

How very good and pleasant it is
    when kindred live together in unity!
It is like the precious oil on the head,
    running down upon the beard,
on the beard of Aaron,
    running down over the collar of his robes.
It is like the dew of Hermon,
    which falls on the mountains of Zion.
For there the LORD ordained his blessing,
    life forevermore. (Ps. 133:1-3)

Additional Readings
1 Samuel 20:1-23, 35-42
The love of David and Jonathan

Acts 11:19-26
Christians in Antioch

Hymn: Blest Be the Tie That Binds, ELW 656

Lord God, you created us to live with each other in unity. Thank you for the kindred you have given us with whom living is easy. Help us to experience unity among those who are not easy to live with.

Tuesday, May 21, 2019
Week of Easter 5

Helena, mother of Constantine, died around 330

Acts 11:27-30
Love embodied in care for others

At that time prophets came down from Jerusalem to Antioch. One of them named Agabus stood up and predicted by the Spirit that there would be a severe famine over all the world; and this took place during the reign of Claudius. The disciples determined that according to their ability, each would send relief to the believers living in Judea; this they did, sending it to the elders by Barnabas and Saul. (Acts 11:27-30)

Psalm
Psalm 133
How good it is to live in unity

Additional Reading
2 Samuel 1:4-27
David mourns Jonathan's death

Hymn: Lord, Whose Love in Humble Service, ELW 712

Caring God, you call your people to care for others as you have cared for us according to our abilities. Help us to share your love with others through acts of loving care.

Wednesday, May 22, 2019
Week of Easter 5

Leviticus 19:9-18
Love your neighbor

You shall not hate in your heart anyone of your kin; you shall reprove your neighbor, or you will incur guilt yourself. You shall not take vengeance or bear a grudge against any of your people, but you shall love your neighbor as yourself: I am the LORD. (Lev. 19:17-18)

Psalm
Psalm 133
How good it is to live in unity

Additional Reading
Luke 10:25-28
Love your neighbor

Hymn: Joyful, Joyful We Adore Thee, ELW 836

O Lord, often we are overcome by hate and judgmental thoughts about others. You call us to a better way of love and caring community. Grant us the wisdom, patience, and grace to not take vengeance, bear a grudge, or hate.

Thursday, May 23, 2019
Week of Easter 5

Psalm 67
Let the nations be glad

May God be gracious to us and bless us
    and make his face to shine upon us,
that your way may be known upon earth,
    your saving power among all nations.
Let the peoples praise you, O God;
    let all the peoples praise you.

Let the nations be glad and sing for joy,
    for you judge the peoples with equity
    and guide the nations upon earth.
Let the peoples praise you, O God;
    let all the peoples praise you. (Ps. 67:1-5)

Additional Readings
Acts 15:36-41
Paul and Barnabas part company

Proverbs 2:1-5
Knowledge of God like silver

Hymn: You Servants of God, ELW 825

Good and gracious God, you judge the people of this world with equity. Be gracious to us and bless us as we join with all your people in singing your praises.

Friday, May 24, 2019
Week of Easter 5

Nicolaus Copernicus, died 1543; Leonhard Euler, died 1783; scientists

Proverbs 2:6-8
God gives wisdom

For the LORD gives wisdom;
> from his mouth come knowledge and understanding;
he stores up sound wisdom for the upright;
> he is a shield to those who walk blamelessly,
guarding the paths of justice
> and preserving the way of his faithful ones. (Prov. 2:6-8)

Psalm
Psalm 67
Let the nations be glad

Additional Reading
Acts 16:1-8
Timothy accompanies Paul

Hymn: Earth and All Stars! ELW 731

God of wisdom, you provide us with knowledge about the ways you desire us to live. Be our shield and source of graceful living. Guard our paths as we walk the roads of life.

Saturday, May 25, 2019
Week of Easter 5

Proverbs 2:9-15
Wisdom makes a home in your heart

Then you will understand righteousness and justice
> and equity, every good path;
for wisdom will come into your heart,
> and knowledge will be pleasant to your soul;
prudence will watch over you;
> and understanding will guard you. (Prov. 2:9-11)

Psalm
Psalm 67
Let the nations be glad

Additional Reading
Luke 19:1-10
Salvation makes a home with Zacchaeus

Hymn: Evening and Morning, ELW 761

Lord God, you alone are the source of wisdom. Guard over us that we may pursue your paths of righteousness, justice, and equity instead of wandering in bad directions.

Sunday, May 26, 2019
Sixth Sunday of Easter

John 14:23-29

The Father will send the Holy Spirit

[Jesus said,] "I have said these things to you while I am still with you. But the Advocate, the Holy Spirit, whom the Father will send in my name, will teach you everything, and remind you of all that I have said to you. Peace I leave with you; my peace I give to you. I do not give to you as the world gives. Do not let your hearts be troubled, and do not let them be afraid." (John 14:25-27)

Psalm

Psalm 67
Let the nations be glad

Additional Readings

Acts 16:9-15
Lydia and her household are baptized

Revelation 21:10, 22—22:5
The Lamb is the light of God's city

Hymn: Alleluia! Jesus Is Risen! ELW 377

Bountiful God, you gather your people into your realm, and you promise us food from your tree of life. Nourish us with your word, that empowered by your Spirit we may love one another and the world you have made, through Jesus Christ, our Savior and Lord, who lives and reigns with you and the Holy Spirit, one God, now and forever.

Monday, May 27, 2019
Week of Easter 6

John Calvin, renewer of the church, died 1564

Psalm 93
God reigns above the floods

The LORD is king, he is robed in majesty;
>the LORD is robed, he is girded with strength.
He has established the world; it shall never be moved;
>your throne is established from of old;
>you are from everlasting.

The floods have lifted up, O LORD,
>the floods have lifted up their voice;
>the floods lift up their roaring.
More majestic than the thunders of mighty waters,
>more majestic than the waves of the sea,
>majestic on high is the LORD!

Your decrees are very sure;
>holiness befits your house,
>O LORD, forevermore. (Ps. 93:1-5)

Additional Readings
1 Chronicles 12:16-22
The spirit of God on Amasai

Revelation 21:5-14
Vision of the holy city

Hymn: Come, Thou Almighty King, ELW 408

Ruler of creation, you reign over all creation and your kingdom will have no end. Just as the waters praise you with their roaring, enliven us so we praise you today with every sound we make.

Tuesday, May 28, 2019
Week of Easter 6

Revelation 21:15-22
Vision of the holy city

The angel who talked to me had a measuring rod of gold to measure the city and its gates and walls. . . . The foundations of the wall of the city are adorned with every jewel; the first was jasper, the second sapphire, the third agate, the fourth emerald, the fifth onyx, the sixth carnelian, the seventh chrysolite, the eighth beryl, the ninth topaz, the tenth chrysoprase, the eleventh jacinth, the twelfth amethyst. And the twelve gates are twelve pearls, each of the gates is a single pearl, and the street of the city is pure gold, transparent as glass.

I saw no temple in the city, for its temple is the Lord God the Almighty and the Lamb. (Rev. 21:15, 19-22)

Psalm
Psalm 93
God reigns above the floods

Additional Reading
2 Chronicles 15:1-15
The spirit of God on Azariah

Hymn: Crown Him with Many Crowns, ELW 855

Lord God Almighty, you give us a vision of a world restored and your people gathered around you in worship. Inspire us with your beauty when what we see of the world around us looks so distasteful.

Wednesday, May 29, 2019
Week of Easter 6

Jiří Třanovský, hymnwriter, died 1637

2 Chronicles 34:20-33
Josiah consults the prophet Huldah

"But as to the king of Judah, who sent you to inquire of the LORD, thus shall you say to him: Thus says the LORD, the God of Israel: Regarding the words that you have heard, because your heart was penitent and you humbled yourself before God when you heard his words against this place and its inhabitants, and you have humbled yourself before me, and have torn your clothes and wept before me, I also have heard you, says the LORD. I will gather you to your ancestors and you shall be gathered to your grave in peace; your eyes shall not see all the disaster that I will bring on this place and its inhabitants." (2 Chron. 34:26-28)

Psalm
Psalm 93
God reigns above the floods

Additional Reading
Luke 2:25-38
The spirit of God on Simeon and Anna

Hymn: Lord Jesus, Think on Me, ELW 599

Lord God, you promise us forgiveness whenever we humble ourselves and turn back to you. Support us as we admit our failures and ask for forgiveness. Supply us with the hope of your loving grace.

Thursday, May 30, 2019
Ascension of Our Lord

Acts 1:1-11

Jesus sends the apostles

When [the disciples] had come together, they asked [Jesus], "Lord, is this the time when you will restore the kingdom to Israel?" He replied, "It is not for you to know the times or periods that the Father has set by his own authority. But you will receive power when the Holy Spirit has come upon you; and you will be my witnesses in Jerusalem, in all Judea and Samaria, and to the ends of the earth." When he had said this, as they were watching, he was lifted up, and a cloud took him out of their sight. While he was going and they were gazing up toward heaven, suddenly two men in white robes stood by them. They said, "Men of Galilee, why do you stand looking up toward heaven? This Jesus, who has been taken up from you into heaven, will come in the same way as you saw him go into heaven." (Acts 1:6-11)

Psalm

Psalm 47
God has gone up with a shout

Additional Readings

Ephesians 1:15-23
Seeing the risen and ascended Christ

Luke 24:44-53
Christ present in all times and places

Hymn: A Hymn of Glory Let Us Sing! ELW 393

Almighty God, your blessed Son, our Savior Jesus Christ, ascended far above all heavens that he might fill all things. Mercifully give us faith to trust that, as he promised, he abides with us on earth to the end of time, who lives and reigns with you and the Holy Spirit, one God, now and forever.

Friday, May 31, 2019
Visit of Mary to Elizabeth

Luke 1:39-57
Mary greets Elizabeth

In those days Mary set out and went with haste to a Judean town in the hill country, where she entered the house of Zechariah and greeted Elizabeth. When Elizabeth heard Mary's greeting, the child leaped in her womb. And Elizabeth was filled with the Holy Spirit and exclaimed with a loud cry, "Blessed are you among women, and blessed is the fruit of your womb." (Luke 1:39-42)

Psalm
Psalm 113
God, the helper of the needy

Additional Readings
1 Samuel 2:1-10
Hannah's thanksgiving

Romans 12:9-16b
Rejoice with those who rejoice

Hymn: Unexpected and Mysterious, ELW 258

Mighty God, by whose grace Elizabeth rejoiced with Mary and greeted her as the mother of the Lord: look with favor on your lowly servants that, with Mary, we may magnify your holy name and rejoice to acclaim her Son as our Savior, who lives and reigns with you and the Holy Spirit, one God, now and forever.

Prayer List for June

- Pray for immigrants and refugees
- Pray for our environment
- Pray for Amelia
- Pray for those without access to good education
- Pray for those who are bullied
- Pray for lonely people
- Pray for Grampy
- Pray for Sandra

Saturday, June 1, 2019
Week of Easter 6

Justin, martyr at Rome, died around 165

Exodus 33:18-23

Moses asks to see God's glory

Moses said, "Show me your glory, I pray." And [the LORD] said, "I will make all my goodness pass before you, and will proclaim before you the name, 'The LORD'; and I will be gracious to whom I will be gracious, and will show mercy on whom I will show mercy. But," he said, "you cannot see my face; for no one shall see me and live." And the LORD continued, "See, there is a place by me where you shall stand on the rock; and while my glory passes by I will put you in a cleft of the rock, and I will cover you with my hand until I have passed by; then I will take away my hand, and you shall see my back; but my face shall not be seen." (Exod. 33:18-23)

Psalm
Psalm 97
Light dawns for the righteous

Additional Reading
John 1:14-18
We have seen the glory of God

Hymn: Rock of Ages, Cleft for Me, ELW 623

Gracious and merciful God, we see your glory in the resurrected Christ. Although we cannot look upon your face, help us to see you in all we encounter in our daily lives.

Sunday, June 2, 2019
Seventh Sunday of Easter

John 17:20-26
Christ's prayer for his disciples

"I ask not only on behalf of these, but also on behalf of those who will believe in me through their word, that they may all be one. As you, Father, are in me and I am in you, may they also be in us, so that the world may believe that you have sent me. The glory that you have given me I have given them, so that they may be one, as we are one, I in them and you in me, that they may become completely one, so that the world may know that you have sent me and have loved them even as you have loved me. Father, I desire that those also, whom you have given me, may be with me where I am, to see my glory, which you have given me because you loved me before the foundation of the world." (John 17:20-24)

Psalm

Psalm 97
Light dawns for the righteous

Additional Readings

Acts 16:16-34
A jailer is baptized

Revelation 22:12-14, 16-17, 20-21
Blessed are those who wash their robe

Hymn: Thine the Amen, ELW 826

O God, form the minds of your faithful people into your one will. Make us love what you command and desire what you promise, that, amid all the changes of this world, our hearts may be fixed where true joy is found, your Son, Jesus Christ our Lord, who lives and reigns with you and the Holy Spirit, one God, now and forever.

Monday, June 3, 2019
Week of Easter 7

The Martyrs of Uganda, died 1886
John XXIII, Bishop of Rome, died 1963

Psalm 29
The glory of God

Ascribe to the LORD, O heavenly beings,
    ascribe to the LORD glory and strength.
Ascribe to the LORD the glory of his name;
    worship the LORD in holy splendor.

The voice of the LORD is over the waters;
    the God of glory thunders,
    the LORD, over mighty waters.
The voice of the LORD is powerful;
    the voice of the LORD is full of majesty. (Ps. 29:1-4)

Additional Readings
Exodus 40:16-38
God's glory on the tabernacle

Acts 16:35-40
The magistrates apologize to Paul and Silas

Hymn: Praise the Lord! O Heavens, ELW 823

Majestic Creator, your voice moved over the waters and, by your power, brought life into being. As we lift our own voices in praise, inspire us that we might share the good news of what you have done.

Tuesday, June 4, 2019
Week of Easter 7

2 Chronicles 5:2-14
God's glory in the temple

Now when the priests came out of the holy place (for all the priests who were present had sanctified themselves, without regard to their divisions), all the levitical singers, Asaph, Heman, and Jeduthun, their sons and kindred, arrayed in fine linen, with cymbals, harps, and lyres, stood east of the altar with one hundred twenty priests who were trumpeters. It was the duty of the trumpeters and singers to make themselves heard in unison in praise and thanksgiving to the LORD, and when the song was raised, with trumpets and cymbals and other musical instruments, in praise to the LORD,

"For he is good,
for his steadfast love endures forever,"

the house, the house of the LORD, was filled with a cloud, so that the priests could not stand to minister because of the cloud; for the glory of the LORD filled the house of God. (2 Chron. 5:11-14)

Psalm
Psalm 29
The glory of God

Additional Reading
Acts 26:19-29
Proclaim the light of the resurrection

Hymn: Come, All You People, ELW 819

God of all, your glory is present whenever your people gather. As we raise the song of your steadfast love for all people, keep us united despite our many differences.

Wednesday, June 5, 2019
Week of Easter 7

Boniface, Bishop of Mainz, missionary to Germany, martyr, died 754

Ezekiel 3:12-21
God's glory commissions the prophet

At the end of seven days, the word of the LORD came to me: Mortal, I have made you a sentinel for the house of Israel; whenever you hear a word from my mouth, you shall give them warning from me. If I say to the wicked, "You shall surely die," and you give them no warning, or speak to warn the wicked from their wicked way, in order to save their life, those wicked persons shall die for their iniquity; but their blood I will require at your hand. But if you warn the wicked, and they do not turn from their wickedness, or from their wicked way, they shall die for their iniquity; but you will have saved your life. (Ezek. 3:16-19)

Psalm
Psalm 29
The glory of God

Additional Reading
Luke 9:18-27
God's glory and discipleship

Hymn: My Lord, What a Morning, ELW 438

Holy God, through the life, death, and resurrection of your Son you offer eternal and abundant life to all. Strengthen us to serve as sentinels, announcing the words you have given us to proclaim.

Thursday, June 6, 2019
Week of Easter 7

Psalm 104:24-34, 35b
Renewing the face of the earth

O LORD, how manifold are your works!
    In wisdom you have made them all;
    the earth is full of your creatures.
Yonder is the sea, great and wide,
    creeping things innumerable are there,
    living things both small and great.
There go the ships,
    and Leviathan that you formed to sport in it.

These all look to you
    to give them their food in due season;
when you give to them, they gather it up;
    when you open your hand, they are filled with good things.
(Ps. 104:24-28)

Additional Readings
Isaiah 32:11-17
The spirit poured out to renew the earth

Galatians 5:16-25
The fruit of the Spirit

Hymn: God of the Sparrow, ELW 740

Lord of every creature, you provide for your people out of the abundance of your wondrous and varied creation. Open your hand and fill us with good things, sending your Spirit on all that you have made.

Friday, June 7, 2019
Week of Easter 7

Seattle, chief of the Duwamish Confederacy, died 1866

Galatians 6:7-10
Reaping eternal life from the Spirit

Do not be deceived; God is not mocked, for you reap whatever you sow. If you sow to your own flesh, you will reap corruption from the flesh; but if you sow to the Spirit, you will reap eternal life from the Spirit. So let us not grow weary in doing what is right, for we will reap at harvest time, if we do not give up. So then, whenever we have an opportunity, let us work for the good of all, and especially for those of the family of faith. (Gal. 6:7-10)

Psalm
Psalm 104:24-34, 35b
Renewing the face of the earth

Additional Reading
Isaiah 44:1-4
The spirit poured out to renew the faithful

Hymn: Lord of All Hopefulness, ELW 765

Enduring God, we offer you thanks for the gift of eternal life we receive through your Spirit. Support us in our work, that we might do what is right and not grow weary.

Saturday, June 8, 2019
Vigil of Pentecost

John 7:37-39
Jesus, the true living water

On the last day of the festival, the great day, while Jesus was standing there, he cried out, "Let anyone who is thirsty come to me, and let the one who believes in me drink. As the scripture has said, 'Out of the believer's heart shall flow rivers of living water.'" Now he said this about the Spirit, which believers in him were to receive; for as yet there was no Spirit, because Jesus was not yet glorified. (John 7:37-39)

Psalm
Psalm 33:12-22
The Lord is our helper and our shield

Additional Readings
Exodus 19:1-9
The covenant at Sinai

Romans 8:14-17, 22-27
Praying with the Spirit

Hymn: Like the Murmur of the Dove's Song, ELW 403

Almighty and ever-living God, you fulfilled the promise of Easter by sending the gift of your Holy Spirit. Look upon your people gathered in prayer, open to receive the Spirit's flame. May it come to rest in our hearts and heal the divisions of word and tongue, that with one voice and one song we may praise your name in joy and thanksgiving; through Jesus Christ, our Savior and Lord, who lives and reigns with you and the Holy Spirit, one God, now and forever.

Pentecost

Christians pray to God "in the power of the Spirit." The gifts of the Spirit are faith, hope, and love. Whenever two or more gather in Jesus' name, the Spirit is present. At every baptism and communion, we pray for the Spirit's presence to forgive and strengthen, inspire and refresh. In the household, we pray for the Spirit's guidance, for the deepening of faith, hope, and love, for the patience and wisdom to live in peace with each other and our neighbors.

Table Prayer for Pentecost

Blessed are you, O Lord our God,
who gathers the whole world into the Spirit of your Son.
You have given us food for another day:
blessed be God forever!
We beg you to pour out food for the needy,
that all peoples and languages may praise your name,
through Jesus Christ our Lord. Amen.

Thanksgiving for the Holy Spirit

Use this prayer during the week following Pentecost Sunday.

O Spirit of God, seek us;
Good Spirit, pray with us;
Spirit of counsel, inform us;
Spirit of might, free us;
Spirit of truth, enlighten us;
Spirit of Christ, raise us;
O Holy Spirit, dwell in us. Amen.

Sunday, June 9, 2019
Day of Pentecost

Columba, died 597; Aidan, died 651; Bede, died 735; renewers of the church

Acts 2:1-21
Filled with the Spirit

When the day of Pentecost had come, [the believers] were all together in one place. And suddenly from heaven there came a sound like the rush of a violent wind, and it filled the entire house where they were sitting. Divided tongues, as of fire, appeared among them, and a tongue rested on each of them. All of them were filled with the Holy Spirit and began to speak in other languages, as the Spirit gave them ability. (Acts 2:1-4)

Psalm
Psalm 104:24-34, 35b
Send forth your spirit

Additional Readings
Romans 8:14-17
The Spirit makes us children of God

John 14:8-17 [25-27]
The Spirit of truth

Hymn: Come, Gracious Spirit, Heavenly Dove, ELW 404

God our creator, the resurrection of your Son offers life to all the peoples of earth. By your Holy Spirit, kindle in us the fire of your love, empowering our lives for service and our tongues for praise, through Jesus Christ, our Savior and Lord, who lives and reigns with you and the Holy Spirit, one God, now and forever.

Monday, June 10, 2019
Time after Pentecost

Psalm 48
The God of Zion

Walk about Zion, go all around it,
    count its towers,
consider well its ramparts;
    go through its citadels,
that you may tell the next generation
    that this is God,
our God forever and ever.
    He will be our guide forever. (Ps. 48:12-14)

Additional Readings

Joel 2:18-29
God's spirit poured out

1 Corinthians 2:1-11
About the Spirit of God

Hymn: O Day Full of Grace, ELW 627

God of all time, from the beginning you have loved us, and your love endures forever. Guide us in our living and enliven us with your Spirit, that we might tell every generation of your grace and mercy.

Tuesday, June 11, 2019
Barnabas, Apostle

Acts 11:19-30; 13:1-3
Barnabas and Saul are set apart

Now in the church at Antioch there were prophets and teachers: Barnabas, Simeon who was called Niger, Lucius of Cyrene, Manaen a member of the court of Herod the ruler, and Saul. While they were worshiping the Lord and fasting, the Holy Spirit said, "Set apart for me Barnabas and Saul for the work to which I have called them." Then after fasting and praying they laid their hands on them and sent them off. (Acts 13:1-3)

Psalm

Psalm 112
Happy are the God-fearing

Additional Readings

Isaiah 42:5-12
The Lord calls us in righteousness

Matthew 10:7-16
Jesus sends out the Twelve

Hymn: Lord, You Give the Great Commission, ELW 579

We praise you, O God, for the life of your faithful servant Barnabas, who, seeking not his own renown but the well-being of your church, gave generously of his life and possessions for the relief of the poor and the spread of the gospel. Grant that we may follow his example and by our actions give glory to you, Father, Son, and Holy Spirit, now and forever.

Wednesday, June 12, 2019
Time after Pentecost

Luke 1:26-38
God's Spirit comes on Mary

The angel said to her, "Do not be afraid, Mary, for you have found favor with God. And now, you will conceive in your womb and bear a son, and you will name him Jesus. He will be great, and will be called the Son of the Most High, and the Lord God will give to him the throne of his ancestor David. He will reign over the house of Jacob forever, and of his kingdom there will be no end." Mary said to the angel, "How can this be, since I am a virgin?" The angel said to her, "The Holy Spirit will come upon you, and the power of the Most High will overshadow you; therefore the child to be born will be holy; he will be called Son of God." (Luke 1:30-35)

Psalm
Psalm 48
The God of Zion

Additional Reading
Numbers 24:1-14
Balaam speaks with God's spirit

Hymn: Spirit of Gentleness, ELW 396

Almighty God, you looked with favor on Mary and chose her to bear the incarnate Christ. Send your Holy Spirit to us, that we might also bear your Word into the world.

Thursday, June 13, 2019
Time after Pentecost

Psalm 8
Your majesty is praised above the heavens

O LORD, our Sovereign,
>	how majestic is your name in all the earth!

You have set your glory above the heavens.
>	Out of the mouths of babes and infants
you have founded a bulwark because of your foes,
>	to silence the enemy and the avenger.

When I look at your heavens, the work of your fingers,
>	the moon and the stars that you have established;
what are human beings that you are mindful of them,
>	mortals that you care for them?

Yet you have made them a little lower than God,
>	and crowned them with glory and honor. (Ps. 8:1-5)

Additional Readings
Proverbs 3:13-18
Wisdom is a tree of life

Ephesians 1:17-19
Wisdom in the Trinity

Hymn: Glorious Things of You Are Spoken, ELW 647

Sovereign Lord, your glory is greater than we can name. Help us remember that you hold all of humanity in the same incredible regard, that we be encouraged to care for and to love one another.

Friday, June 14, 2019
Time after Pentecost

Basil the Great, Bishop of Caesarea, died 379; Gregory, Bishop of Nyssa, died around 385; Gregory of Nazianzus, Bishop of Constantinople, died around 389; Macrina, teacher, died around 379

Ephesians 4:1-6
Life in the Trinity

I therefore, the prisoner in the Lord, beg you to lead a life worthy of the calling to which you have been called, with all humility and gentleness, with patience, bearing with one another in love, making every effort to maintain the unity of the Spirit in the bond of peace. There is one body and one Spirit, just as you were called to the one hope of your calling, one Lord, one faith, one baptism, one God and Father of all, who is above all and through all and in all. (Eph. 4:1-6)

Psalm
Psalm 8
Your majesty is praised above the heavens

Additional Reading
Proverbs 3:19-26
By wisdom God creates and preserves

Hymn: Many and Great, O God, ELW 837

Holy Three in One, you have called us into communion with you. Give us every good thing we need to be worthy of that calling, that we may join with one another in an everlasting bond of peace.

Saturday, June 15, 2019
Time after Pentecost

Proverbs 4:1-9
Choose God's wisdom

"The beginning of wisdom is this: Get wisdom,
  and whatever else you get, get insight.
Prize her highly, and she will exalt you;
  she will honor you if you embrace her.
She will place on your head a fair garland;
  she will bestow on you a beautiful crown." (Prov. 4:7-9)

Psalm
Psalm 8
Your majesty is praised above the heavens

Additional Reading
Luke 2:41-52
Jesus increases in wisdom

Hymn: O God of Mercy, God of Light, ELW 714

God of wisdom, you have guided your people throughout the ages. Teach us to love your judgments and lead us to compassionate discernment, that we might embrace your insights and faithfully participate in your holy work.

Time after Pentecost
Summer

The weeks and months following the Day of Pentecost coincide with the natural seasons of summer, autumn, and late autumn/November. Christian communities refer to this time in different ways. Whatever time is used to describe the many weeks between Pentecost and Christ the King (the last Sunday of the year), the seasons and calendars of North America offer some distinctive periods through which we may shape prayer in the household.

The Day of Pentecost is celebrated close to the end of the school year. A connection exists between graduations/new beginnings and our prayer for the Spirit's guidance in new endeavors. For many people, the months of June, July, and August signal a slightly altered schedule attuned to the weather, harvests, and vacations. Summer months offer their unique grace to those who spend time in discerning the many images which link the scriptures and the patient growth of the seed in the soil.

Table Prayer for Summer

The earth is the Lord's and all that is in it,
the world, and those who live in it. (Ps. 24:1)

All here gathered, food from the land,
all is gift from your gracious hand.
Feed us today; feed all those who hunger;
teach us to feed one another.
We ask this in the name of the one who is our bread, Jesus Christ.
Amen.

Sunday, June 16, 2019
The Holy Trinity

John 16:12-15

The Spirit will guide you into the truth

[Jesus said,] "I still have many things to say to you, but you cannot bear them now. When the Spirit of truth comes, he will guide you into all the truth; for he will not speak on his own, but will speak whatever he hears, and he will declare to you the things that are to come. He will glorify me, because he will take what is mine and declare it to you. All that the Father has is mine. For this reason I said that he will take what is mine and declare it to you." (John 16:12-15)

Psalm

Psalm 8
Your majesty is praised above the heavens

Additional Readings

Proverbs 8:1-4, 22-31
Wisdom rejoices in the creation

Romans 5:1-5
God's love poured into our hearts

Hymn: Father Most Holy, ELW 415

God of heaven and earth, before the foundation of the universe and the beginning of time you are the triune God: Author of creation, eternal Word of salvation, life-giving Spirit of wisdom. Guide us to all truth by your Spirit, that we may proclaim all that Christ has revealed and rejoice in the glory he shares with us. Glory and praise to you, Father, Son, and Holy Spirit, now and forever.

Monday, June 17, 2019
Time after Pentecost

Psalm 124
We have escaped like a bird

If it had not been the LORD who was on our side
    —let Israel now say—
if it had not been the LORD who was on our side,
    when our enemies attacked us,
then they would have swallowed us up alive,
    when their anger was kindled against us;
then the flood would have swept us away,
    the torrent would have gone over us;
then over us would have gone
    the raging waters. (Ps. 124:1-5)

Additional Readings
Proverbs 7:1-4
Wisdom is your sister

Ephesians 4:7-16
Building up the body of Christ

Hymn: Eternal Father, Strong to Save, ELW 756

Faithful God, you are always beside us, protecting us from all enemies. Give us a bold confidence in your presence and bolster our courage, that we might stand firm in the presence of doubt, hardship, and adversity.

Tuesday, June 18, 2019
Time after Pentecost

Ephesians 5:15-20
Living as wise ones in the Trinity

Be careful then how you live, not as unwise people but as wise, making the most of the time, because the days are evil. So do not be foolish, but understand what the will of the Lord is. Do not get drunk with wine, for that is debauchery; but be filled with the Spirit, as you sing psalms and hymns and spiritual songs among yourselves, singing and making melody to the Lord in your hearts, giving thanks to God the Father at all times and for everything in the name of our Lord Jesus Christ. (Eph. 5:15-20)

Psalm
Psalm 124
We have escaped like a bird

Additional Reading
Proverbs 8:4-21
Wisdom's riches

Hymn: Praise the Almighty! ELW 877

Eternal Trinity, you come to us and fill us with your Spirit. Make us wise and give us thankful hearts, that we might seek to do your will and sing a song of praise for all that you have done.

Wednesday, June 19, 2019
Time after Pentecost

Daniel 1:1-21
Daniel's wisdom

At the end of the time that the king had set for them to be brought in, the palace master brought them into the presence of Nebuchadnezzar, and the king spoke with them. And among them all, no one was found to compare with Daniel, Hananiah, Mishael, and Azariah; therefore they were stationed in the king's court. In every matter of wisdom and understanding concerning which the king inquired of them, he found them ten times better than all the magicians and enchanters in his whole kingdom. And Daniel continued there until the first year of King Cyrus. (Dan. 1:18-21)

Psalm
Psalm 124
We have escaped like a bird

Additional Reading
Luke 1:46b-55
Mary sings of God

Hymn: Canticle of the Turning, ELW 723

Almighty God, in ancient days you granted your servant Daniel great wisdom. Enlighten your people today and give us the talents to steadfastly serve you, that we might proclaim your goodness in every word and deed.

Thursday, June 20, 2019
Time after Pentecost

Psalm 22:19-28
I will praise you

But you, O LORD, do not be far away!
> O my help, come quickly to my aid!
Deliver my soul from the sword,
> my life from the power of the dog!
> Save me from the mouth of the lion!

From the horns of the wild oxen you have rescued me.
I will tell of your name to my brothers and sisters;
> in the midst of the congregation I will praise you:
You who fear the LORD, praise him!
> All you offspring of Jacob, glorify him;
> stand in awe of him, all you offspring of Israel! (Ps. 22:19-23)

Additional Readings
Isaiah 56:9-12
Israel's leaders are corrupt

Romans 2:17-29
Real circumcision is a matter of the heart

Hymn: Dear Christians, One and All, Rejoice, ELW 594

Gracious deliverer, you come quickly to the aid of your people and deliver them from harm. Encourage us to follow your example, that we might help our neighbors in times of distress and proclaim to the world your saving word.

Friday, June 21, 2019
Time after Pentecost

Onesimos Nesib, translator, evangelist, died 1931

Galatians 3:15-22
The purpose of the law

Brothers and sisters, I give an example from daily life: once a person's will has been ratified, no one adds to it or annuls it. Now the promises were made to Abraham and to his offspring; it does not say, "And to offsprings," as of many; but it says, "And to your offspring," that is, to one person, who is Christ. My point is this: the law, which came four hundred thirty years later, does not annul a covenant previously ratified by God, so as to nullify the promise. For if the inheritance comes from the law, it no longer comes from the promise; but God granted it to Abraham through the promise. (Gal. 3:15-18)

Psalm
Psalm 22:19-28
I will praise you

Additional Reading
Isaiah 57:1-13
The righteous perish and no one cares

Hymn: Give to Our God Immortal Praise! ELW 848

God of promise, you made your covenant with Abraham and remain faithful to your word. Keep us ever mindful of your commitment to us, that we might be inspired to serve one another with that same dedication.

Saturday, June 22, 2019
Time after Pentecost

Isaiah 59:1-8

Sin creates barriers

See, the LORD's hand is not too short to save,
    nor his ear too dull to hear.
Rather, your iniquities have been barriers
    between you and your God,
and your sins have hidden his face from you
    so that he does not hear.
For your hands are defiled with blood,
    and your fingers with iniquity;
your lips have spoken lies,
    your tongue mutters wickedness. (Isa. 59:1-3)

Psalm
Psalm 22:19-28
I will praise you

Additional Reading
Matthew 9:27-34
Healing the blind, casting out a demon

Hymn: Forgive Our Sins As We Forgive, ELW 605

Saving God, through the death and resurrection of Jesus Christ you have reconciled all peoples to yourself. Hear our sins and forgive us, that we might be made new and forgive others who sin against us.

Sunday, June 23, 2019
Time after Pentecost

Luke 8:26-39

Jesus casts out demons

When the swineherds saw what had happened, they ran off and told it in the city and in the country. Then people came out to see what had happened, and when they came to Jesus, they found the man from whom the demons had gone sitting at the feet of Jesus, clothed and in his right mind. And they were afraid. Those who had seen it told them how the one who had been possessed by demons had been healed. (Luke 8:34-36)

Psalm

Psalm 22:19-28
I will praise you

Additional Readings

Isaiah 65:1-9
The prophet sent to a rebellious people

Galatians 3:23-29
Clothed with Christ in baptism

Hymn: Rise, Shine, You People! ELW 665

O Lord God, we bring before you the cries of a sorrowing world. In your mercy set us free from the chains that bind us, and defend us from everything that is evil, through Jesus Christ, our Savior and Lord.

Monday, June 24, 2019
John the Baptist

Luke 1:57-67 [68-80]
The birth and naming of John

On the eighth day [Elizabeth and her neighbors and relatives] came to circumcise the child, and they were going to name him Zechariah after his father. But his mother said, "No; he is to be called John." They said to her, "None of your relatives has this name." Then they began motioning to his father to find out what name he wanted to give him. He asked for a writing tablet and wrote, "His name is John." And all of them were amazed. Immediately his mouth was opened and his tongue freed, and he began to speak, praising God. (Luke 1:59-64)

Psalm
Psalm 141
My eyes are turned to God

Additional Readings
Malachi 3:1-4
My messenger, a refiner and purifier

Acts 13:13-26
The gospel for the descendants of Abraham

Hymn: Christ, Whose Glory Fills the Skies, ELW 553

Almighty God, by your gracious providence your servant John the Baptist was born to Elizabeth and Zechariah. Grant to your people the wisdom to see your purpose and the openness to hear your will, that the light of Christ may increase in us, through Jesus Christ, our Savior and Lord, who lives and reigns with you and the Holy Spirit, one God, now and forever.

Tuesday, June 25, 2019
Time after Pentecost

Presentation of the Augsburg Confession, 1530
Philipp Melanchthon, renewer of the church, died 1560

Psalm 64

Prayer for protection

Hear my voice, O God, in my complaint;
      preserve my life from the dread enemy.
Hide me from the secret plots of the wicked,
      from the scheming of evildoers,
who whet their tongues like swords,
      who aim bitter words like arrows,
shooting from ambush at the blameless;
      they shoot suddenly and without fear. (Ps. 64:1-4)

Additional Readings

Job 19:1-22
Job questions God's ways

Ephesians 2:11-22
One new humanity in Christ

Hymn: Jesus, Priceless Treasure, ELW 775

O God, you hear every plea and cry of our hearts. Keep us from all harm and protect us from any who may work against us, that we might continue to proclaim your good news without fear.

Wednesday, June 26, 2019
Time after Pentecost

Luke 9:37-43a

Jesus heals a boy with a demon

On the next day, when [Jesus, Peter and John and James] had come down from the mountain, a great crowd met [Jesus]. Just then a man from the crowd shouted, "Teacher, I beg you to look at my son; he is my only child. Suddenly a spirit seizes him, and all at once he shrieks. It convulses him until he foams at the mouth; it mauls him and will scarcely leave him. I begged your disciples to cast it out, but they could not." Jesus answered, "You faithless and perverse generation, how much longer must I be with you and bear with you? Bring your son here." While he was coming, the demon dashed him to the ground in convulsions. But Jesus rebuked the unclean spirit, healed the boy, and gave him back to his father. And all were astounded at the greatness of God. (Luke 9:37-43a)

Psalm
Psalm 64
Prayer for protection

Additional Reading
Ezekiel 32:1-10
Evil like a dragon will be destroyed

Hymn: O Christ, the Healer, We Have Come, ELW 610

Compassionate God, you offer healing and wholeness to all who call upon you. Have mercy on us and free us from those things that possess us and keep us from you, that we may joyfully serve you without constraint.

Thursday, June 27, 2019
Time after Pentecost

Cyril, Bishop of Alexandria, died 444

Psalm 16
Protect me, O God

Protect me, O God, for in you I take refuge.
I say to the LORD, "You are my Lord;
>   I have no good apart from you."

As for the holy ones in the land, they are the noble,
>   in whom is all my delight.

Those who choose another god multiply their sorrows;
>   their drink offerings of blood I will not pour out
>   or take their names upon my lips.

The LORD is my chosen portion and my cup;
>   you hold my lot. (Ps. 16:1-5)

Additional Readings

Leviticus 9:22—10:11
God's fire consumes Aaron's sons

2 Corinthians 13:5-10
Examine yourselves concerning the faith

Hymn: Just a Closer Walk with Thee, ELW 697

O God, our defender, you protect us and hold our lives in your hands. Keep our hearts committed to you and give us refuge, that we might be strengthened in ardent service to you and to one another.

Friday, June 28, 2019
Time after Pentecost

Irenaeus, Bishop of Lyons, died around 202

Galatians 4:8-20

Paul reproves the hearers

Formerly, when you did not know God, you were enslaved to beings that by nature are not gods. Now, however, that you have come to know God, or rather to be known by God, how can you turn back again to the weak and beggarly elemental spirits? How can you want to be enslaved to them again? You are observing special days, and months, and seasons, and years. I am afraid that my work for you may have been wasted. (Gal. 4:8-11)

Psalm

Psalm 16
Protect me, O God

Additional Reading

2 Kings 1:1-16
God's fire consumes the king's men

Hymn: Sing Praise to God, the Highest Good, ELW 871

Liberating God, you have freed us from sin and all forces that seek to keep us bound. Make your consistent presence known to us, that we might never forget what you have done and faithfully live as your disciples.

Saturday, June 29, 2019
Peter and Paul, Apostles

John 21:15-19

Jesus says to Peter: Tend my sheep

When they had finished breakfast, Jesus said to Simon Peter, "Simon son of John, do you love me more than these?" He said to him, "Yes, Lord; you know that I love you." Jesus said to him, "Feed my lambs." A second time he said to him, "Simon son of John, do you love me?" He said to him, "Yes, Lord; you know that I love you." Jesus said to him, "Tend my sheep." He said to him the third time, "Simon son of John, do you love me?" Peter felt hurt because he said to him the third time, "Do you love me?" And he said to him, "Lord, you know everything; you know that I love you." Jesus said to him, "Feed my sheep. Very truly, I tell you, when you were younger, you used to fasten your own belt and to go wherever you wished. But when you grow old, you will stretch out your hands, and someone else will fasten a belt around you and take you where you do not wish to go." (He said this to indicate the kind of death by which he would glorify God.) After this he said to him, "Follow me." (John 21:15-19)

Psalm

Psalm 87:1-3, 5-7
Glorious things are spoken of you

Additional Readings

Acts 12:1-11
Peter released from prison

2 Timothy 4:6-8, 17-18
The good fight of faith

Hymn: We All Are One in Mission, ELW 576

Almighty God, we praise you that your blessed apostles Peter and Paul glorified you by their martyrdoms. Grant that your church throughout the world may always be instructed by their teaching and example, be knit together in unity by your Spirit, and ever stand firm upon the one foundation who is Jesus Christ our Lord, for he lives and reigns with you and the Holy Spirit, one God, now and forever.

Sunday, June 30, 2019
Time after Pentecost

Luke 9:51-62

Jesus says, Follow me

As [Jesus and his disciples] were going along the road, someone said to him, "I will follow you wherever you go." And Jesus said to him, "Foxes have holes, and birds of the air have nests; but the Son of Man has nowhere to lay his head." To another he said, "Follow me." But he said, "Lord, first let me go and bury my father." But Jesus said to him, "Let the dead bury their own dead; but as for you, go and proclaim the kingdom of God." (Luke 9:57-60)

Psalm

Psalm 16
Protect me, O God

Additional Readings

1 Kings 19:15-16, 19-21
Elijah says, Follow me

Galatians 5:1, 13-25
Love is the whole of the law

Hymn: O Jesus, I Have Promised, ELW 810

Sovereign God, ruler of all hearts, you call us to obey you, and you favor us with true freedom. Keep us faithful to the ways of your Son, that, leaving behind all that hinders us, we may steadfastly follow your paths, through Jesus Christ, our Savior and Lord.

Prayer List for July

- Pray for Leah, Sal, and all others with mental illnesses
- Pray for people making minimum wage
- Pray for my family, near & far.
- Pray for those making the world a better place

Monday, July 1, 2019
Time after Pentecost

Catherine Winkworth, died 1878; John Mason Neale, died 1866; hymn translators

Psalm 140
Prayer for deliverance

I say to the LORD, "You are my God;
>> give ear, O LORD, to the voice of my supplications."

O LORD, my Lord, my strong deliverer,
>> you have covered my head in the day of battle.

Do not grant, O LORD, the desires of the wicked;
>> do not further their evil plot. (Ps. 140:6-8)

Additional Readings
Genesis 24:34-41, 50-67
Rebekah follows Abraham's servant

1 John 2:7-11
Living in the light of love

Hymn: Thee We Adore, O Savior, ELW 476

God of the nations, you teach us to seek peace and to live in love. We pray that wars may cease and that political leaders will turn from violence and pursue outcomes that benefit all.

Tuesday, July 2, 2019
Time after Pentecost

Jeremiah 3:15-18
Nations cease to follow their own will

I will give you shepherds after my own heart, who will feed you with knowledge and understanding. And when you have multiplied and increased in the land, in those days, says the LORD, they shall no longer say, "The ark of the covenant of the LORD." It shall not come to mind, or be remembered, or missed; nor shall another one be made. At that time Jerusalem shall be called the throne of the LORD, and all nations shall gather to it, to the presence of the LORD in Jerusalem, and they shall no longer stubbornly follow their own evil will. In those days the house of Judah shall join the house of Israel, and together they shall come from the land of the north to the land that I gave your ancestors for a heritage. (Jer. 3:15-18)

Psalm
Psalm 140
Prayer for deliverance

Additional Reading
Ephesians 5:6-20
The fruit of the light

Hymn: O God of Every Nation, ELW 713

Lord, you are our good shepherd. We give you thanks for watching over us in all our ventures, and we pray that you will provide shepherds after your own heart to guide your people.

Wednesday, July 3, 2019
Thomas, Apostle

John 14:1-7
Jesus, the way, the truth, the life

Thomas said to [Jesus], "Lord, we do not know where you are going. How can we know the way?" Jesus said to him, "I am the way, and the truth, and the life. No one comes to the Father except through me. If you know me, you will know my Father also. From now on you do know him and have seen him." (John 14:5-7)

Psalm
Psalm 136:1-4, 23-26
God's mercy endures forever

Additional Readings
Judges 6:36-40
God affirms Gideon's calling

Ephesians 4:11-16
The body of Christ has various gifts

Hymn: Come, My Way, My Truth, My Life, ELW 816

Ever-living God, you strengthened your apostle Thomas with firm and certain faith in the resurrection of your Son. Grant that we too may confess our faith in Jesus Christ, our Lord and our God, who lives and reigns with you and the Holy Spirit, one God, now and forever.

Thursday, July 4, 2019
Time after Pentecost

Psalm 66:1-9
God holds our souls in life

Come and see what God has done:
> he is awesome in his deeds among mortals.
He turned the sea into dry land;
> they passed through the river on foot.
There we rejoiced in him,
> who rules by his might forever,
whose eyes keep watch on the nations—
> let the rebellious not exalt themselves.

Bless our God, O peoples,
> let the sound of his praise be heard,
who has kept us among the living,
> and has not let our feet slip. (Ps. 66:5-9)

Additional Readings
2 Kings 21:1-15
God will wipe Jerusalem as a dish

Romans 7:14-25
I do not do the good I want

Hymn: Lead Me, Guide Me, ELW 768

God of land and sea, you led your people through mighty waters and kept them safe from their enemies. Grant safety to all your creatures from wildfires, floods, earthquakes, and other disasters.

Friday, July 5, 2019
Time after Pentecost

Jeremiah 51:47-58

Let Jerusalem come into your mind

Assuredly, the days are coming
    when I will punish the images of Babylon;
her whole land shall be put to shame,
    and all her slain shall fall in her midst.
Then the heavens and the earth,
    and all that is in them,
shall shout for joy over Babylon;
    for the destroyers shall come against them out of the north,
says the LORD.
Babylon must fall for the slain of Israel,
    as the slain of all the earth have fallen because of Babylon.

You survivors of the sword,
    go, do not linger!
Remember the LORD in a distant land,
    and let Jerusalem come into your mind. (Jer. 51:47-50)

Psalm

Psalm 66:1-9
God holds our souls in life

Additional Reading

2 Corinthians 8:1-7
Poverty overflows in generosity

Hymn: Come, We That Love the Lord, ELW 625

Living God, you have taught us to worship you alone and not to honor false idols. When we go astray, correct us gently and guide us back to you, our source and salvation.

Saturday, July 6, 2019
Time after Pentecost

Jan Hus, martyr, died 1415

Zechariah 14:10-21
Jerusalem shall abide in security

The whole land shall be turned into a plain from Geba to Rimmon south of Jerusalem. But Jerusalem shall remain aloft on its site from the Gate of Benjamin to the place of the former gate, to the Corner Gate, and from the Tower of Hananel to the king's wine presses. And it shall be inhabited, for never again shall it be doomed to destruction; Jerusalem shall abide in security. (Zech. 14:10-11)

Psalm
Psalm 66:1-9
God holds our souls in life

Additional Reading
Luke 9:1-6
The mission of the Twelve

Hymn: Jerusalem, My Happy Home, ELW 628

God of peace, we long for the day when all peoples may live in harmony. We pray that our daily living and the tools of our hands may become holy and consecrated to you, as we worship you with our whole beings.

Sunday, July 7, 2019
Time after Pentecost

Luke 10:1-11, 16-20
Jesus sends out seventy disciples

After this the Lord appointed seventy others and sent them on ahead of him in pairs to every town and place where he himself intended to go. He said to them, "The harvest is plentiful, but the laborers are few; therefore ask the Lord of the harvest to send out laborers into his harvest. Go on your way. See, I am sending you out like lambs into the midst of wolves. Carry no purse, no bag, no sandals; and greet no one on the road. Whatever house you enter, first say, 'Peace to this house!' " (Luke 10:1-5)

Psalm
Psalm 66:1-9
God holds our souls in life

Additional Readings
Isaiah 66:10-14
Jerusalem, a nursing mother

Galatians 6:[1-6] 7-16
Do what is right now

Hymn: Spread, Oh, Spread, Almighty Word, ELW 663

O God, the Father of our Lord Jesus, you are the city that shelters us, the mother who comforts us. With your Spirit accompany us on our life's journey, that we may spread your peace in all the world, through your Son, Jesus Christ, our Savior and Lord.

Monday, July 8, 2019
Time after Pentecost

Psalm 119:73-80
Living in faithfulness

Your hands have made and fashioned me;
　　give me understanding that I may learn your commandments.
Those who fear you shall see me and rejoice,
　　because I have hoped in your word.
I know, O LORD, that your judgments are right,
　　and that in faithfulness you have humbled me.
Let your steadfast love become my comfort
　　according to your promise to your servant.
Let your mercy come to me, that I may live;
　　for your law is my delight. (Ps. 119:73-77)

Additional Readings
Jeremiah 6:10-19
Call to faithfulness

Acts 19:21-27
Demetrius opposes Paul

Hymn: O God, My Faithful God, ELW 806

Blessed Creator, you formed us from simple dust and you sustain us with your own life-giving breath. Place your wisdom in our minds and your instruction on our hearts, that we may always follow you.

Tuesday, July 9, 2019
Time after Pentecost

Jeremiah 8:4-13
Call to faithfulness

You shall say to them, Thus says the LORD:
When people fall, do they not get up again?
> If they go astray, do they not turn back?
Why then has this people turned away
> in perpetual backsliding?
They have held fast to deceit,
> they have refused to return.
I have given heed and listened,
> but they do not speak honestly;
no one repents of wickedness,
> saying, "What have I done!"
All of them turn to their own course,
> like a horse plunging headlong into battle. (Jer. 8:4-6)

Psalm
Psalm 119:73-80
Living in faithfulness

Additional Reading
Acts 19:28-41
A riot follows Paul's preaching

Hymn: Word of God, Come Down on Earth, ELW 510

Gracious God, you abound in steadfast love. You forgive us when we repent. You accept us when we turn to you. Grant that we may always follow your wisdom and guide us on your right paths.

Wednesday, July 10, 2019
Time after Pentecost

Joshua 23:1-16
Joshua urges faithfulness

A long time afterward, when the Lord had given rest to Israel from all their enemies all around, and Joshua was old and well advanced in years, Joshua summoned all Israel, their elders and heads, their judges and officers, and said to them, "I am now old and well advanced in years; and you have seen all that the Lord your God has done to all these nations for your sake, for it is the Lord your God who has fought for you. I have allotted to you as an inheritance for your tribes those nations that remain, along with all the nations that I have already cut off, from the Jordan to the Great Sea in the west. The Lord your God will push them back before you, and drive them out of your sight; and you shall possess their land, as the Lord your God promised you." (Josh. 23:1-5)

Psalm
Psalm 119:73-80
Living in faithfulness

Additional Reading
Luke 10:13-16
Woe to unrepentant cities

Hymn: Amazing Grace, How Sweet the Sound, ELW 779

Blessed are you, God of eternity. Your faithfulness endures from age to age. We praise you with all the saints who rest in you, and we pray for the day when we are all united in your resurrection life.

Thursday, July 11, 2019
Time after Pentecost

Benedict of Nursia, Abbot of Monte Cassino, died around 540

Psalm 25:1-10

Show me your ways

To you, O Lord, I lift up my soul.
O my God, in you I trust;
>   do not let me be put to shame;
>   do not let my enemies exult over me.
Do not let those who wait for you be put to shame;
>   let them be ashamed who are wantonly treacherous.

Make me to know your ways, O Lord;
>   teach me your paths.
Lead me in your truth, and teach me,
>   for you are the God of my salvation;
>   for you I wait all day long. (Ps. 25:1-5)

Additional Readings

Genesis 41:14-36
Joseph plans to feed Egypt

James 2:14-26
Faith produces good works

Hymn: Guide Me Ever, Great Redeemer, ELW 618

God of justice and mercy, you do not desire empty praise but a living faith that shows itself in our actions. Teach us your ways and lead us in your truth, that we may act according to your desire.

Friday, July 12, 2019
Time after Pentecost

Nathan Söderblom, Bishop of Uppsala, died 1931

Genesis 41:37-49
God saves Egypt from starvation

Joseph was thirty years old when he entered the service of Pharaoh king of Egypt. And Joseph went out from the presence of Pharaoh, and went through all the land of Egypt. During the seven plenteous years the earth produced abundantly. He gathered up all the food of the seven years when there was plenty in the land of Egypt, and stored up food in the cities; he stored up in every city the food from the fields around it. So Joseph stored up grain in such abundance—like the sand of the sea—that he stopped measuring it; it was beyond measure. (Gen. 41:46-49)

Psalm
Psalm 25:1-10
Show me your ways

Additional Reading
Acts 7:9-16
Egypt's food rescues Israel

Hymn: Praise and Thanksgiving, ELW 689

Lord God, shower us with abundance. Bless the planting and the harvest, that there may be food for all the world. Inspire us to show generosity to others and to ensure that none go hungry.

Saturday, July 13, 2019
Time after Pentecost

Leviticus 19:1-4, 32-37
Mercy to the alien

You shall rise before the aged, and defer to the old; and you shall fear your God: I am the LORD.

When an alien resides with you in your land, you shall not oppress the alien. The alien who resides with you shall be to you as the citizen among you; you shall love the alien as yourself, for you were aliens in the land of Egypt: I am the LORD your God. (Lev. 19:32-34)

Psalm
Psalm 25:1-10
Show me your ways

Additional Reading
John 3:16-21
God's Son saves the world

Hymn: In Christ There Is No East or West, ELW 650

God of wanderers, you love and care for all people, including those who are refugees, immigrants, or otherwise far from their native lands. Help us to show compassion to the stranger in our midst, just as you have taught us.

Sunday, July 14, 2019
Time after Pentecost

Luke 10:25-37
The parable of the merciful Samaritan

[Jesus said,] "But a Samaritan while traveling came near him; and when he saw him, he was moved with pity. He went to him and bandaged his wounds, having poured oil and wine on them. Then he put him on his own animal, brought him to an inn, and took care of him. The next day he took out two denarii, gave them to the innkeeper, and said, 'Take care of him; and when I come back, I will repay you whatever more you spend.' Which of these three, do you think, was a neighbor to the man who fell into the hands of the robbers?" [The lawyer] said, "The one who showed him mercy." Jesus said to him, "Go and do likewise." (Luke 10:33-37)

Psalm
Psalm 25:1-10
Show me your ways

Additional Readings
Deuteronomy 30:9-14
God delights in your fruitfulness

Colossians 1:1-14
The gospel is bearing fruit

Hymn: Lord of All Nations, Grant Me Grace, ELW 716

O Lord God, your mercy delights us, and the world longs for your loving care. Hear the cries of everyone in need, and turn our hearts to love our neighbors with the love of your Son, Jesus Christ, our Savior and Lord.

Monday, July 15, 2019
Time after Pentecost

Psalm 25:11-20
I take refuge in you, O God

Turn to me and be gracious to me,
    for I am lonely and afflicted.
Relieve the troubles of my heart,
    and bring me out of my distress.
Consider my affliction and my trouble,
    and forgive all my sins.

Consider how many are my foes,
    and with what violent hatred they hate me.
O guard my life, and deliver me;
    do not let me be put to shame, for I take refuge in you.
(Ps. 25:16-20)

Additional Readings
Job 24:1-8
The needy are thrust off the road

James 2:1-7
God has chosen the poor

Hymn: My Faith Looks Up to Thee, ELW 759

Lord God, you call us away from injustice. Where people are hungry, help us to feed them. Where people are naked, lead us to clothe them. Where people are homeless, guide us to shelter them. May everyone receive your blessings.

Tuesday, July 16, 2019
Time after Pentecost

Proverbs 19:1-17
Kindness to the poor

Laziness brings on deep sleep;
     an idle person will suffer hunger.
Those who keep the commandment will live;
     those who are heedless of their ways will die.
Whoever is kind to the poor lends to the LORD,
     and will be repaid in full. (Prov. 19:15-17)

Psalm
Psalm 25:11-20
I take refuge in you, O God

Additional Reading
1 John 3:11-17
Do not refuse one in need

Hymn: Lord of Glory, You Have Bought Us, ELW 707

God of abundance, teach us to live our days for one another, just as Christ laid down his life for us. Give us a spirit of generosity to share with the poor.

Wednesday, July 17, 2019
Time after Pentecost

Bartolomé de Las Casas, missionary to the Indies, died 1566

Ecclesiastes 9:13-18

One bungler destroys much good

There was a little city with few people in it. A great king came against it and besieged it, building the great siegeworks against it. Now there was found in it a poor wise man, and he by his wisdom delivered the city. Yet no one remembered that poor man. So I said, "Wisdom is better than might; yet the poor man's wisdom is despised, and his words are not heeded."

> The quiet words of the wise are more to be heeded
> > than the shouting of a ruler among fools.
> Wisdom is better than weapons of war,
> > but one bungler destroys much good. (Eccles. 9:14-18)

Psalm
Psalm 25:11-20
I take refuge in you, O God

Additional Reading
Matthew 25:31-46
As you did it to one of the least of these

Hymn: Lord of Light, ELW 688

In every time and place, O God, your concern is for those who have the least. Give us the wisdom to see the face of Christ in our neighbor and to provide care and comfort for all in need.

Thursday, July 18, 2019
Time after Pentecost

Psalm 15
Leading a blameless life

O Lord, who may abide in your tent?
   Who may dwell on your holy hill?

Those who walk blamelessly, and do what is right,
   and speak the truth from their heart;
who do not slander with their tongue,
   and do no evil to their friends,
      nor take up a reproach against their neighbors;
in whose eyes the wicked are despised,
   but who honor those who fear the Lord;
who stand by their oath even to their hurt;
who do not lend money at interest,
   and do not take a bribe against the innocent.

Those who do these things shall never be moved. (Ps. 15:1-5)

Additional Readings
Genesis 12:10-20
Pharaoh offers hospitality to Sarai

Hebrews 5:1-6
Christ did not glorify himself

Hymn: Son of God, Eternal Savior, ELW 655

God of steadfast love, grant that we may enter into your holy presence.
Direct our thoughts and actions that we may live according to your will,
walking blamelessly and doing what is right.

Friday, July 19, 2019
Time after Pentecost

Ephesians 3:14-21
The love of Christ surpasses knowledge

For this reason I bow my knees before the Father, from whom every family in heaven and on earth takes its name. I pray that, according to the riches of his glory, he may grant that you may be strengthened in your inner being with power through his Spirit, and that Christ may dwell in your hearts through faith, as you are being rooted and grounded in love. I pray that you may have the power to comprehend, with all the saints, what is the breadth and length and height and depth, and to know the love of Christ that surpasses knowledge, so that you may be filled with all the fullness of God. (Eph. 3:14-19)

Psalm
Psalm 15
Leading a blameless life

Additional Reading
Genesis 13:1-18
Abram and Lot separate peacefully

Hymn: Our Father, by Whose Name, ELW 640

God our parent, we give you thanks that you name us your beloved children. Let our brother, Jesus Christ, dwell in our hearts so we may be rooted and grounded in love.

Saturday, July 20, 2019
Time after Pentecost

Genesis 14:1-16

Lot is rescued

When Abram heard that his nephew had been taken captive, he led forth his trained men, born in his house, three hundred eighteen of them, and went in pursuit as far as Dan. He divided his forces against them by night, he and his servants, and routed them and pursued them to Hobah, north of Damascus. Then he brought back all the goods, and also brought back his nephew Lot with his goods, and the women and the people. (Gen. 14:14-16)

Psalm
Psalm 15
Leading a blameless life

Additional Reading
Luke 8:4-10
Jesus speaks in parables

Hymn: On Our Way Rejoicing, ELW 537

Lord, you are king above all kings. Guide the leaders of nations to pursue justice and peace for all people. Give those in authority ears to hear and hearts of truth.

Sunday, July 21, 2019
Time after Pentecost

Luke 10:38-42
Choosing the better part

Now as [Jesus and his disciples] went on their way, he entered a certain village, where a woman named Martha welcomed him into her home. She had a sister named Mary, who sat at the Lord's feet and listened to what he was saying. But Martha was distracted by her many tasks; so she came to him and asked, "Lord, do you not care that my sister has left me to do all the work by myself? Tell her then to help me." But the Lord answered her, "Martha, Martha, you are worried and distracted by many things; there is need of only one thing. Mary has chosen the better part, which will not be taken away from her." (Luke 10:38-42)

Psalm

Psalm 15
Leading a blameless life

Additional Readings

Genesis 18:1-10a
The hospitality of Abraham and Sarah

Colossians 1:15-28
A hymn to Christ

Hymn: Lord, Thee I Love with All My Heart, ELW 750

Eternal God, you draw near to us in Christ, and you make yourself our guest. Amid the cares of our lives, make us attentive to your presence, that we may treasure your word above all else, through Jesus Christ, our Savior and Lord.

Monday, July 22, 2019
Mary Magdalene, Apostle

John 20:1-2, 11-18
Mary Magdalene meets Jesus in the garden

Jesus said to [Mary Magdalene], "Woman, why are you weeping? Whom are you looking for?" Supposing him to be the gardener, she said to him, "Sir, if you have carried him away, tell me where you have laid him, and I will take him away." Jesus said to her, "Mary!" She turned and said to him in Hebrew, "Rabbouni!" (which means Teacher). Jesus said to her, "Do not hold on to me, because I have not yet ascended to the Father. But go to my brothers and say to them, 'I am ascending to my Father and your Father, to my God and your God.'" Mary Magdalene went and announced to the disciples, "I have seen the Lord"; and she told them that he had said these things to her. (John 20:15-18)

Psalm
Psalm 73:23-28
I will speak of all God's works

Additional Readings
Ruth 1:6-18
Ruth stays with Naomi

Acts 13:26-33a
The raising of Jesus fulfills God's promise

Hymn: For All the Faithful Women, stanza 9, ELW 419

Almighty God, your Son first entrusted the apostle Mary Magdalene with the joyful news of his resurrection. Following the example of her witness, may we proclaim Christ as our living Lord and one day see him in glory, for he lives and reigns with you and the Holy Spirit, one God, now and forever.

Tuesday, July 23, 2019
Time after Pentecost

Birgitta of Sweden, renewer of the church, died 1373

Psalm 119:97-104
God's word like honey

I hold back my feet from every evil way,
    in order to keep your word.
I do not turn away from your ordinances,
    for you have taught me.
How sweet are your words to my taste,
    sweeter than honey to my mouth!
Through your precepts I get understanding;
    therefore I hate every false way. (Ps. 119:101-104)

Additional Readings
Proverbs 9:1-18
The wise and foolish women

1 John 2:1-6
Walking as Christ walked

Hymn: Let Us Ever Walk with Jesus, ELW 802

God, you offer your instruction to all those seeking wisdom. Teach us your wisdom, understanding, and knowledge. Make these blessings as sweet as honey in our mouths.

Wednesday, July 24, 2019
Time after Pentecost

John 6:41-51

Whoever eats this bread will live forever

[Jesus answered,] "Very truly, I tell you, whoever believes has eternal life. I am the bread of life. Your ancestors ate the manna in the wilderness, and they died. This is the bread that comes down from heaven, so that one may eat of it and not die. I am the living bread that came down from heaven. Whoever eats of this bread will live forever; and the bread that I will give for the life of the world is my flesh." (John 6:47-51)

Psalm

Psalm 119:97-104
God's word like honey

Additional Reading

Deuteronomy 12:1-12
The promise to eat before God

Hymn: Bread of Life, Our Host and Meal, ELW 464

Generous God, you sent to us Jesus, the living bread from heaven. May we come again and again to your bountiful table, to be fed and sustained by the bread of life.

Thursday, July 25, 2019
James, Apostle

Mark 10:35-45
Whoever wishes to be great must serve

James and John, the sons of Zebedee, came forward to [Jesus] and said to him, "Teacher, we want you to do for us whatever we ask of you." And he said to them, "What is it you want me to do for you?" And they said to him, "Grant us to sit, one at your right hand and one at your left, in your glory." But Jesus said to them, "You do not know what you are asking. Are you able to drink the cup that I drink, or be baptized with the baptism that I am baptized with?" They replied, "We are able." Then Jesus said to them, "The cup that I drink you will drink; and with the baptism with which I am baptized, you will be baptized; but to sit at my right hand or at my left is not mine to grant, but it is for those for whom it has been prepared." (Mark 10:35-40)

Psalm
Psalm 7:1-10
God, my shield and defense

Additional Readings
1 Kings 19:9-18
Elijah hears God in the midst of silence

Acts 11:27—12:3a
James is killed by Herod

Hymn: Jesu, Jesu, Fill Us with Your Love, ELW 708

Gracious God, we remember before you today your servant and apostle James, the first among the twelve to be martyred for the name of Jesus Christ. Pour out on the leaders of your church that spirit of self-denying service which is the true mark of authority among your people, through Jesus Christ our servant, who lives and reigns with you and the Holy Spirit, one God, now and forever.

Friday, July 26, 2019
Time after Pentecost

Psalm 138
Your love endures forever

All the kings of the earth shall praise you, O LORD,
　　for they have heard the words of your mouth.
They shall sing of the ways of the LORD,
　　for great is the glory of the LORD.
For though the LORD is high, he regards the lowly;
　　but the haughty he perceives from far away.

Though I walk in the midst of trouble,
　　you preserve me against the wrath of my enemies;
you stretch out your hand,
　　and your right hand delivers me.
The LORD will fulfill his purpose for me;
　　your steadfast love, O LORD, endures forever.
　　Do not forsake the work of your hands. (Ps. 138:4-8)

Additional Readings
Esther 3:7-15　　　　　　　　　　　　**Acts 2:22-36**
Haman's plot to kill the Jews　　　　　*The Messiah is handed over to death*

Hymn: O God beyond All Praising, ELW 880

Great is your glory, O Lord; though you are on high, you have regard for the lowly. When we walk in the midst of trouble, be with us. Protect us and preserve us.

Saturday, July 27, 2019
Time after Pentecost

Esther 4:1-17

Royal dignity for such a time as this

Then Esther said in reply to Mordecai, "Go, gather all the Jews to be found in Susa, and hold a fast on my behalf, and neither eat nor drink for three days, night or day. I and my maids will also fast as you do. After that I will go to the king, though it is against the law; and if I perish, I perish." Mordecai then went away and did everything as Esther had ordered him. (Esther 4:15-17)

Psalm

Psalm 138
Your love endures forever

Additional Reading

Luke 8:22-25
Jesus' disciples cry out for safety

Hymn: Lost in the Night, ELW 243

God of justice, you preserved your people through the courage of Esther. Raise up leaders in our own time who are willing to risk their lives for the sake of the most vulnerable people.

Sunday, July 28, 2019
Time after Pentecost

Johann Sebastian Bach, died 1750; Heinrich Schütz, died 1672;
George Frederick Handel, died 1759; musicians

Luke 11:1-13

Jesus teaches prayer

[Jesus] was praying in a certain place, and after he had finished, one of his disciples said to him, "Lord, teach us to pray, as John taught his disciples." He said to them, "When you pray, say:

Father, hallowed be your name.

Your kingdom come.

Give us each day our daily bread.

And forgive us our sins,

for we ourselves forgive everyone indebted to us.

And do not bring us to the time of trial." (Luke 11:1-4)

Psalm

Psalm 138
Your love endures forever

Additional Readings

Genesis 18:20-32
Abraham bargains with God

Colossians 2:6-15 [16-19]
Buried with Christ in baptism

Hymn: Our Father, God in Heaven Above, ELW 746

Almighty and ever-living God, you are always more ready to hear than we are to pray, and you gladly give more than we either desire or deserve. Pour upon us your abundant mercy. Forgive us those things that weigh on our conscience, and give us those good things that come only through your Son, Jesus Christ, our Savior and Lord.

Monday, July 29, 2019
Time after Pentecost

Mary, Martha, and Lazarus of Bethany
Olaf, King of Norway, martyr, died 1030

Psalm 55:16-23
Cast your burden on God

My companion laid hands on a friend
    and violated a covenant with me
with speech smoother than butter,
    but with a heart set on war;
with words that were softer than oil,
    but in fact were drawn swords.

Cast your burden on the LORD,
    and he will sustain you;
he will never permit
    the righteous to be moved.

But you, O God, will cast them down
    into the lowest pit;
the bloodthirsty and treacherous
    shall not live out half their days.
But I will trust in you. (Ps. 55:20-23)

Additional Readings

Esther 5:1-14
A banquet guest with a murderous heart

Colossians 2:16—3:1
About false regulations

Hymn: What a Friend We Have in Jesus, ELW 742

God, you hear our prayers morning and evening. When we struggle under the weight of our burdens, teach us to cast those burdens on you and trust in your sustaining love.

Tuesday, July 30, 2019
Time after Pentecost

Romans 9:30—10:4
Christ is the end of the law

Brothers and sisters, my heart's desire and prayer to God for [Israel] is that they may be saved. I can testify that they have a zeal for God, but it is not enlightened. For, being ignorant of the righteousness that comes from God, and seeking to establish their own, they have not submitted to God's righteousness. For Christ is the end of the law so that there may be righteousness for everyone who believes. (Rom. 10:1-4)

Psalm
Psalm 55:16-23
Cast your burden on God

Additional Reading
Esther 6:1—7:6
A royal reversal of fortunes

Hymn: All Depends on Our Possessing, ELW 589

God of all peoples, through Christ you opened the possibility of righteousness to all, while remaining faithful to your chosen people. May we who come to you as adopted children rely on Christ for our salvation.

Wednesday, July 31, 2019
Time after Pentecost

Matthew 5:43-48

Pray for those who persecute you

[Jesus said,] "You have heard that it was said, 'You shall love your neighbor and hate your enemy.' But I say to you, Love your enemies and pray for those who persecute you, so that you may be children of your Father in heaven; for he makes his sun rise on the evil and on the good, and sends rain on the righteous and on the unrighteous. For if you love those who love you, what reward do you have? Do not even the tax collectors do the same? And if you greet only your brothers and sisters, what more are you doing than others? Do not even the Gentiles do the same? Be perfect, therefore, as your heavenly Father is perfect." (Matt. 5:43-48)

Psalm

Psalm 55:16-23
Cast your burden on God

Additional Reading

Esther 7:7—8:17
Esther saves her people

Hymn: O Spirit of Life, ELW 405

Compassionate God, you have taught us that it is not enough to love our neighbors but that we must also love our enemies. Give us your Spirit of love so we may pray even for those who persecute us.

Prayer List for August

- Pray for those making efforts to save the planet
- Pray for those who are unloved
- Pray for those struggling with addiction
- Pray for those who are true followers of God
- Pray for those unable to access clean water

Thursday, August 1, 2019
Time after Pentecost

Psalm 49:1-12
The folly of trust in riches

Why should I fear in times of trouble,
>   when the iniquity of my persecutors surrounds me,
those who trust in their wealth
>   and boast of the abundance of their riches?
Truly, no ransom avails for one's life,
>   there is no price one can give to God for it.
For the ransom of life is costly,
>   and can never suffice
that one should live on forever
>   and never see the grave. (Ps. 49:5-9)

Additional Readings
Proverbs 23:1-11
Resist the allure of becoming rich

Romans 11:33-36
God's riches, wisdom, and knowledge

Hymn: Jesus Calls Us; o'er the Tumult, ELW 696

Saving God, you come to us in times of trouble, reminding us that our very lives rest in you. Guide us to trust in the abundance of your grace, that our hands may be opened in generosity to others.

Friday, August 2, 2019
Time after Pentecost

Proverbs 24:1-12
By wisdom a house is built

Do not envy the wicked,
    nor desire to be with them;
for their minds devise violence,
    and their lips talk of mischief.

By wisdom a house is built,
    and by understanding it is established;
by knowledge the rooms are filled
    with all precious and pleasant riches. (Prov. 24:1-4)

Psalm
Psalm 49:1-12
The folly of trust in riches

Additional Reading
Ephesians 4:17-24
A new self in the likeness of God

Hymn: Abide, O Dearest Jesus, ELW 539

Lord God, you know the desires of our hearts, and you long for us to live in freedom from the bitterness of envy. Draw us to desire wisdom and knowledge, that our lives may be shaped by thankfulness.

Saturday, August 3, 2019
Time after Pentecost

Ecclesiastes 1:1-11
Nothing new under the sun

What has been is what will be,
> and what has been done is what will be done;
> there is nothing new under the sun.
Is there a thing of which it is said,
> "See, this is new"?
It has already been,
> in the ages before us.
The people of long ago are not remembered,
> nor will there be any remembrance
of people yet to come
> by those who come after them. (Eccles. 1:9-11)

Psalm	Additional Reading
Psalm 49:1-12	Mark 10:17-22
The folly of trust in riches	*Treasure in heaven*

Hymn: I Want to Walk as a Child of the Light, ELW 815

God of the ages, you are with us from generation to generation; and when your people grow weary and afraid, you offer newness of life in Jesus Christ. Help us to learn from the past and hope for the future.

Sunday, August 4, 2019
Time after Pentecost

Luke 12:13-21

Be rich toward God, your treasure

Then [Jesus] told them a parable: "The land of a rich man produced abundantly. And he thought to himself, 'What should I do, for I have no place to store my crops?' Then he said, 'I will do this: I will pull down my barns and build larger ones, and there I will store all my grain and my goods. And I will say to my soul, 'Soul, you have ample goods laid up for many years; relax, eat, drink, be merry.' But God said to him, 'You fool! This very night your life is being demanded of you. And the things you have prepared, whose will they be?' So it is with those who store up treasures for themselves but are not rich toward God." (Luke 12:16-21)

Psalm

Psalm 49:1-12
The folly of trust in riches

Additional Readings

Ecclesiastes 1:2, 12-14; 2:18-23
Search out wisdom

Colossians 3:1-11
Clothed in Christ

Hymn: God, Whose Giving Knows No Ending, ELW 678

Benevolent God, you are the source, the guide, and the goal of our lives. Teach us to love what is worth loving, to reject what is offensive to you, and to treasure what is precious in your sight, through Jesus Christ, our Savior and Lord.

Monday, August 5, 2019
Time after Pentecost

Psalm 127
Unless the Lord builds the house

Unless the LORD builds the house,
    those who build it labor in vain.
Unless the LORD guards the city,
    the guard keeps watch in vain.
It is in vain that you rise up early
    and go late to rest,
eating the bread of anxious toil;
    for he gives sleep to his beloved.

Sons are indeed a heritage from the LORD,
    the fruit of the womb a reward.
Like arrows in the hand of a warrior
    are the sons of one's youth.
Happy is the man who has
    his quiver full of them.
He shall not be put to shame
    when he speaks with his enemies in the gate. (Ps. 127:1-5)

Additional Readings
Ecclesiastes 2:1-17   **Colossians 3:18—4:1**
The fool accumulates wealth   *A household code*

Hymn: In Thee Is Gladness, ELW 867

Gracious God, you create us to live in community and you call us into relationships with loved ones and strangers alike. Strengthen our hearts in steadfast love, that young and old may joyfully and patiently care for one another.

Tuesday, August 6, 2019
Time after Pentecost

Colossians 4:2-6
Wise conduct toward outsiders

Devote yourselves to prayer, keeping alert in it with thanksgiving. At the same time pray for us as well that God will open to us a door for the word, that we may declare the mystery of Christ, for which I am in prison, so that I may reveal it clearly, as I should.

Conduct yourselves wisely toward outsiders, making the most of the time. Let your speech always be gracious, seasoned with salt, so that you may know how you ought to answer everyone. (Col. 4:2-6)

Psalm
Psalm 127
Unless the Lord builds the house

Additional Reading
Ecclesiastes 3:16—4:8
Death comes to all

Hymn: Lord, Teach Us How to Pray Aright, ELW 745

Holy God, in baptism you make us members of the body of Christ and send us into the world. May your Spirit reveal Christ's face in our neighbors, that we may in turn embody Christ's love for those we meet.

Wednesday, August 7, 2019
Time after Pentecost

Ecclesiastes 12:1-8, 13-14
Remember God

Fear God, and keep his commandments; for that is the whole duty of everyone. For God will bring every deed into judgment, including every secret thing, whether good or evil. (Eccles. 12:13b-14)

Psalm
Psalm 127
Unless the Lord builds the house

Additional Reading
Luke 12:22-31
Trust in God

Hymn: Be Thou My Vision, ELW 793

God of justice, nothing is hidden from you. You know all we have done and left undone. Forgive our sins and guide us always, that we may keep your commandments as we love and serve you and our neighbors.

Thursday, August 8, 2019
Time after Pentecost

Dominic, founder of the Order of Preachers (Dominicans), died 1221

Psalm 33:12-22

Let your loving kindness be upon us

Our soul waits for the Lord;
> he is our help and shield.
Our heart is glad in him,
> because we trust in his holy name.
Let your steadfast love, O Lord, be upon us,
> even as we hope in you. (Ps. 33:20-22)

Additional Readings

Job 21:1-16
The rich blessed with children despise God

Romans 9:1-9
True descendants of Abraham

Hymn: O God, Our Help in Ages Past, ELW 632

God of understanding and compassion, you know our anxious restlessness when we wait for signs of hope. Grant us patience and perseverance through your Holy Spirit to trust in your guidance and to follow where you lead.

Friday, August 9, 2019
Time after Pentecost

Ecclesiastes 6:1-6

Those who waste life

There is an evil that I have seen under the sun, and it lies heavy upon humankind: those to whom God gives wealth, possessions, and honor, so that they lack nothing of all that they desire, yet God does not enable them to enjoy these things, but a stranger enjoys them. This is vanity; it is a grievous ill. A man may beget a hundred children, and live many years; but however many are the days of his years, if he does not enjoy life's good things, or has no burial, I say that a stillborn child is better off than he. For it comes into vanity and goes into darkness, and in darkness its name is covered; moreover it has not seen the sun or known anything; yet it finds rest rather than he. Even though he should live a thousand years twice over, yet enjoy no good—do not all go to one place? (Eccles. 6:1-6)

Psalm
Psalm 33:12-22
Let your loving kindness be upon us

Additional Reading
Acts 7:1-8
Descendants promised to Abraham

Hymn: O Master, Let Me Walk with You, ELW 818

God of truth, you know how we long for joy and are easily tempted by empty promises of happiness. Help us to discern what is false and choose what is true, that we may find real life in you.

Saturday, August 10, 2019
Time after Pentecost

Lawrence, deacon, martyr, died 258

Matthew 6:19-24

Treasures and masters

[Jesus said,] "Do not store up for yourselves treasures on earth, where moth and rust consume and where thieves break in and steal; but store up for yourselves treasures in heaven, where neither moth nor rust consumes and where thieves do not break in and steal. For where your treasure is, there your heart will be also." (Matt. 6:19-21)

Psalm

Psalm 33:12-22
Let your loving kindness be upon us

Additional Reading

Genesis 11:27-32
The ancestors of Abram and Sarai

Hymn: Children of the Heavenly Father, ELW 781

God of wisdom, you sent Jesus into the world to give us abundant life. Help us to strive not for the wealth of material possessions but for the richness of generosity, so that all might be fed, nurtured, and loved.

Sunday, August 11, 2019
Time after Pentecost

Clare, Abbess of San Damiano, died 1253

Luke 12:32-40

The treasure of the kingdom

[Jesus said,] "Do not be afraid, little flock, for it is your Father's good pleasure to give you the kingdom. Sell your possessions, and give alms. Make purses for yourselves that do not wear out, an unfailing treasure in heaven, where no thief comes near and no moth destroys. For where your treasure is, there your heart will be also." (Luke 12:32-34)

Psalm

Psalm 33:12-22
Let your loving kindness be upon us

Additional Readings

Genesis 15:1-6
God's promise of a child

Hebrews 11:1-3, 8-16
Abraham's faith

Hymn: Lord Jesus, You Shall Be My Song, ELW 808

Almighty God, you sent your Holy Spirit to be the life and light of your church. Open our hearts to the riches of your grace, that we may be ready to receive you wherever you appear, through Jesus Christ, our Savior and Lord.

Monday, August 12, 2019
Time after Pentecost

Psalm 89:1-18
God's covenant with David

I will sing of your steadfast love, O LORD, forever;
> with my mouth I will proclaim your faithfulness to all generations.
I declare that your steadfast love is established forever;
> your faithfulness is as firm as the heavens.

You said, "I have made a covenant with my chosen one,
> I have sworn to my servant David:
'I will establish your descendants forever,
> and build your throne for all generations.'" (Ps. 89:1-4)

Additional Readings
2 Chronicles 33:1-17
Manasseh returns to God

Hebrews 11:1-7
The ancestors' faith

Hymn: You Servants of God, ELW 825

Faithful God, your promises do not fail. You are present with us in every time and place. Inspire us to share your story in our lives, that together with our ancestors we may sing your love for all generations.

Tuesday, August 13, 2019
Time after Pentecost

Florence Nightingale, died 1910; Clara Maass, died 1901; renewers of society

Hebrews 11:17-28
The faith of Abraham's descendants

By faith Abraham, when put to the test, offered up Isaac. He who had received the promises was ready to offer up his only son, of whom he had been told, "It is through Isaac that descendants shall be named for you." He considered the fact that God is able even to raise someone from the dead—and figuratively speaking, he did receive him back. (Heb. 11:17-19)

Psalm
Psalm 89:1-18
God's covenant with David

Additional Reading
2 Chronicles 34:22-33
Huldah preaches the covenant

Hymn: Faith of Our Fathers, ELW 812/813

God of the covenant, the stories of our ancestors tell us of your promises for us, and your love is faithful even when we are not. Let your steadfast love grant us courage to entrust our whole lives to you.

Wednesday, August 14, 2019
Time after Pentecost

Maximilian Kolbe, died 1941; Kaj Munk, died 1944; martyrs

Luke 12:41-48
A parable of the slaves

Peter said, "Lord, are you telling this parable for us or for everyone?" And the Lord said, "Who then is the faithful and prudent manager whom his master will put in charge of his slaves, to give them their allowance of food at the proper time? Blessed is that slave whom his master will find at work when he arrives. Truly I tell you, he will put that one in charge of all his possessions." (Luke 12:41-44)

Psalm
Psalm 89:1-18
God's covenant with David

Additional Reading
Jeremiah 33:14-26
God remembers the covenant

Hymn: We Are an Offering, ELW 692

Trusting God, you call us by name and entrust your holy work to our hands. Lead us in joyful service and equip us for our vocations, that together we may build your kingdom of justice and peace on earth.

Thursday, August 15, 2019
Mary, Mother of Our Lord

Luke 1:46-55
Mary's thanksgiving

And Mary said,

"My soul magnifies the Lord,

and my spirit rejoices in God my Savior,

for he has looked with favor on the lowliness of his servant.

Surely, from now on all generations will call me blessed;

for the Mighty One has done great things for me,

and holy is his name." (Luke 1:46-49)

Psalm

Psalm 34:1-9
O magnify the Lord with me

Additional Readings

Isaiah 61:7-11
God will cause righteousness to spring up

Galatians 4:4-7
We are no longer slaves, but children

Hymn: Signs and Wonders, ELW 672

Almighty God, in choosing the virgin Mary to be the mother of your Son, you made known your gracious regard for the poor, the lowly, and the despised. Grant us grace to receive your word in humility, and so to be made one with your Son, Jesus Christ our Savior and Lord, who lives and reigns with you and the Holy Spirit, one God, now and forever.

Friday, August 16, 2019
Time after Pentecost

Psalm 82
O God, rule the earth

God has taken his place in the divine council;
   in the midst of the gods he holds judgment:
"How long will you judge unjustly
   and show partiality to the wicked?
Give justice to the weak and the orphan;
   maintain the right of the lowly and the destitute.
Rescue the weak and the needy;
   deliver them from the hand of the wicked." (Ps. 82:1-4)

Additional Readings
1 Samuel 5:1-12
The Philistines punished

Hebrews 10:32-39
Do not abandon your confidence

Hymn: Peace, to Soothe Our Bitter Woes, ELW 381

God of tender care for the vulnerable, your heart breaks when your people suffer unjustly. Turn our thoughts and our actions toward help for those who are poor, orphaned, and in need, that your justice may reign for all people.

Saturday, August 17, 2019
Time after Pentecost

1 Samuel 6:1-16
The Philistines atone for sacrilege

Now the people of Beth-shemesh were reaping their wheat harvest in the valley. When they looked up and saw the ark, they went with rejoicing to meet it. The cart came into the field of Joshua of Beth-shemesh, and stopped there. A large stone was there; so they split up the wood of the cart and offered the cows as a burnt offering to the LORD. The Levites took down the ark of the LORD and the box that was beside it, in which were the gold objects, and set them upon the large stone. Then the people of Beth-shemesh offered burnt offerings and presented sacrifices on that day to the LORD. When the five lords of the Philistines saw it, they returned that day to Ekron. (1 Sam. 6:13-16)

Psalm
Psalm 82
O God, rule the earth

Additional Reading
Matthew 24:15-27
The desolating sacrilege

Hymn: Accept, O Lord, the Gifts We Bring, ELW 691

Almighty God, your presence makes all places holy ground, and your glory transforms the ordinary moments of our lives. Help us to be attentive to your Spirit, that in awe and thankfulness we may offer our lives to your service.

Sunday, August 18, 2019
Time after Pentecost

Luke 12:49-56
Jesus brings fire on earth

[Jesus said,] "I came to bring fire to the earth, and how I wish it were already kindled! I have a baptism with which to be baptized, and what stress I am under until it is completed! Do you think that I have come to bring peace to the earth? No, I tell you, but rather division! From now on five in one household will be divided, three against two and two against three; they will be divided:

father against son
    and son against father,
mother against daughter
    and daughter against mother,
mother-in-law against her daughter-in-law
    and daughter-in-law against mother-in-law." (Luke 12:49-53)

Psalm
Psalm 82
O God, rule the earth

Additional Readings
Jeremiah 23:23-29
God's word is like fire

Hebrews 11:29—12:2
The faith of the Hebrew people

Hymn: We've Come This Far by Faith, ELW 633

O God, judge eternal, you love justice and hate oppression, and you call us to share your zeal for truth. Give us courage to take our stand with all victims of bloodshed and greed, and, following your servants and prophets, to look to the pioneer and perfecter of our faith, your Son, Jesus Christ, our Savior and Lord.

Monday, August 19, 2019
Time after Pentecost

Psalm 32
Prayer for forgiveness

Happy are those whose transgression is forgiven,
>   whose sin is covered.
Happy are those to whom the LORD imputes no iniquity,
>   and in whose spirit there is no deceit.

While I kept silence, my body wasted away
>   through my groaning all day long.
For day and night your hand was heavy upon me;
>   my strength was dried up as by the heat of summer.

Then I acknowledged my sin to you,
>   and I did not hide my iniquity;
I said, "I will confess my transgressions to the LORD,"
>   and you forgave the guilt of my sin. (Ps. 32:1-5)

Additional Readings
Jeremiah 23:30-40
False prophets

1 John 4:1-6
False prophets are in the world

Hymn: O Christ, Our Hope, ELW 604

Merciful God, when in guilt and shame we hide our faces from you, you gently turn us back and we find grace in you. Free us to boldly confess our sins to you and to one another, giving and receiving forgiveness.

Tuesday, August 20, 2019
Time after Pentecost

Bernard, Abbot of Clairvaux, died 1153

Acts 7:44-53

Our ancestors persecuted true prophets

[Stephen replied to the high priest:] "You stiff-necked people, uncircumcised in heart and ears, you are forever opposing the Holy Spirit, just as your ancestors used to do. Which of the prophets did your ancestors not persecute? They killed those who foretold the coming of the Righteous One, and now you have become his betrayers and murderers. You are the ones that received the law as ordained by angels, and yet you have not kept it." (Acts 7:51-53)

Psalm

Psalm 32
Prayer for forgiveness

Additional Reading

Jeremiah 25:15-29
The cup of God's wrath

Hymn: O Jesus, Joy of Loving Hearts, ELW 658

Wise and patient God, your faithful word of life too often finds us unwilling to listen. Soften our stubborn hearts to hear the holy wisdom of the prophets in every age, that we may discern your will and follow Christ.

Wednesday, August 21, 2019
Time after Pentecost

Jeremiah 25:30-38

The peaceful flock is devastated

Wail, you shepherds, and cry out;
> roll in ashes, you lords of the flock,
for the days of your slaughter have come—and your dispersions,
> and you shall fall like a choice vessel.
Flight shall fail the shepherds,
> and there shall be no escape for the lords of the flock.
Hark! the cry of the shepherds,
> and the wail of the lords of the flock!
For the LORD is despoiling their pasture,
> and the peaceful folds are devastated,
> because of the fierce anger of the LORD.
Like a lion he has left his covert;
> for their land has become a waste
because of the cruel sword,
> and because of his fierce anger. (Jer. 25:34-38)

Psalm

Psalm 32
Prayer for forgiveness

Additional Reading

Luke 19:45-48
Jesus cleanses the temple

Hymn: O Lord, Hear My Prayer, ELW 751

God of fierce love for the world, your anger is kindled by injustice and your mighty arm sweeps away all evil, including the evil in our own hearts. Restore us as your children, that we may love one another.

Thursday, August 22, 2019
Time after Pentecost

Psalm 103:1-8
Crowned with mercy

Bless the LORD, O my soul,
 and all that is within me,
 bless his holy name.
Bless the LORD, O my soul,
 and do not forget all his benefits—
who forgives all your iniquity,
 who heals all your diseases,
who redeems your life from the Pit,
 who crowns you with steadfast love and mercy,
who satisfies you with good as long as you live
 so that your youth is renewed like the eagle's. (Ps. 103:1-5)

Additional Readings
Numbers 15:32-41
The severity of breaking sabbath law

Hebrews 12:3-17
Call for endurance

Hymn: Praise to the Lord, the Almighty, ELW 858

God of blessing, your saving grace finds us at our lowest points; in our struggle you are already nearer to us than we are to ourselves. Through your Holy Spirit, raise us up, renewing us in faith and hope.

Friday, August 23, 2019
Time after Pentecost

2 Chronicles 8:12-15
Solomon honors sabbaths

Then Solomon offered up burnt offerings to the LORD on the altar of the LORD that he had built in front of the vestibule, as the duty of each day required, offering according to the commandment of Moses for the sabbaths, the new moons, and the three annual festivals—the festival of unleavened bread, the festival of weeks, and the festival of booths. According to the ordinance of his father David, he appointed the divisions of the priests for their service, and the Levites for their offices of praise and ministry alongside the priests as the duty of each day required, and the gatekeepers in their divisions for the several gates; for so David the man of God had commanded. They did not turn away from what the king had commanded the priests and Levites regarding anything at all, or regarding the treasuries. (2 Chron. 8:12-15)

Psalm
Psalm 103:1-8
Crowned with mercy

Additional Reading
Acts 17:1-9
Paul preaches Christ on the sabbath

Hymn: Let All Things Now Living, ELW 881

God of every day, you show us what is good for life: time for celebration, work, and rest. Grant that all your people may find this balance, to better serve you and others in wholeness, health, and joy.

Saturday, August 24, 2019
Bartholomew, Apostle

John 1:43-51

Jesus says, Follow me

When Jesus saw Nathanael coming toward him, he said of him, "Here is truly an Israelite in whom there is no deceit!" Nathanael asked him, "Where did you get to know me?" Jesus answered, "I saw you under the fig tree before Philip called you." Nathanael replied, "Rabbi, you are the Son of God! You are the King of Israel!" Jesus answered, "Do you believe because I told you that I saw you under the fig tree? You will see greater things than these." And he said to him, "Very truly, I tell you, you will see heaven opened and the angels of God ascending and descending upon the Son of Man." (John 1:47-51)

Psalm

Psalm 12
A plea for help in evil times

Additional Readings

Exodus 19:1-6
Israel is God's priestly kingdom

1 Corinthians 12:27-31a
The body of Christ

Hymn: Listen, God Is Calling, ELW 513

Almighty and everlasting God, you gave to your apostle Bartholomew grace truly to believe and courageously to preach your word. Grant that your church may proclaim the good news to the ends of the earth, through Jesus Christ, our Savior and Lord, who lives and reigns with you and the Holy Spirit, one God, now and forever.

Sunday, August 25, 2019
Time after Pentecost

Luke 13:10-17
Jesus heals on the sabbath

And just then there appeared a woman with a spirit that had crippled her for eighteen years. She was bent over and was quite unable to stand up straight. When Jesus saw her, he called her over and said, "Woman, you are set free from your ailment.". . . But the leader of the synagogue, indignant because Jesus had cured on the sabbath, kept saying to the crowd, "There are six days on which work ought to be done; come on those days and be cured, and not on the sabbath day." But the Lord answered him and said, "You hypocrites! Does not each of you on the sabbath untie his ox or his donkey from the manger, and lead it away to give it water? And ought not this woman, a daughter of Abraham whom Satan bound for eighteen long years, be set free from this bondage on the sabbath day?" (Luke 13:11-12, 14-16)

Psalm
Psalm 103:1-8
Crowned with mercy

Additional Readings
Isaiah 58:9b-14
Do not trample the sabbath

Hebrews 12:18-29
Coming to the city of the living God

Hymn: Praise the One Who Breaks the Darkness, ELW 843

O God, mighty and immortal, you know that as fragile creatures surrounded by great dangers, we cannot by ourselves stand upright. Give us strength of mind and body, so that even when we suffer because of human sin, we may rise victorious through your Son, Jesus Christ, our Savior and Lord.

Psalm 109:21-31

Praise for healing

Help me, O LORD my God!
>   Save me according to your steadfast love. . . .
May my accusers be clothed with dishonor;
>   may they be wrapped in their own shame as in a mantle.
With my mouth I will give great thanks to the LORD;
>   I will praise him in the midst of the throng.
For he stands at the right hand of the needy,
>   to save them from those who would condemn them to death.
(Ps. 109:26, 29-31)

Additional Readings

Ezekiel 20:1-17
The people profaned the sabbath

Hebrews 3:7—4:11
Sabbath rest of God's people

Hymn: O Savior, Precious Savior, ELW 820

Steadfast God, your justice reigns. Vindicate us when we are wrongfully accused and correct us when we act unjustly and cause others pain. Place the truth in our hearts and guide our feet to stand with those in need.

Tuesday, August 27, 2019
Time after Pentecost

Ezekiel 20:18-32
Israel become like the nations

I said to their children in the wilderness, Do not follow the statutes of your parents, nor observe their ordinances, nor defile yourselves with their idols. I the LORD am your God; follow my statutes, and be careful to observe my ordinances, and hallow my sabbaths that they may be a sign between me and you, so that you may know that I the LORD am your God. (Ezek. 20:18-20)

Psalm
Psalm 109:21-31
Praise for healing

Additional Reading
Revelation 3:7-13
The new Jerusalem from heaven

Hymn: We Are Marching in the Light, ELW 866

God of the wilderness, you always find a way. When we do not know which way to go or whose advice to take, be our guide and help, that in following your direction we may find the right path.

Wednesday, August 28, 2019
Time after Pentecost

Augustine, Bishop of Hippo, died 430
Moses the Black, monk, martyr, died around 400

Luke 6:6-11
Jesus heals on the sabbath

On another sabbath [Jesus] entered the synagogue and taught, and there was a man there whose right hand was withered. The scribes and the Pharisees watched him to see whether he would cure on the sabbath, so that they might find an accusation against him. Even though he knew what they were thinking, he said to the man who had the withered hand, "Come and stand here." He got up and stood there. Then Jesus said to them, "I ask you, is it lawful to do good or to do harm on the sabbath, to save life or to destroy it?" After looking around at all of them, he said to him, "Stretch out your hand." He did so, and his hand was restored. (Luke 6:6-10)

Psalm
Psalm 109:21-31
Praise for healing

Additional Reading
Ezekiel 20:33-44
God restores rebellious Israel

Hymn: Jesus Lives, My Sure Defense, ELW 621

God of healing, in Jesus you stretched out your hand to restore all people to life. Strengthen our bodies, enliven our minds, and mend our broken hearts, that we may also work for the healing of the world.

Thursday, August 29, 2019
Time after Pentecost

Psalm 112
The righteous are merciful

Praise the LORD!
> Happy are those who fear the LORD,
> who greatly delight in his commandments.
Their descendants will be mighty in the land;
> the generation of the upright will be blessed.
Wealth and riches are in their houses,
> and their righteousness endures forever. (Ps. 112:1-3)

Additional Readings
Proverbs 15:13-17
A continual feast for the poor

1 Peter 3:8-12
Repay abuse with a blessing

Hymn: Praise and Thanks and Adoration, ELW 783

Righteous God, your commandments are for the sake of the world, that all people and the earth might flourish in your love. Inspire and empower us to live in kindness and to work for justice and mercy all our days.

Friday, August 30, 2019
Time after Pentecost

1 Peter 4:7-11
Be hospitable to one another

The end of all things is near; therefore be serious and discipline yourselves for the sake of your prayers. Above all, maintain constant love for one another, for love covers a multitude of sins. Be hospitable to one another without complaining. Like good stewards of the manifold grace of God, serve one another with whatever gift each of you has received. Whoever speaks must do so as one speaking the very words of God; whoever serves must do so with the strength that God supplies, so that God may be glorified in all things through Jesus Christ. To him belong the glory and the power forever and ever. Amen. (1 Peter 4:7-11)

Psalm
Psalm 112
The righteous are merciful

Additional Reading
Proverbs 18:6-12
Humility precedes honor

Hymn: We Give Thee but Thine Own, ELW 686

God of beloved community, you remind us that every life is precious and you give each of us gifts to use together for the sake of the world. Make us good stewards of all we have and all we are.

Saturday, August 31, 2019
Time after Pentecost

Proverbs 21:1-4, 24-26
The righteous give and do not hold back

The proud, haughty person, named "Scoffer,"
    acts with arrogant pride.
The craving of the lazy person is fatal,
    for lazy hands refuse to labor.
All day long the wicked covet,
    but the righteous give and do not hold back. (Prov. 21:24-26)

Psalm

Psalm 112
The righteous are merciful

Additional Reading

Matthew 20:20-28
A request for seats of honor

Hymn: Awake, My Soul, and with the Sun, ELW 557

Generous God, you urge us to find our pride in humility and our peace in faithful service. Help us to give and not hold back, trusting that you will provide what we need for our work and for our living.

Prayer List for September

- Pray for those who went to make a difference
- Pray for the creatures native to the Amazon Rainforest
- Pray for those making minimum wage
- Pray for Leah
- Pray for those struggling academically
- Pray for marine creatures

Time after Pentecost

Autumn

The days of early autumn (September and October) herald the resumption of a more regular schedule: school begins, church education programs commence, and the steady rhythms of work are accompanied by cooling breezes and the changing colors of the landscape. During these months, various crops are harvested and appear on roadside stands and in grocery stores. In many countries the harvest days of September and October are marked with prayer, feasting, and special care for the poor and hungry.

Table Prayer for Autumn

We praise you and bless you, O God,
for autumn days,
and for the gifts of this table.
Grant us grace to share your goodness,
until all people are fed by the harvest of the earth.
We ask this through Christ our Lord. Amen.

Sunday, September 1, 2019
Time after Pentecost

Luke 14:1, 7-14

Invite the poor to your banquet

[Jesus] said also to the one who had invited him, "When you give a luncheon or a dinner, do not invite your friends or your brothers or your relatives or rich neighbors, in case they may invite you in return, and you would be repaid. But when you give a banquet, invite the poor, the crippled, the lame, and the blind. And you will be blessed, because they cannot repay you, for you will be repaid at the resurrection of the righteous." (Luke 14:12-14)

Psalm

Psalm 112
The righteous are merciful

Additional Readings

Proverbs 25:6-7
Do not put yourself forward

Hebrews 13:1-8, 15-16
God is with us

Hymn: Let Us Go Now to the Banquet, ELW 523

O God, you resist those who are proud and give grace to those who are humble. Give us the humility of your Son, that we may embody the generosity of Jesus Christ, our Savior and Lord.

Monday, September 2, 2019
Time after Pentecost

Nikolai Frederik Severin Grundtvig, bishop, renewer of the church, died 1872

Psalm 119:65-72
God blesses the humble

You have dealt well with your servant,
    O Lord, according to your word.
Teach me good judgment and knowledge,
    for I believe in your commandments.
Before I was humbled I went astray,
    but now I keep your word.
You are good and do good;
    teach me your statutes. (Ps. 119:65-68)

Additional Readings
2 Chronicles 12:1-12   Hebrews 13:7-21
King Rehoboam humbles himself   *Call for faithfulness*

Hymn: God's Word Is Our Great Heritage, ELW 509

Lord God, you deal with each of us patiently, meeting us where we go astray. It is by your example that we learn to live faithful, humble lives. Be with us this day and every day that we may live according to your word.

Tuesday, September 3, 2019
Time after Pentecost

Titus 1:1-9
Humble and hospitable leaders

I left you behind in Crete for this reason, so that you should put in order what remained to be done, and should appoint elders in every town, as I directed you: someone who is blameless, married only once, whose children are believers, not accused of debauchery and not rebellious. For a bishop, as God's steward, must be blameless; he must not be arrogant or quick-tempered or addicted to wine or violent or greedy for gain; but he must be hospitable, a lover of goodness, prudent, upright, devout, and self-controlled. He must have a firm grasp of the word that is trustworthy in accordance with the teaching, so that he may be able both to preach with sound doctrine and to refute those who contradict it. (Titus 1:5-9)

Psalm
Psalm 119:65-72
God blesses the humble

Additional Reading
Isaiah 2:12-17
Pride shall be brought low

Hymn: Lord, Whose Love in Humble Service, ELW 712

Holy God, you've invited us to be your stewards in the world. Help us put in order the tasks to which you've called us. Help us carry out your will with humility, hospitality, and love.

Wednesday, September 4, 2019
Time after Pentecost

Isaiah 57:14-21
God blesses the humble

It shall be said,
"Build up, build up, prepare the way,
    remove every obstruction from my people's way."
For thus says the high and lofty one
    who inhabits eternity, whose name is Holy:
I dwell in the high and holy place,
    and also with those who are contrite and humble in spirit,
to revive the spirit of the humble,
    and to revive the heart of the contrite.
For I will not continually accuse,
    nor will I always be angry;
for then the spirits would grow faint before me,
    even the souls that I have made. (Isa. 57:14-16)

Psalm
Psalm 119:65-72
God blesses the humble

Additional Reading
Luke 14:15-24
God's hospitality to the humble

Hymn: Built on a Rock, ELW 652

Creator God, you dwell in the high and holy place, yet you are also with us in each step here on earth. Let the vastness of your love for your creation overwhelm us, that we may grow in humility with every breath.

Thursday, September 5, 2019
Time after Pentecost

Psalm 1
Delight in the law

Happy are those
>who do not follow the advice of the wicked,
or take the path that sinners tread,
>or sit in the seat of scoffers;
but their delight is in the law of the Lord,
>and on his law they meditate day and night.
They are like trees
>planted by streams of water,
which yield their fruit in its season,
>and their leaves do not wither.
In all that they do, they prosper. (Ps. 1:1-3)

Additional Readings

Genesis 39:1-23
Joseph does not sin against God

Philippians 2:25-30
Welcome a faithful servant home

Hymn: Great Is Thy Faithfulness, ELW 733

Loving God, like trees planted by streams of water, our lives are nourished when we are rooted in you. Help us not forget that we flourish in you, bearing fruit that sustains your reign on earth.

Friday, September 6, 2019
Time after Pentecost

Colossians 4:7-17
A faithful and beloved brother

Tychicus will tell you all the news about me; he is a beloved brother, a faithful minister, and a fellow servant in the Lord. I have sent him to you for this very purpose, so that you may know how we are and that he may encourage your hearts; he is coming with Onesimus, the faithful and beloved brother, who is one of you. They will tell you about everything here. (Col. 4:7-9)

Psalm
Psalm 1
Delight in the law

Additional Reading
Deuteronomy 7:12-26
The way of obedience

Hymn: We All Are One in Mission, ELW 576

Lord, it is in fellowship with your people that we build one another up and encourage one another along our journeys. Thank you for the gift of friends and neighbors, people who are witnesses to us of your love, mercy, compassion, and grace.

Saturday, September 7, 2019
Time after Pentecost

Deuteronomy 29:2-20

A renewed covenant

You stand assembled today, all of you, before the LORD your God—the leaders of your tribes, your elders, and your officials, all the men of Israel, your children, your women, and the aliens who are in your camp, both those who cut your wood and those who draw your water—to enter into the covenant of the LORD your God, sworn by an oath, which the LORD your God is making with you today; in order that he may establish you today as his people, and that he may be your God, as he promised you and as he swore to your ancestors, to Abraham, to Isaac, and to Jacob. (Deut. 29:10-13)

Psalm	Additional Reading
Psalm 1	**Matthew 10:34-42**
Delight in the law	*The cost of discipleship*

Hymn: On My Heart Imprint Your Image, ELW 811

Almighty God, we join the long lineage of people whom you have called your own from all walks of life, backgrounds, and corners of the earth. Help us not to forget that our neighbors are our family, that every person is your child, and that we are all yours.

Sunday, September 8, 2019
Time after Pentecost

Luke 14:25-33
Give up your possessions

[Jesus said,] "What king, going out to wage war against another king, will not sit down first and consider whether he is able with ten thousand to oppose the one who comes against him with twenty thousand? If he cannot, then, while the other is still far away, he sends a delegation and asks for the terms of peace. So therefore, none of you can become my disciple if you do not give up all your possessions." (Luke 14:31-33)

Psalm
Psalm 1
Delight in the law

Additional Readings
Deuteronomy 30:15-20
Walk in the way of life

Philemon 1-21
Paul says, Receive Onesimus

Hymn: Jesus, Keep Me Near the Cross, ELW 335

Direct us, O Lord God, in all our doings with your continual help, that in all our works, begun, continued, and ended in you, we may glorify your holy name; and finally, by your mercy, bring us to everlasting life, through Jesus Christ, our Savior and Lord.

Monday, September 9, 2019
Time after Pentecost

Peter Claver, priest, missionary to Colombia, died 1654

Psalm 101
Choosing God's law

I will sing of loyalty and of justice;
    to you, O Lord, I will sing.
I will study the way that is blameless.
    When shall I attain it?

I will walk with integrity of heart
    within my house;
I will not set before my eyes
    anything that is base.

I hate the work of those who fall away;
    it shall not cling to me. (Ps. 101:1-3)

Additional Readings
2 Kings 17:24-41
The Assyrians worship other gods

1 Timothy 3:14—4:5
Behavior in the church

Hymn: How Marvelous God's Greatness, ELW 830

Merciful God, you call us to set our eyes on justice and to tune our hearts to your will for the world. Help us to hear the voices of those who grieve, who hunger for righteousness, and who cry out for comfort, that we may surround them with hope.

Tuesday, September 10, 2019
Time after Pentecost

1 Timothy 4:6-16
Being a servant of Christ

If you put these instructions before the brothers and sisters, you will be a good servant of Christ Jesus, nourished on the words of the faith and of the sound teaching that you have followed. Have nothing to do with profane myths and old wives' tales. Train yourself in godliness, for, while physical training is of some value, godliness is valuable in every way, holding promise for both the present life and the life to come. (1 Tim. 4:6-8)

Psalm
Psalm 101
Choosing God's law

Additional Reading
2 Kings 18:9-18
Transgressing the covenant

Hymn: O Christ, Your Heart, Compassionate, ELW 722

Lord of all, in your Son Jesus Christ you trained us in godliness, setting an example of peace, love, and grace for us to follow. Grant us the courage to continue living in this example and to choose the way of Christ regardless of the cost.

Wednesday, September 11, 2019
Time after Pentecost

Luke 18:18-30
The rich ruler

A certain ruler asked [Jesus], "Good Teacher, what must I do to inherit eternal life?" Jesus said to him, "Why do you call me good? No one is good but God alone. You know the commandments: 'You shall not commit adultery; You shall not murder; You shall not steal; You shall not bear false witness; Honor your father and mother.'" He replied, "I have kept all these since my youth." When Jesus heard this, he said to him, "There is still one thing lacking. Sell all that you own and distribute the money to the poor, and you will have treasure in heaven; then come, follow me." (Luke 18:18-22)

Psalm
Psalm 101
Choosing God's law

Additional Reading
2 Kings 18:19-25; 19:1-7
A king repents, the nation is saved

Hymn: Will You Come and Follow Me, ELW 798

Good and loving God, you've commanded us to care for our neighbors the way you've cared for us. Help us remember that it is not our treasure on earth that matters to you but that we treasure what matters to you in our hearts.

Thursday, September 12, 2019
Time after Pentecost

Psalm 51:1-10
Have mercy upon me, O God

Have mercy on me, O God,
> according to your steadfast love;
according to your abundant mercy
> blot out my transgressions.
Wash me thoroughly from my iniquity,
> and cleanse me from my sin.

For I know my transgressions,
> and my sin is ever before me.
Against you, you alone, have I sinned,
> and done what is evil in your sight,
so that you are justified in your sentence
> and blameless when you pass judgment. (Ps. 51:1-4)

Additional Readings
Genesis 6:1-6
Sinful humanity forgets God

1 Timothy 1:1-11
About false teachers

Hymn: Chief of Sinners Though I Be, ELW 609

Eternal God, you love us regardless of our past mistakes. Whatever our histories, we are made new when we call on you. Thank you for your forgiveness, for your grace, and for unending opportunities to begin again.

Friday, September 13, 2019
Time after Pentecost

John Chrysostom, Bishop of Constantinople, died 407

Genesis 7:6-10; 8:1-5
God remembers faithful Noah

Noah was six hundred years old when the flood of waters came on the earth. And Noah with his sons and his wife and his sons' wives went into the ark to escape the waters of the flood. Of clean animals, and of animals that are not clean, and of birds, and of everything that creeps on the ground, two and two, male and female, went into the ark with Noah, as God had commanded Noah. And after seven days the waters of the flood came on the earth. (Gen. 7:6-10)

Psalm
Psalm 51:1-10
Have mercy upon me, O God

Additional Reading
2 Peter 2:1-10a
God judges and rescues

Hymn: God of the Sparrow, ELW 740

Lord, as you looked over Noah when the rains covered the earth, you look over us. Grant that by Noah's example we will remember the promise of your grace: that there is nowhere we can go where we are not covered by your love.

Saturday, September 14, 2019
Holy Cross Day

John 3:13-17
The Son of Man will be lifted up

[Jesus said to Nicodemus,] "No one has ascended into heaven except the one who descended from heaven, the Son of Man. And just as Moses lifted up the serpent in the wilderness, so must the Son of Man be lifted up, that whoever believes in him may have eternal life.

"For God so loved the world that he gave his only Son, so that everyone who believes in him may not perish but may have eternal life.

"Indeed, God did not send the Son into the world to condemn the world, but in order that the world might be saved through him." (John 3:13-17)

Psalm

Psalm 98:1-4
God has done marvelous things

Additional Readings

Numbers 21:4b-9
A bronze serpent in the wilderness

1 Corinthians 1:18-24
The cross is the power of God

Hymn: When I Survey the Wondrous Cross, ELW 803

Almighty God, your Son Jesus Christ was lifted high upon the cross so that he might draw the whole world to himself. To those who look upon the cross, grant your wisdom, healing, and eternal life, through Jesus Christ, our Savior and Lord, who lives and reigns with you and the Holy Spirit, one God, now and forever.

Sunday, September 15, 2019
Time after Pentecost

Luke 15:1-10
Lost sheep and lost coin

[Jesus] told them this parable: "Which one of you, having a hundred sheep and losing one of them, does not leave the ninety-nine in the wilderness and go after the one that is lost until he finds it? When he has found it, he lays it on his shoulders and rejoices. And when he comes home, he calls together his friends and neighbors, saying to them, 'Rejoice with me, for I have found my sheep that was lost.' Just so, I tell you, there will be more joy in heaven over one sinner who repents than over ninety-nine righteous persons who need no repentance." (Luke 15:3-7)

Psalm
Psalm 51:1-10
Have mercy upon me, O God

Additional Readings
Exodus 32:7-14
Moses begs forgiveness

1 Timothy 1:12-17
Christ Jesus came for sinners

Hymn: Beloved, God's Chosen, ELW 648

O God, overflowing with mercy and compassion, you lead back to yourself all those who go astray. Preserve your people in your loving care, that we may reject whatever is contrary to you and may follow all things that sustain our life in your Son, Jesus Christ, our Savior and Lord.

Monday, September 16, 2019
Time after Pentecost

Cyprian, Bishop of Carthage, martyr, died around 258

Psalm 73
God is my portion

My flesh and my heart may fail,
> but God is the strength of my heart and my portion forever.

Indeed, those who are far from you will perish;
> you put an end to those who are false to you.
But for me it is good to be near God;
> I have made the Lord GOD my refuge,
> to tell of all your works. (Ps. 73:26-28)

Additional Readings
Amos 7:1-6
God relents from punishing Israel

1 Timothy 1:18-20
The danger of rejecting conscience

Hymn: A Mighty Fortress Is Our God, ELW 503/504

Lord God, we know that you are never far from us, that you always hear us when we call. When we stray from this truth, help us to return and to find comfort in your closeness, for it is in you that we will find our strength.

Tuesday, September 17, 2019
Time after Pentecost

Hildegard, Abbess of Bingen, died 1179

Jonah 3:1-10
God relents from punishing Nineveh

When the news reached the king of Nineveh, he rose from his throne, removed his robe, covered himself with sackcloth, and sat in ashes. Then he had a proclamation made in Nineveh: "By the decree of the king and his nobles: No human being or animal, no herd or flock, shall taste anything. They shall not feed, nor shall they drink water. Human beings and animals shall be covered with sackcloth, and they shall cry mightily to God. All shall turn from their evil ways and from the violence that is in their hands. Who knows? God may relent and change his mind; he may turn from his fierce anger, so that we do not perish."

When God saw what they did, how they turned from their evil ways, God changed his mind about the calamity that he had said he would bring upon them; and he did not do it. (Jonah 3:6-10)

Psalm
Psalm 73
God is my portion

Additional Reading
2 Peter 3:8-13
That all may come to repentance

Hymn: There's a Wideness in God's Mercy, ELW 587/588

Almighty God, you rejoice when we repent from wickedness. Thank you for your patience with us when we forget the things to which you've called us: faithfulness, kindness, mercy, and justice. Continue to be patient with us as we journey in your grace.

Wednesday, September 18, 2019
Time after Pentecost

Dag Hammarskjöld, renewer of society, died 1961

Job 40:6-14; 42:1-6
Job repents

Then the LORD answered Job out of the whirlwind:
"Deck yourself with majesty and dignity;
    clothe yourself with glory and splendor.
Pour out the overflowings of your anger,
    and look on all who are proud, and abase them.
Look on all who are proud, and bring them low;
    tread down the wicked where they stand.
Hide them all in the dust together;
    bind their faces in the world below.
Then I will also acknowledge to you
    that your own right hand can give you victory." (Job 40:6, 10-14)

Psalm
Psalm 73
God is my portion

Additional Reading
Luke 22:31-33, 54-62
Peter denies Jesus

Hymn: Soul, Adorn Yourself with Gladness, ELW 488

Merciful Lord, you sent your prophets with sharp words for those who sinned against you. Help us to continue to hear your holy scripture and the work of the Holy Spirit around us. May we never cease to learn from those you've called to preach in your name.

Thursday, September 19, 2019
Time after Pentecost

Psalm 113
Our God lifts up the poor

Who is like the LORD our God,
>who is seated on high,
who looks far down
>on the heavens and the earth?
He raises the poor from the dust,
>and lifts the needy from the ash heap,
to make them sit with princes,
>with the princes of his people. (Ps. 113:5-8)

Additional Readings
Exodus 23:1-9
Justice for all

Romans 3:1-8
The justice of God

Hymn: Hear I Am, Lord, ELW 574

No other is like you, Lord. You flip the order of this world upside down so that the last shall be first and the small shall be great. Help us live out your vision for reversing the world's ills each day.

Friday, September 20, 2019
Time after Pentecost

Romans 8:31-39
It is God who justifies

What then are we to say about these things? If God is for us, who is against us? He who did not withhold his own Son, but gave him up for all of us, will he not with him also give us everything else? Who will bring any charge against God's elect? It is God who justifies. Who is to condemn? It is Christ Jesus, who died, yes, who was raised, who is at the right hand of God, who indeed intercedes for us. (Rom. 8:31-34)

Psalm
Psalm 113
Our God lifts up the poor

Additional Reading
Ezekiel 22:17-31
Israel becomes dross to God

Hymn: Neither Death nor Life, ELW 622

Almighty God, you did not send your Son to condemn us but to free us. Help us to walk in the footsteps of Jesus, remembering that he offers us the way to be made right with you.

Saturday, September 21, 2019
Matthew, Apostle and Evangelist

Matthew 9:9-13
Jesus calls to Matthew, Follow me

As Jesus was walking along, he saw a man called Matthew sitting at the tax booth; and he said to him, "Follow me." And he got up and followed him.

And as he sat at dinner in the house, many tax collectors and sinners came and were sitting with him and his disciples. When the Pharisees saw this, they said to his disciples, "Why does your teacher eat with tax collectors and sinners?" But when he heard this, he said, "Those who are well have no need of a physician, but those who are sick. Go and learn what this means, 'I desire mercy, not sacrifice.' For I have come to call not the righteous but sinners." (Matt. 9:9-13)

Psalm
Psalm 119:33-40
Give me understanding

Additional Readings
Ezekiel 2:8—3:11
A prophet to the house of Israel

Ephesians 2:4-10
By grace you have been saved

Hymn: Come, Follow Me, the Savior Spake, ELW 799

Almighty God, your Son our Savior called a despised tax collector to become one of his apostles. Help us, like Matthew, to respond to the transforming call of Jesus Christ, who lives and reigns with you and the Holy Spirit, one God, now and forever.

Sunday, September 22, 2019
Time after Pentecost

Luke 16:1-13

Serving God or wealth

[Jesus said,] "Whoever is faithful in a very little is faithful also in much; and whoever is dishonest in a very little is dishonest also in much. If then you have not been faithful with the dishonest wealth, who will entrust to you the true riches? And if you have not been faithful with what belongs to another, who will give you what is your own? No slave can serve two masters; for a slave will either hate the one and love the other, or be devoted to the one and despise the other. You cannot serve God and wealth." (Luke 16:10-13)

Psalm

Psalm 113
Our God lifts up the poor

Additional Readings

Amos 8:4-7
Those who trample the needy

1 Timothy 2:1-7
One God, one mediator

Hymn: When the Poor Ones, ELW 725

God among us, we gather in the name of your Son to learn love for one another. Keep our feet from evil paths. Turn our minds to your wisdom and our hearts to the grace revealed in your Son, Jesus Christ, our Savior and Lord.

Monday, September 23, 2019
Time after Pentecost

Psalm 12

Help for the poor

"Because the poor are despoiled, because the needy groan,
> I will now rise up," says the LORD;
> "I will place them in the safety for which they long."
The promises of the LORD are promises that are pure,
> silver refined in a furnace on the ground,
> purified seven times.

You, O LORD, will protect us;
> you will guard us from this generation forever. (Ps. 12:5-7)

Additional Readings

Proverbs 14:12-31
Oppressing the poor

Acts 4:1-12
Salvation through Jesus Christ

Hymn: Goodness Is Stronger than Evil, ELW 721

God of every generation, like silver refined in the furnace, you mold our lives into something beautiful. In you we find respite but also challenge. Help us see ourselves as you see us: brimming with potential, called by you.

Tuesday, September 24, 2019
Time after Pentecost

1 Corinthians 9:19-23

A servant of the gospel

For though I am free with respect to all, I have made myself a slave to all, so that I might win more of them. To the Jews I became as a Jew, in order to win Jews. To those under the law I became as one under the law (though I myself am not under the law) so that I might win those under the law. To those outside the law I became as one outside the law (though I am not free from God's law but am under Christ's law) so that I might win those outside the law. To the weak I became weak, so that I might win the weak. I have become all things to all people, that I might by all means save some. I do it all for the sake of the gospel, so that I may share in its blessings. (1 Cor. 9:19-23)

Psalm
Psalm 12
Help for the poor

Additional Reading
Proverbs 17:1-5
Oppressing the poor

Hymn: Send Me, Jesus, ELW 549

Lord God, you have written your laws in our hearts, commanding us to love you and our neighbors. Help us to be servants of the gospel you've given us in your Son Jesus Christ, sharing your saving mercy with the world.

Wednesday, September 25, 2019
Time after Pentecost

Proverbs 21:10-16

Ears closed to the cry of the poor

The souls of the wicked desire evil;
    their neighbors find no mercy in their eyes.
When a scoffer is punished, the simple become wiser;
    when the wise are instructed, they increase in knowledge.
The Righteous One observes the house of the wicked;
    he casts the wicked down to ruin.
If you close your ear to the cry of the poor,
    you will cry out and not be heard. (Prov. 21:10-13)

Psalm

Psalm 12
Help for the poor

Additional Reading

Luke 20:45—21:4
The rich versus the poor

Hymn: Where Cross the Crowded Ways of Life, ELW 719

Everlasting God, you've always heard the cries of the poor, the hurting, and those in need. Though you've never promised that our lives would be easy, you've promised to be with us. Thank you for not leaving us alone.

Thursday, September 26, 2019
Time after Pentecost

Psalm 146
Justice to the oppressed

Happy are those whose help is the God of Jacob,
     whose hope is in the LORD their God,
who made heaven and earth,
     the sea, and all that is in them;
who keeps faith forever;
who executes justice for the oppressed;
     who gives food to the hungry. (Ps. 146:5-7a)

Additional Readings
Proverbs 22:2-16   **2 Corinthians 8:8-15**
The rich versus the poor   *Christ became poor*

Hymn: We Come to the Hungry Feast, ELW 479

Creator God, just as you made the sun and the stars, the earth and the water, you've made each of us in your wonderful image. Help us not to take for granted what you've given us and to recognize your fingerprints on everyone we meet.

Friday, September 27, 2019
Time after Pentecost

Proverbs 28:3-10
The rich versus the poor

Better to be poor and walk in integrity
    than to be crooked in one's ways even though rich.
Those who keep the law are wise children,
    but companions of gluttons shame their parents.
One who augments wealth by exorbitant interest
    gathers it for another who is kind to the poor. (Prov. 28:6-8)

Psalm
Psalm 146
Justice to the oppressed

Additional Reading
Ephesians 2:1-10
God is rich in mercy

Hymn: We Are Called, ELW 720

Lord, it is easy to be swept up in the riches of this earth, desiring material treasures rather than keeping our eyes on you. Be with us when we struggle with greed and jealousy. Set our eyes on what is right and true.

Saturday, September 28, 2019
Time after Pentecost

Proverbs 28:11-28

Helpers of the poor lack nothing

The greedy person stirs up strife,
>but whoever trusts in the LORD will be enriched.
Those who trust in their own wits are fools;
>but those who walk in wisdom come through safely.
Whoever gives to the poor will lack nothing,
>but one who turns a blind eye will get many a curse.
When the wicked prevail, people go into hiding;
>but when they perish, the righteous increase. (Prov. 28:25-28)

Psalm

Psalm 146
Justice to the oppressed

Additional Reading

Luke 9:43b-48
Welcoming little ones

Hymn: O God of Mercy, God of Light, ELW 714

Loving God, in your kingdom those who lose themselves find themselves, those who give everything have much, and those who give nothing have little. Help us to trust in you for everything and to give of ourselves without fear.

Sunday, September 29, 2019
Time after Pentecost

Michael and All Angels (transferred to September 30)

Luke 16:19-31

Poor Lazarus and the rich man

[Jesus said,] "There was a rich man who was dressed in purple and fine linen and who feasted sumptuously every day. And at his gate lay a poor man named Lazarus, covered with sores, who longed to satisfy his hunger with what fell from the rich man's table; even the dogs would come and lick his sores. The poor man died and was carried away by the angels to be with Abraham. The rich man also died and was buried. In Hades, where he was being tormented, he looked up and saw Abraham far away with Lazarus by his side." (Luke 16:19-23)

Psalm

Psalm 146
Justice to the oppressed

Additional Readings

Amos 6:1a, 4-7
Warnings to the wealthy

1 Timothy 6:6-19
Pursuing God's justice

Hymn: Will You Let Me Be Your Servant, ELW 659

O God, rich in mercy, you look with compassion on this troubled world. Feed us with your grace, and grant us the treasure that comes only from you, through Jesus Christ, our Savior and Lord.

Monday, September 30, 2019
Michael and All Angels (transferred)

Jerome, translator, teacher, died 420

Revelation 12:7-12
Michael defeats Satan in a cosmic battle

War broke out in heaven; Michael and his angels fought against the dragon. The dragon and his angels fought back, but they were defeated, and there was no longer any place for them in heaven. The great dragon was thrown down, that ancient serpent, who is called the Devil and Satan, the deceiver of the whole world—he was thrown down to the earth, and his angels were thrown down with him. (Rev. 12:7-9)

Psalm
Psalm 103:1-5, 20-22
Bless the Lord, you angels

Additional Readings
Daniel 10:10-14; 12:1-3
Michael shall arise

Luke 10:17-20
Jesus gives his followers authority

Hymn: Ye Watchers and Ye Holy Ones, ELW 424

Everlasting God, you have wonderfully established the ministries of angels and mortals. Mercifully grant that as Michael and the angels contend against the cosmic forces of evil, so by your direction they may help and defend us here on earth, through your Son, Jesus Christ our Lord, who lives and reigns with you and the Holy Spirit, one God whom we worship and praise with angels and archangels and all the company of heaven, now and forever.

Prayer List for October

_____

_____

_____

_____

_____

_____

_____

_____

Tuesday, October 1, 2019
Time after Pentecost

Psalm 62
I wait on God

For God alone my soul waits in silence,
    for my hope is from him.
He alone is my rock and my salvation,
    my fortress; I shall not be shaken.
On God rests my deliverance and my honor;
    my mighty rock, my refuge is in God.

Trust in him at all times, O people;
    pour out your heart before him;
        God is a refuge for us. (Ps. 62:5-8)

Additional Readings
James 5:1-6
Riches that rot

Hosea 10:9-15
Reaping injustice

Hymn: Christ, Be Our Light, ELW 715

God our rock and our salvation, you are our refuge. Shelter us during the storms of life. Strengthen our faith in times of trouble. Sit with us in the silence. Surround us with hope all the days of our lives.

Wednesday, October 2, 2019
Time after Pentecost

Hosea 12:2-14

I have gained wealth for myself

The LORD has an indictment against Judah,
>   and will punish Jacob according to his ways,
>   and repay him according to his deeds.
In the womb he tried to supplant his brother,
>   and in his manhood he strove with God.
He strove with the angel and prevailed,
>   he wept and sought his favor;
he met him at Bethel,
>   and there he spoke with him.
The LORD the God of hosts,
>   the LORD is his name!
But as for you, return to your God,
>   hold fast to love and justice,
>   and wait continually for your God. (Hosea 12:2-6)

Psalm

Psalm 62
I wait on God

Additional Reading

Matthew 19:16-22
Treasure in heaven

Hymn: Come Now, O Prince of Peace, ELW 247

Waiting is hard, eternal Lord. We desire your kingdom to come, but turn away as we await its arrival. Open our eyes to see your kingdom come. Open our hearts to be your kingdom come. Turn our waiting into serving.

Thursday, October 3, 2019
Time after Pentecost

Psalm 37:1-9
Commit your way to the Lord

Do not fret because of the wicked;
    do not be envious of wrongdoers,
for they will soon fade like the grass,
    and wither like the green herb.

Trust in the LORD, and do good;
    so you will live in the land, and enjoy security.
Take delight in the LORD,
    and he will give you the desires of your heart.

Commit your way to the LORD;
    trust in him, and he will act. (Ps. 37:1-5)

Additional Readings
2 Kings 18:1-8, 28-36   **Revelation 2:8-11**
King Hezekiah trusts in God   *Be faithful until death*

Hymn: Have No Fear, Little Flock, ELW 764

*Alpha and Omega, you are the beginning and the end. Sometimes
life overwhelms us and we forget this truth. Surround us with a faith
community that reminds us to trust in you. In Christ's name we pray.*

Friday, October 4, 2019
Time after Pentecost

Francis of Assisi, renewer of the church, died 1226

Theodor Fliedner, renewer of society, died 1864

2 Kings 19:8-20, 35-37
God saves the people

And Hezekiah prayed before the LORD, and said: "O LORD the God of Israel, who are enthroned above the cherubim, you are God, you alone, of all the kingdoms of the earth; you have made heaven and earth. Incline your ear, O LORD, and hear; open your eyes, O LORD, and see; hear the words of Sennacherib, which he has sent to mock the living God. Truly, O LORD, the kings of Assyria have laid waste the nations and their lands, and have hurled their gods into the fire, though they were no gods but the work of human hands—wood and stone—and so they were destroyed. So now, O LORD our God, save us, I pray you, from his hand, so that all the kingdoms of the earth may know that you, O LORD, are God alone." (2 Kings 19:15-19)

Psalm	Additional Reading
Psalm 37:1-9	Revelation 2:12-29
Commit your way to the Lord	*Call to faithfulness*

Hymn: Before You, Lord, We Bow, ELW 893

Holy One of Israel, you alone are God. Save us from the false gods of this age we have created and inherited. Redeem us from the golden calves we worship. Restore us to the holiness of your kingdom.

Saturday, October 5, 2019
Time after Pentecost

Matthew 20:29-34

Mercy on persistent blind men

As [Jesus and the disciples] were leaving Jericho, a large crowd followed him. There were two blind men sitting by the roadside. When they heard that Jesus was passing by, they shouted, "Lord, have mercy on us, Son of David!" The crowd sternly ordered them to be quiet; but they shouted even more loudly, "Have mercy on us, Lord, Son of David!" Jesus stood still and called them, saying, "What do you want me to do for you?" They said to him, "Lord, let our eyes be opened." Moved with compassion, Jesus touched their eyes. Immediately they regained their sight and followed him. (Matt. 20:29-34)

Psalm
Psalm 37:1-9
Commit your way to the Lord

Additional Reading
Isaiah 7:1-9
Standing firm in faith

Hymn: Amazing Grace, How Sweet the Sound, ELW 779

Gracious God, your mercy is endless. We sit with the blind men on the roadside and cry out. Do you hear us? We are broken. We cannot see. We are desperate for your vision. Give it to us.

Sunday, October 6, 2019
Time after Pentecost

William Tyndale, translator, martyr, died 1536

Luke 17:5-10

Faith the size of a mustard seed

The apostles said to the Lord, "Increase our faith!" The Lord replied, "If you had faith the size of a mustard seed, you could say to this mulberry tree, 'Be uprooted and planted in the sea,' and it would obey you." (Luke 17:5-6)

Psalm

Psalm 37:1-9
Commit your way to the Lord

Additional Readings

Habakkuk 1:1-4; 2:1-4
The wicked surround the righteous

2 Timothy 1:1-14
Guard the treasure entrusted to you

Hymn: O Spirit of Life, ELW 405

Benevolent, merciful God: When we are empty, fill us. When we are weak in faith, strengthen us. When we are cold in love, warm us, that with fervor we may love our neighbors and serve them for the sake of your Son, Jesus Christ, our Savior and Lord.

Monday, October 7, 2019
Time after Pentecost

Henry Melchior Muhlenberg, pastor in North America, died 1787

Psalm 3
Deliverance comes from God

I lie down and sleep;
> I wake again, for the LORD sustains me.
I am not afraid of ten thousands of people
> who have set themselves against me all around.

Rise up, O LORD!
> Deliver me, O my God!
For you strike all my enemies on the cheek;
> you break the teeth of the wicked.

Deliverance belongs to the LORD;
> may your blessing be on your people! (Ps. 3:5-8)

Additional Readings
Habakkuk 1:5-17
The wicked swallow the righteous

James 1:2-11
Faith produces endurance

Hymn: God, Who Made the Earth and Heaven, ELW 564

Sustaining Lord, you hear the cries of all who call upon you. Deliver us in our time of need. Take away our fear. Turn our hatred into empathy. Transform our enemies into neighbors and strangers into friends.

Tuesday, October 8, 2019
Time after Pentecost

1 John 5:1-5, 13-21
Faith overcomes the world

Everyone who believes that Jesus is the Christ has been born of God, and everyone who loves the parent loves the child. By this we know that we love the children of God, when we love God and obey his commandments. For the love of God is this, that we obey his commandments. And his commandments are not burdensome, for whatever is born of God conquers the world. And this is the victory that conquers the world, our faith. Who is it that conquers the world but the one who believes that Jesus is the Son of God? (1 John 5:1-5)

Psalm
Psalm 3
Deliverance comes from God

Additional Reading
Habakkuk 2:5-11
Those who heap up what is not theirs

Hymn: You Are the Way, ELW 758

Mothering God, you love us and care for us. Write your commandments on our hearts. Give us joy in following your way. Teach us how to share this joy with all people. Send us out to make disciples.

Wednesday, October 9, 2019
Time after Pentecost

Habakkuk 2:12-20
Knowledge of the glory of God

"Alas for you who build a town by bloodshed,
    and found a city on iniquity!"
Is it not from the LORD of hosts
    that peoples labor only to feed the flames,
    and nations weary themselves for nothing?
But the earth will be filled
    with the knowledge of the glory of the LORD,
    as the waters cover the sea. (Hab. 2:12-14)

Psalm
Psalm 3
Deliverance comes from God

Additional Reading
Mark 11:12-14, 20-24
Faith that moves mountains

Hymn: God, Who Stretched the Spangled Heavens, ELW 771

Creator God, you separated the waters and called forth life. How beautiful is your creation! Fill us with the knowledge of your glory. Move us to work for food that satisfies. Send us out to share your word with all.

Thursday, October 10, 2019
Time after Pentecost

Psalm 111
I give thanks with my whole heart

Praise the LORD!
I will give thanks to the LORD with my whole heart,
    in the company of the upright, in the congregation.
Great are the works of the LORD,
    studied by all who delight in them.
Full of honor and majesty is his work,
    and his righteousness endures forever. (Ps. 111:1-3)

Additional Readings
Leviticus 14:33-53
Cleansing a leprous house

2 Timothy 1:13-18
Paul in prison

Hymn: Voices Raised to You, ELW 845

Love Eternal, you are holy and worthy of praise. Your righteousness endures forever. For the beauty of creation, we give you thanks. For the gift of salvation, we rejoice. Compose our lives into songs of eternal praise.

Friday, October 11, 2019
Time after Pentecost

Numbers 4:34—5:4
A census and the exclusion of lepers

The LORD spoke to Moses, saying: Command the Israelites to put out of the camp everyone who is leprous, or has a discharge, and everyone who is unclean through contact with a corpse; you shall put out both male and female, putting them outside the camp; they must not defile their camp, where I dwell among them. The Israelites did so, putting them outside the camp; as the LORD had spoken to Moses, so the Israelites did. (Num. 5:1-4)

Psalm
Psalm 111
I give thanks with my whole heart

Additional Reading
2 Timothy 2:1-7
Share in suffering

Hymn: All Are Welcome, ELW 641

Heavenly Father, you sent Jesus your Son to heal us. Restore us to your presence. Mend the brokenness within the body of Christ. When we exclude people, stir up your Spirit within us to welcome and include all people.

Saturday, October 12, 2019
Time after Pentecost

Luke 5:12-16
A leper healed

Once, when [Jesus] was in one of the cities, there was a man covered with leprosy. When he saw Jesus, he bowed with his face to the ground and begged him, "Lord, if you choose, you can make me clean." Then Jesus stretched out his hand, touched him, and said, "I do choose. Be made clean." Immediately the leprosy left him. And he ordered him to tell no one. "Go," he said, "and show yourself to the priest, and, as Moses commanded, make an offering for your cleansing, for a testimony to them." But now more than ever the word about Jesus spread abroad; many crowds would gather to hear him and to be cured of their diseases. But he would withdraw to deserted places and pray. (Luke 5:12-16)

Psalm
Psalm 111
I give thanks with my whole heart

Additional Reading
Numbers 12:1-15
Miriam contracts leprosy

Hymn: There Is a Balm in Gilead, ELW 614

Holy Trinity, in you is healing and wholeness. Bind up our broken hearts. Cure our diseases. Ease our pain and sorrow. Move us to speak with joy about the many ways you restore us to health and community.

Sunday, October 13, 2019
Time after Pentecost

Luke 17:11-19

One leper gives thanks to God

As [Jesus] entered a village, ten lepers approached him. Keeping their distance, they called out, saying, "Jesus, Master, have mercy on us!" When he saw them, he said to them, "Go and show yourselves to the priests." And as they went, they were made clean. Then one of them, when he saw that he was healed, turned back, praising God with a loud voice. He prostrated himself at Jesus' feet and thanked him. And he was a Samaritan. (Luke 17:12-16)

Psalm

Psalm 111
I give thanks with my whole heart

Additional Readings

2 Kings 5:1-3, 7-15c
Naaman is cleansed

2 Timothy 2:8-15
We will live with Christ

Hymn: Baptized in Water, ELW 456

Almighty and most merciful God, your bountiful goodness fills all creation. Keep us safe from all that may hurt us, that, whole and well in body and spirit, we may with grateful hearts accomplish all that you would have us do, through Jesus Christ, our Savior and Lord.

Monday, October 14, 2019
Time after Pentecost

Day of Thanksgiving (Canada)

A Blessing of the Household for Thanksgiving Day is provided on page 362.

Psalm 61

Prayer for a long life

Hear my cry, O God;
>   listen to my prayer.
From the end of the earth I call to you,
>   when my heart is faint.

Lead me to the rock
>   that is higher than I;
for you are my refuge,
>   a strong tower against the enemy.

Let me abide in your tent forever,
>   find refuge under the shelter of your wings. (Ps. 61:1-4)

Additional Readings

2 Kings 5:15-19a
Naaman seeks to repay Elisha

Acts 26:24-29
Except for these chains

Hymn: O Lord, Hear My Prayer, ELW 751

God of the faint-hearted, you care for the weary and the worn. Shelter our neighbors without housing. Comfort our neighbors who mourn. Surround us with love. Gather us under your protective wings now and forever.

Tuesday, October 15, 2019
Time after Pentecost

Teresa of Avila, teacher, renewer of the church, died 1582

Ephesians 6:10-20

An ambassador in chains

Finally, be strong in the Lord and in the strength of his power. Put on the whole armor of God, so that you may be able to stand against the wiles of the devil. For our struggle is not against enemies of blood and flesh, but against the rulers, against the authorities, against the cosmic powers of this present darkness, against the spiritual forces of evil in the heavenly places. (Eph. 6:10-12)

Psalm

Psalm 61
Prayer for a long life

Additional Reading

2 Kings 5:19b-27
Greed brings leprosy to Gehazi

Hymn: I Bind unto Myself Today, ELW 450

Mighty Lord, you are our strength and our power. When the devil tempts us, root us in your Word. When Satan calls out, turn our ears to your voice. Deliver us from evil today and always.

Wednesday, October 16, 2019
Time after Pentecost

Matthew 10:5-15
Cure without payment

These twelve Jesus sent out with the following instructions: "Go nowhere among the Gentiles, and enter no town of the Samaritans, but go rather to the lost sheep of the house of Israel. As you go, proclaim the good news, 'The kingdom of heaven has come near.' Cure the sick, raise the dead, cleanse the lepers, cast out demons. You received without payment; give without payment." (Matt. 10:5-8)

Psalm
Psalm 61
Prayer for a long life

Additional Reading
2 Kings 15:1-7
A leprous king lives in isolation

Hymn: The Son of God, Our Christ, ELW 584

Good Shepherd, you sent out the disciples to share the good news. Move our feet to visit people who are homebound. Guide our hands to cook for the hungry. Send us out to live your love each day.

Thursday, October 17, 2019
Time after Pentecost

Ignatius, Bishop of Antioch, martyr, died around 115

Psalm 121

My help is from the Lord

I lift up my eyes to the hills—
    from where will my help come?
My help comes from the LORD,
    who made heaven and earth.

He will not let your foot be moved;
    he who keeps you will not slumber.
He who keeps Israel
    will neither slumber nor sleep. (Ps. 121:1-4)

Additional Readings

Isaiah 54:11-17
God will vindicate the faithful

Acts 17:22-34
God has fixed a day of judgment

Hymn: All Praise to Thee, My God, This Night, ELW 565

Creator of the universe, you are always with us. Hold the sleepless in your care. Sustain the weary worker. Energize the exhausted parent. Guide the wandering youth. Comfort the dying. Remind us we are never alone.

Friday, October 18, 2019

Luke, Evangelist

Luke 1:1-4; 24:44-53

Luke witnesses to the ministry of Jesus

Since many have undertaken to set down an orderly account of the events that have been fulfilled among us, just as they were handed on to us by those who from the beginning were eyewitnesses and servants of the word, I too decided, after investigating everything carefully from the very first, to write an orderly account for you, most excellent Theophilus, so that you may know the truth concerning the things about which you have been instructed. (Luke 1:1-4)

Psalm

Psalm 124
Our help is in God

Additional Readings

Isaiah 43:8-13
You are my witness

2 Timothy 4:5-11
The good fight of faith

Hymn: Oh, for a Thousand Tongues to Sing, ELW 886

Almighty God, you inspired your servant Luke to reveal in his gospel the love and healing power of your Son. Give your church the same love and power to heal, and to proclaim your salvation among the nations to the glory of your name, through Jesus Christ, your Son, our healer, who lives and reigns with you and the Holy Spirit, one God, now and forever.

Saturday, October 19, 2019
Time after Pentecost

Mark 10:46-52

A man who would not be silenced

[Jesus and the disciples] came to Jericho. As he and his disciples and a large crowd were leaving Jericho, Bartimaeus son of Timaeus, a blind beggar, was sitting by the roadside. When he heard that it was Jesus of Nazareth, he began to shout out and say, "Jesus, Son of David, have mercy on me!" . . . Then Jesus said to him, "What do you want me to do for you?" The blind man said to him, "My teacher, let me see again." Jesus said to him, "Go; your faith has made you well." Immediately he regained his sight and followed him on the way. (Mark 10:46-47, 51-52)

Psalm
Psalm 121
My help is from the Lord

Additional Reading
Genesis 32:3-21
Jacob sends gifts to Esau

Hymn: Be Thou My Vision, ELW 793

Open our eyes, Lord. Help us to see ourselves as you see us. Correct our vision. Train us to see our neighbors as you see them. Send us out with fresh eyes to live and serve in your name.

Sunday, October 20, 2019
Time after Pentecost

Luke 18:1-8
A widow begs for justice

Then Jesus told them a parable about their need to pray always and not to lose heart. He said, "In a certain city there was a judge who neither feared God nor had respect for people. In that city there was a widow who kept coming to him and saying, 'Grant me justice against my opponent.' For a while he refused; but later he said to himself, 'Though I have no fear of God and no respect for anyone, yet because this widow keeps bothering me, I will grant her justice, so that she may not wear me out by continually coming.' " (Luke 18:1-5)

Psalm

Psalm 121
My help is from the Lord

Additional Readings

Genesis 32:22-31
Jacob's struggle with the angel

2 Timothy 3:14—4:5
Christ the judge

Hymn: Lord, Listen to Your Children Praying, ELW 752

O Lord God, tireless guardian of your people, you are always ready to hear our cries. Teach us to rely day and night on your care. Inspire us to seek your enduring justice for all this suffering world, through Jesus Christ, our Savior and Lord.

Monday, October 21, 2019
Time after Pentecost

Psalm 57
Vindication from God

Be merciful to me, O God, be merciful to me,
    for in you my soul takes refuge;
in the shadow of your wings I will take refuge,
    until the destroying storms pass by.
I cry to God Most High,
    to God who fulfills his purpose for me.
He will send from heaven and save me,
    he will put to shame those who trample on me.
God will send forth his steadfast love and his faithfulness. (Ps. 57:1-3)

Additional Readings

1 Samuel 25:2-22
David judges against Nabal

1 Corinthians 6:1-11
You are washed and sanctified

Hymn: What a Friend We Have in Jesus, ELW 742

God most high, your steadfast love and faithfulness endures forever. Have mercy on us and forgive the sins we committed this day. Save us from our lust for power and money. Turn us from our complacency when injustice reigns.

Tuesday, October 22, 2019
Time after Pentecost

James 5:7-12
The Judge standing at the doors

Be patient, therefore, beloved, until the coming of the Lord. The farmer waits for the precious crop from the earth, being patient with it until it receives the early and the late rains. You also must be patient. Strengthen your hearts, for the coming of the Lord is near. Beloved, do not grumble against one another, so that you may not be judged. See, the Judge is standing at the doors! As an example of suffering and patience, beloved, take the prophets who spoke in the name of the Lord. Indeed we call blessed those who showed endurance. You have heard of the endurance of Job, and you have seen the purpose of the Lord, how the Lord is compassionate and merciful. (James 5:7-11)

Psalm
Psalm 57
Vindication from God

Additional Reading
1 Samuel 25:23-35
Abigail pleads for life

Hymn: Oh, Worship the King, ELW 842

Compassionate God, abundant is your mercy. Steadfast is your love. Give us patience as we struggle to understand the pain and suffering of this world. Strengthen our hearts as we wait for you. Bless us with endurance through your Spirit.

Wednesday, October 23, 2019
Time after Pentecost

James of Jerusalem, martyr, died around 62

Luke 22:39-46
Jesus prays for life

[Jesus] came out and went, as was his custom, to the Mount of Olives;
and the disciples followed him. When he reached the place, he said
to them, "Pray that you may not come into the time of trial." Then he
withdrew from them about a stone's throw, knelt down, and prayed,
"Father, if you are willing, remove this cup from me; yet, not my will but
yours be done." (Luke 22:39-42)

Psalm
Psalm 57
Vindication from God

Additional Reading
1 Samuel 25:36-42
David welcomes Abigail as wife

Hymn: Go to Dark Gethsemane, ELW 347

*Heavenly Father, your Son Jesus taught us to pray and the Holy Spirit
intercedes on our behalf. Enrich our prayer life. Transform your church into
a living prayer, bold to speak and diligent to listen. Let your will be done.*

Thursday, October 24, 2019
Time after Pentecost

Psalm 84:1-7
Happy are they whose strength is in you

How lovely is your dwelling place,
    O LORD of hosts!
My soul longs, indeed it faints
    for the courts of the LORD;
my heart and my flesh sing for joy
    to the living God.

Even the sparrow finds a home,
    and the swallow a nest for herself,
    where she may lay her young,
at your altars, O LORD of hosts,
    my King and my God.
Happy are those who live in your house,
    ever singing your praise.

Happy are those whose strength is in you,
    in whose heart are the highways to Zion. (Ps. 84:1-5)

Additional Readings
Jeremiah 9:1-16
Israel refuses to know God

2 Timothy 3:1-9
Godlessness

Hymn: Beautiful Savior, ELW 838

God our king, you are our home in all times. We thank you for shelter. We praise you for the oceans, trees, and meadows that house fish, birds, and mammals. Bring us with them into your eternal home.

Friday, October 25, 2019
Time after Pentecost

Jeremiah 9:17-26
Israel uncircumcised in heart

Thus says the LORD: Do not let the wise boast in their wisdom, do not let the mighty boast in their might, do not let the wealthy boast in their wealth; but let those who boast boast in this, that they understand and know me, that I am the LORD; I act with steadfast love, justice, and righteousness in the earth, for in these things I delight, says the LORD.

The days are surely coming, says the LORD, when I will attend to all those who are circumcised only in the foreskin: Egypt, Judah, Edom, the Ammonites, Moab, and all those with shaven temples who live in the desert. For all these nations are uncircumcised, and all the house of Israel is uncircumcised in heart. (Jer. 9:23-26)

Psalm
Psalm 84:1-7
Happy are they whose strength is in you

Additional Reading
2 Timothy 3:10-15
The persecution of the godly

Hymn: Joyful, Joyful We Adore Thee, ELW 836

Restore us to you, ever-loving Lord. When our own knowledge enthralls us, turn us to your wisdom. When our strength grips us, turn us to your power. When our wealth consumes us, turn us to your riches.

Saturday, October 26, 2019
Time after Pentecost

Philipp Nicolai, died 1608; Johann Heermann, died 1647;
Paul Gerhardt, died 1676; hymnwriters

Jeremiah 14:1-6

A drought portends destruction

The word of the LORD that came to Jeremiah concerning the drought:
Judah mourns
> and her gates languish;
they lie in gloom on the ground,
> and the cry of Jerusalem goes up.
Her nobles send their servants for water;
> they come to the cisterns,
they find no water,
> they return with their vessels empty.
They are ashamed and dismayed
> and cover their heads,
because the ground is cracked.
> Because there has been no rain on the land
the farmers are dismayed;
> they cover their heads. (Jer. 14:1-4)

Psalm
Psalm 84:1-7
Happy are they whose strength is in you

Additional Reading
Luke 1:46-55
Mary's song

Hymn: O Christ, Our Light, O Radiance True, ELW 675

Mover of the waters, you spoke creation into being. Speak now. Rain down on the cracked earth. Flood barren wells. Overflow dried up lakes. Fill empty vessels. Pour out your living water on all the earth.

Sunday, October 27, 2019
Time after Pentecost

Luke 18:9-14

A Pharisee and tax collector pray

[Jesus said,] "Two men went up to the temple to pray, one a Pharisee and the other a tax collector. The Pharisee, standing by himself, was praying thus, 'God, I thank you that I am not like other people: thieves, rogues, adulterers, or even like this tax collector. I fast twice a week; I give a tenth of all my income.' But the tax collector, standing far off, would not even look up to heaven, but was beating his breast and saying, 'God, be merciful to me, a sinner!' I tell you, this man went down to his home justified rather than the other; for all who exalt themselves will be humbled, but all who humble themselves will be exalted." (Luke 18:10-14)

Psalm

Psalm 84:1-7
Happy are they whose strength is in you

Additional Readings

Jeremiah 14:7-10, 19-22
Jerusalem will be defeated

2 Timothy 4:6-8, 16-18
The good fight of faith

Hymn: Just As I Am, without One Plea, ELW 592

Holy God, our righteous judge, daily your mercy surprises us with everlasting forgiveness. Strengthen our hope in you, and grant that all the peoples of the earth may find their glory in you, through Jesus Christ, our Savior and Lord.

Monday, October 28, 2019
Simon and Jude, Apostles

John 14:21-27

Those who love Jesus will keep his word

[Jesus said,] "They who have my commandments and keep them are those who love me; and those who love me will be loved by my Father, and I will love them and reveal myself to them." Judas (not Iscariot) said to him, "Lord, how is it that you will reveal yourself to us, and not to the world?" Jesus answered him, "Those who love me will keep my word, and my Father will love them, and we will come to them and make our home with them. Whoever does not love me does not keep my words; and the word that you hear is not mine, but is from the Father who sent me." (John 14:21-24)

Psalm

Psalm 11
Take refuge in God

Additional Readings

Jeremiah 26:[1-6] 7-16
Jeremiah promises the judgment of God

1 John 4:1-6
Do not believe every spirit of this world

Hymn: Rejoice in God's Saints, ELW 418

O God, we thank you for the glorious company of the apostles, and especially on this day for Simon and Jude. We pray that, as they were faithful and zealous in your mission, so we may with ardent devotion make known the love and mercy of our Savior Jesus Christ, who lives and reigns with you and the Holy Spirit, one God, now and forever.

Tuesday, October 29, 2019
Time after Pentecost

Psalm 84:8-12
A doorkeeper in God's house

For a day in your courts is better
> than a thousand elsewhere.
I would rather be a doorkeeper in the house of my God
> than live in the tents of wickedness.
For the LORD God is a sun and shield;
> he bestows favor and honor.
No good thing does the LORD withhold
> from those who walk uprightly.
O LORD of hosts,
> happy is everyone who trusts in you. (Ps. 84:10-12)

Additional Readings
Daniel 5:1-12
A hand writing on the wall

1 Peter 5:1-11
The unfading crown of glory

Hymn: Savior, like a Shepherd Lead Us, ELW 789

Wondrous God, heaven and earth are full of your glory. Make us bold to share the joy of your kingdom. Bless our lives with songs of praise. Transform our lives into acts of testimony that speak about your abundant grace.

Wednesday, October 30, 2019
Time after Pentecost

Matthew 21:28-32
Faith of tax collectors and prostitutes

[Jesus said,] "What do you think? A man had two sons; he went to the first and said, 'Son, go and work in the vineyard today.' He answered, 'I will not'; but later he changed his mind and went. The father went to the second and said the same; and he answered, 'I go, sir'; but he did not go. Which of the two did the will of his father?" They said, "The first." Jesus said to them, "Truly I tell you, the tax collectors and the prostitutes are going into the kingdom of God ahead of you. For John came to you in the way of righteousness and you did not believe him, but the tax collectors and the prostitutes believed him; and even after you saw it, you did not change your minds and believe him." (Matt. 21:28-32)

Psalm
Psalm 84:8-12
A doorkeeper in God's house

Additional Reading
Daniel 5:13-31
Daniel urges humility

Hymn: Lord, Dismiss Us with Your Blessing, ELW 545

Merciful God, you seek us out again and again. Turn our "no" into your "yes." Give us courage and endurance to work in your vineyard. Give us joy in serving you through our neighbors. In Christ's name we pray.

Thursday, October 31, 2019
Reformation Day

Romans 3:19-28

Justified by God's grace as a gift

But now, apart from law, the righteousness of God has been disclosed, and is attested by the law and the prophets, the righteousness of God through faith in Jesus Christ for all who believe. For there is no distinction, since all have sinned and fall short of the glory of God; they are now justified by his grace as a gift, through the redemption that is in Christ Jesus, whom God put forward as a sacrifice of atonement by his blood, effective through faith. He did this to show his righteousness, because in his divine forbearance he had passed over the sins previously committed; it was to prove at the present time that he himself is righteous and that he justifies the one who has faith in Jesus. (Rom. 3:21-26)

Psalm

Psalm 46
The God of Jacob is our stronghold

Additional Readings

Jeremiah 31:31-34
I will write my law in their hearts

John 8:31-36
The truth will set you free

Hymn: The Church of Christ, in Every Age, ELW 729

Gracious Father, we pray for your holy catholic church. Fill it with all truth and peace. Where it is corrupt, purify it; where it is in error, direct it; where in anything it is amiss, reform it; where it is right, strengthen it; where it is in need, provide for it; where it is divided, reunite it; for the sake of your Son, Jesus Christ, our Savior, who lives and reigns with you and the Holy Spirit, one God, now and forever.

Prayer List for November

_____

_____

_____

_____

_____

_____

_____

_____

_____

Time after Pentecost
November

The month of November is unique in that it begins with All Saints Day (November 1) and ends with the feast of Christ the King (often the last Sunday of November). The Sunday and daily readings seem to extend the harvest, but in a new way: they speak of God's harvest of human beings into their heavenly home.

Perhaps it is no coincidence that November's scriptural emphasis on the consummation of all things in Christ is reflected in the landscape and the chilling temperatures. Yet in the midst of this turning of the seasons and the reminders of death's presence, Christians hold forth the central feast of the year: the death and resurrection of Christ present in baptism and the holy supper. In these last days of the church's year, Christians are invited to celebrate the reign of Christ, whose death on the cross has transformed our deaths into the gate of everlasting life.

Table Prayer for November
Stay with us, God of life,
as we share the bounty of this food and drink.
We give you thanks for those who have gone before us in faith.
Bring us, with them, to the harvest of everlasting life,
where all people will feast forever at your abundant table.
We ask this through Christ our Lord. Amen.

Remembering Those Who Have Died

Use this prayer in the home or at the grave.

O God, our help in ages past and our hope for years to come:
We give you thanks for all your faithful people
who have followed the light of your word throughout the centuries
into our time and place.

Here individual names may be spoken.

As we remember these people,
strengthen us to follow Christ through this world
until we are carried into the harvest of eternal life,
where suffering and death will be no more.
Hear our prayer in the name of the good and gracious shepherd,
Jesus Christ, our Savior and Lord. Amen.

or

With reverence and affection we remember before you,
O everlasting God,
all our departed friends and relatives.
Keep us in union with them here
through faith and love toward you,
that hereafter we may enter into your presence
and be numbered with those who serve you
and look upon your face in glory everlasting,
through your Son, Jesus Christ our Lord. Amen.

Friday, November 1, 2019
All Saints Day

Luke 6:20-31
Jesus speaks blessings and woes

Then [Jesus] looked up at his disciples and said:

"Blessed are you who are poor,

for yours is the kingdom of God.

"Blessed are you who are hungry now,

for you will be filled.

"Blessed are you who weep now,

for you will laugh.

"Blessed are you when people hate you, and when they exclude you, revile you, and defame you on account of the Son of Man. Rejoice in that day and leap for joy, for surely your reward is great in heaven; for that is what their ancestors did to the prophets." (Luke 6:20-23)

Psalm

Psalm 149
Sing praise for God's goodness

Additional Readings

Daniel 7:1-3, 15-18
The holy ones of the Most High

Ephesians 1:11-23
God made Christ head over all

Hymn: Blest Are They, ELW 728

Almighty God, you have knit your people together in one communion in the mystical body of your Son, Jesus Christ our Lord. Grant us grace to follow your blessed saints in lives of faith and commitment, and to know the inexpressible joys you have prepared for those who love you, through Jesus Christ, our Savior and Lord, who lives and reigns with you and the Holy Spirit, one God, now and forever.

Saturday, November 2, 2019
Time after Pentecost

Isaiah 1:1-9
Sinful Judah

Hear, O heavens, and listen, O earth;
    for the LORD has spoken:
I reared children and brought them up,
    but they have rebelled against me.
The ox knows its owner,
    and the donkey its master's crib;
but Israel does not know,
    my people do not understand.

Ah, sinful nation,
    people laden with iniquity,
offspring who do evil,
    children who deal corruptly,
who have forsaken the LORD,
    who have despised the Holy One of Israel,
    who are utterly estranged! (Isa. 1:2-4)

Psalm
Psalm 32:1-7
Praying in time of trouble

Additional Reading
John 8:39-47
True children of Abraham

Hymn: All Who Love and Serve Your City, ELW 724

Like rebellious children, we too often turn from your ways of justice and mercy. Thank you, God, for being a loving parent even when we stray. Claim us again and again as your children and restore our faithfulness.

Sunday, November 3, 2019
Time after Pentecost

Martín de Porres, renewer of society, died 1639

Luke 19:1-10
Zacchaeus climbs high to see Jesus

When Jesus came to [the place where Zacchaeus was waiting], he looked up and said to [Zacchaeus], "Zacchaeus, hurry and come down; for I must stay at your house today." So he hurried down and was happy to welcome him. All who saw it began to grumble and said, "He has gone to be the guest of one who is a sinner." Zacchaeus stood there and said to the Lord, "Look, half of my possessions, Lord, I will give to the poor; and if I have defrauded anyone of anything, I will pay back four times as much." Then Jesus said to him, "Today salvation has come to this house, because he too is a son of Abraham. For the Son of Man came to seek out and to save the lost." (Luke 19:5-10)

Psalm
Psalm 32:1-7
Praying in time of trouble

Additional Readings
Isaiah 1:10-18
Learn to do good

2 Thessalonians 1:1-4, 11-12
Faith and love amid adversity

Hymn: Blessed Assurance, ELW 638

Merciful God, gracious and benevolent, through your Son you invite all the world to a meal of mercy. Grant that we may eagerly follow his call, and bring us with all your saints into your life of justice and joy, through Jesus Christ, our Savior and Lord.

Monday, November 4, 2019
Time after Pentecost

Psalm 50
A sacrifice of thanksgiving

"Mark this, then, you who forget God,
  or I will tear you apart, and there will be no one to deliver.
Those who bring thanksgiving as their sacrifice honor me;
  to those who go the right way
  I will show the salvation of God." (Ps. 50:22-23)

Additional Readings
Nehemiah 13:1-3, 23-31
Israel separates from foreigners

1 Corinthians 5:9-13
Drive out the wicked

Hymn: Praise, My Soul, the God of Heaven, ELW 864

God of the covenant, you promise to keep and sustain your holy people. Turn our faith outward, to care for all our neighbors. Use us to heal divides and to bridge divisions, for the sake of your love.

Tuesday, November 5, 2019
Time after Pentecost

Jude 5-21
Warning against sinners

But you, beloved, must remember the predictions of the apostles of our Lord Jesus Christ; for they said to you, "In the last time there will be scoffers, indulging their own ungodly lusts." It is these worldly people, devoid of the Spirit, who are causing divisions. But you, beloved, build yourselves up on your most holy faith; pray in the Holy Spirit; keep yourselves in the love of God; look forward to the mercy of our Lord Jesus Christ that leads to eternal life. (Jude 17-21)

Psalm
Psalm 50
A sacrifice of thanksgiving

Additional Readings
Zechariah 7:1-14
Fasting versus justice and mercy

Hymn: Thy Strong Word, ELW 511

Let us hear your voice, again, God of justice. Incite our hearts toward kindness and mercy for all. Where we are now self-centered, give us new ears to hear the cries of the poor, the oppressed, and the stranger.

Wednesday, November 6, 2019
Time after Pentecost

Amos 5:12-24
God desires justice, not offerings

I hate, I despise your festivals,
>   and I take no delight in your solemn assemblies.
Even though you offer me your burnt offerings and grain offerings,
>   I will not accept them;
and the offerings of well-being of your fatted animals
>   I will not look upon.
Take away from me the noise of your songs;
>   I will not listen to the melody of your harps.
But let justice roll down like waters,
>   and righteousness like an ever-flowing stream. (Amos 5:21-24)

Psalm
Psalm 50
A sacrifice of thanksgiving

Additional Reading
Luke 19:11-27
The parable of the pounds

Hymn: Let Justice Flow like Streams, ELW 717

You are a God of blessings. Give us grateful hearts for all that we have been given. Stir our imaginations, that we might use our gifts, big or small, for the good of others and the good of all creation.

Thursday, November 7, 2019
Time after Pentecost

John Christian Frederick Heyer, died 1873; Bartholomaeus Ziegenbalg, died 1719;
Ludwig Nommensen, died 1918; missionaries

Psalm 17:1-9

Keep me as the apple of your eye

I call upon you, for you will answer me, O God;
>   incline your ear to me, hear my words.
Wondrously show your steadfast love,
>   O savior of those who seek refuge
>   from their adversaries at your right hand.

Guard me as the apple of the eye;
>   hide me in the shadow of your wings,
from the wicked who despoil me,
>   my deadly enemies who surround me. (Ps. 17:6-9)

Additional Readings

Deuteronomy 25:5-10
Instructions for levirate marriage

Acts 22:22—23:11
Paul confronts religious leaders

Hymn: What Wondrous Love Is This, ELW 666

Our hearts take refuge in you, God of wondrous things. Give us courage to proclaim your steadfast love to all the ends of the earth. Guard and protect us as we testify to the hope that is in us.

Friday, November 8, 2019
Time after Pentecost

Acts 24:10-23
Paul testifies to the resurrection

When the governor motioned to him to speak, Paul replied:

"I cheerfully make my defense, knowing that for many years you have been a judge over this nation. As you can find out, it is not more than twelve days since I went up to worship in Jerusalem. They did not find me disputing with anyone in the temple or stirring up a crowd either in the synagogues or throughout the city. Neither can they prove to you the charge that they now bring against me. But this I admit to you, that according to the Way, which they call a sect, I worship the God of our ancestors, believing everything laid down according to the law or written in the prophets. I have a hope in God—a hope that they themselves also accept—that there will be a resurrection of both the righteous and the unrighteous." (Acts 24:10-15)

Psalm
Psalm 17:1-9
Keep me as the apple of your eye

Additional Reading
Genesis 38:1-26
Tamar and levirate marriage

Hymn: Holy God, Holy and Glorious, ELW 637

God of our ancestors, you hold and comfort us with your righteousness when we feel forgotten, hurt, or unjustly accused. Incline your ear to us. Bring renewed hope to our hearts through your promise of resurrection.

Saturday, November 9, 2019
Time after Pentecost

Exodus 3:13-20
God appears to Moses

Moses said to God, "If I come to the Israelites and say to them, 'The God of your ancestors has sent me to you,' and they ask me, 'What is his name?' what shall I say to them?" God said to Moses, "I AM WHO I AM." He said further, "Thus you shall say to the Israelites, 'I AM has sent me to you.' " God also said to Moses, "Thus you shall say to the Israelites, 'The LORD, the God of your ancestors, the God of Abraham, the God of Isaac, and the God of Jacob, has sent me to you':

> This is my name forever,
> and this my title for all generations." (Exod. 3:13-15)

Psalm
Psalm 17:1-9
Keep me as the apple of your eye

Additional Reading
Luke 20:1-8
Jesus' teaching authority

Hymn: The God of Abraham Praise, ELW 831

God of Abraham, Isaac, and Jacob: you are the Holy One. In the burning bush you revealed the mystery of your power. In Christ you reveal the depths of your compassion. We praise you for your strength and mercy.

Sunday, November 10, 2019
Time after Pentecost

Luke 20:27-38

Jesus speaks of the resurrection

Jesus said to [the Sadducees], "Those who belong to this age marry and are given in marriage; but those who are considered worthy of a place in that age and in the resurrection from the dead neither marry nor are given in marriage. Indeed they cannot die anymore, because they are like angels and are children of God, being children of the resurrection. And the fact that the dead are raised Moses himself showed, in the story about the bush, where he speaks of the Lord as the God of Abraham, the God of Isaac, and the God of Jacob. Now he is God not of the dead, but of the living; for to him all of them are alive." (Luke 20:34-38)

Psalm

Psalm 17:1-9
Keep me as the apple of your eye

Additional Readings

Job 19:23-27a
I know that my Redeemer lives

2 Thessalonians 2:1-5, 13-17
The coming of Christ Jesus

Hymn: Sing with All the Saints in Glory, ELW 426

O God, our eternal redeemer, by the presence of your Spirit you renew and direct our hearts. Keep always in our mind the end of all things and the day of judgment. Inspire us for a holy life here, and bring us to the joy of the resurrection, through Jesus Christ, our Savior and Lord.

Monday, November 11, 2019
Time after Pentecost

Martin, Bishop of Tours, died 397
Søren Aabye Kierkegaard, teacher, died 1855

Psalm 123

Our eyes look to God

To you I lift up my eyes,
>   O you who are enthroned in the heavens!
As the eyes of servants
>   look to the hand of their master,
as the eyes of a maid
>   to the hand of her mistress,
so our eyes look to the LORD our God,
>   until he has mercy upon us.

Have mercy upon us, O LORD, have mercy upon us,
>   for we have had more than enough of contempt.
Our soul has had more than its fill
>   of the scorn of those who are at ease,
>   of the contempt of the proud. (Ps. 123:1-4)

Additional Readings

Job 20:1-11
Mortals fly away like a dream

2 Peter 1:16-21
Prophecy comes not by human will

Hymn: Kyrie! God, Father, ELW 409

We have had more than enough of contempt, O Lord. Let the dawn of peace rise upon us and the morning star of your reconciling love shine upon our world. Show us your never-ending mercy.

Tuesday, November 12, 2019
Time after Pentecost

2 John 1-13
Be on your guard

Many deceivers have gone out into the world, those who do not confess that Jesus Christ has come in the flesh; any such person is the deceiver and the antichrist! Be on your guard, so that you do not lose what we have worked for, but may receive a full reward. Everyone who does not abide in the teaching of Christ, but goes beyond it, does not have God; whoever abides in the teaching has both the Father and the Son. Do not receive into the house or welcome anyone who comes to you and does not bring this teaching; for to welcome is to participate in the evil deeds of such a person. (2 John 7-11)

Psalm
Psalm 123
Our eyes look to God

Additional Reading
Job 21:1, 17-34
Poor and rich lie down in the dust

Hymn: Jesus, Still Lead On, ELW 624

Saving God, in life and in death we abide in you. Teach us to number our days and to live with resurrection hope. Remind us that our reward is not in the stuff of this world but in you.

Wednesday, November 13, 2019
Time after Pentecost

John 5:19-29
The authority of the Son

[Jesus said,] "Very truly, I tell you, the hour is coming, and is now here, when the dead will hear the voice of the Son of God, and those who hear will live. For just as the Father has life in himself, so he has granted the Son also to have life in himself; and he has given him authority to execute judgment, because he is the Son of Man. Do not be astonished at this; for the hour is coming when all who are in their graves will hear his voice and will come out—those who have done good, to the resurrection of life, and those who have done evil, to the resurrection of condemnation." (John 5:25-29)

Psalm
Psalm 123
Our eyes look to God

Additional Reading
Job 25:1—26:14
Even Sheol is naked before God

Hymn: On Jordan's Stormy Bank I Stand, ELW 437

Nothing is a mystery to you, O God. Your voice calls beyond the boundaries of life and death, light and shadow, earth and sky. Search our hearts. Look upon us with mercy instead of judgment. Bring all things to life.

Thursday, November 14, 2019
Time after Pentecost

Psalm 98

God judges the world

Let the sea roar, and all that fills it;
    the world and those who live in it.
Let the floods clap their hands;
    let the hills sing together for joy
at the presence of the LORD, for he is coming
    to judge the earth.
He will judge the world with righteousness,
    and the peoples with equity. (Ps. 98:7-9)

Additional Readings

1 Samuel 28:3-19
Saul warned of God's judgment

Romans 1:18-25
The revealing of God's wrath

Hymn: Light Dawns on a Weary World, ELW 726

God our creator, the universe reflects your glory. Open our eyes to see beyond the beauty of this world into the holy beauty of your heart. Free our hearts to leap for joy and our tongues to sing praise.

Friday, November 15, 2019
Time after Pentecost

2 Thessalonians 1:3-12
God's judgment

This is evidence of the righteous judgment of God, and is intended to make you worthy of the kingdom of God, for which you are also suffering. For it is indeed just of God to repay with affliction those who afflict you, and to give relief to the afflicted as well as to us, when the Lord Jesus is revealed from heaven with his mighty angels in flaming fire, inflicting vengeance on those who do not know God and on those who do not obey the gospel of our Lord Jesus. (2 Thess. 1:5-8)

Psalm
Psalm 98
God judges the world

Additional Reading
2 Samuel 21:1-14
Violence comes on Saul's household

Hymn: O Day of Peace, ELW 711

In all our griefs and afflictions, we turn to you, O Lord, for relief. Spare us from violence and destruction. Turn our hearts from vengeance and retribution. Release us from our suffering and embrace us again with peace.

Saturday, November 16, 2019
Time after Pentecost

Luke 17:20-37
The judgment coming

Then [Jesus] said to the disciples, "The days are coming when you will long to see one of the days of the Son of Man, and you will not see it. They will say to you, 'Look there!' or 'Look here!' Do not go, do not set off in pursuit. For as the lightning flashes and lights up the sky from one side to the other, so will the Son of Man be in his day." (Luke 17:22-24)

Psalm
Psalm 98
God judges the world

Additional Reading
Ezekiel 10:1-19
God's glory leaves Jerusalem

Hymn: Soon and Very Soon, ELW 439

Our hearts long for the day of your redemption, O God. Sustain us in our daily work. Give us patience and perseverance through all trials, until the full glory of your kingdom is revealed among us.

Sunday, November 17, 2019
Time after Pentecost

Elizabeth of Hungary, renewer of society, died 1231

Luke 21:5-19
Suffering for Jesus' sake

[Jesus said,] "You will be betrayed even by parents and brothers, by relatives and friends; and they will put some of you to death. You will be hated by all because of my name. But not a hair of your head will perish. By your endurance you will gain your souls." (Luke 21:16-19)

Psalm

Psalm 98
God judges the world

Additional Readings

Malachi 4:1-2a
A day of healing for the righteous

2 Thessalonians 3:6-13
Do what is right

Hymn: Through the Night of Doubt and Sorrow, ELW 327

O God, the protector of all who trust in you, without you nothing is strong, nothing is holy. Embrace us with your mercy, that with you as our ruler and guide, we may live through what is temporary without losing what is eternal, through Jesus Christ, our Savior and Lord.

Monday, November 18, 2019
Time after Pentecost

Psalm 141
God is my refuge

But my eyes are turned toward you, O GOD, my Lord;
> in you I seek refuge; do not leave me defenseless.

Keep me from the trap that they have laid for me,
> and from the snares of evildoers.

Let the wicked fall into their own nets,
> while I alone escape. (Ps. 141:8-10)

Additional Readings

Ezekiel 11:14-25
Judgment and promised restoration

Ephesians 4:25—5:2
Be imitators of God

Hymn: My Hope Is Built on Nothing Less, ELW 596/597

God our rescuer, gather us from our scattered places and give us new hearts. Turn our eyes toward you and lead us in kindness, tenderness, and faithfulness. Help us to live in love, following the example of Christ.

Tuesday, November 19, 2019
Time after Pentecost

1 Corinthians 10:23—11:1
Do all to the glory of God

So, whether you eat or drink, or whatever you do, do everything for the glory of God. Give no offense to Jews or to Greeks or to the church of God, just as I try to please everyone in everything I do, not seeking my own advantage, but that of many, so that they may be saved. Be imitators of me, as I am of Christ. (1 Cor. 10:31—11:1)

Psalm
Psalm 141
God is my refuge

Additional Reading
Ezekiel 39:21—40:4
Mercy on the house of Israel

Hymn: Awake, My Soul, and with the Sun, ELW 557

Restore us to yourself, Lord God, and restore us to one another. Help us to teach the faith in word and in deed. Give us open minds and hearts to see Christ in the face of our neighbors.

Wednesday, November 20, 2019
Time after Pentecost

Ezekiel 43:1-12
Divine glory returns to the temple

As for you, mortal, describe the temple to the house of Israel, and let them measure the pattern; and let them be ashamed of their iniquities. When they are ashamed of all that they have done, make known to them the plan of the temple, its arrangement, its exits and its entrances, and its whole form—all its ordinances and its entire plan and all its laws; and write it down in their sight, so that they may observe and follow the entire plan and all its ordinances. This is the law of the temple: the whole territory on the top of the mountain all around shall be most holy. This is the law of the temple. (Ezek. 43:10-12)

Psalm
Psalm 141
God is my refuge

Additional Reading
Matthew 23:37—24:14
The last things

Hymn: In His Temple Now Behold Him, ELW 417

When the earth shakes, the nations tremble, and all of our temples begin to crumble, visit us again with your presence, Holy One. Rebuild our faith and protect us always in the shadow of your wings.

Thursday, November 21, 2019
Time after Pentecost

Psalm 46
The God of Jacob is our stronghold

There is a river whose streams make glad the city of God,
> the holy habitation of the Most High.
God is in the midst of the city; it shall not be moved;
> God will help it when the morning dawns.
The nations are in an uproar, the kingdoms totter;
> he utters his voice, the earth melts.
The LORD of hosts is with us;
> the God of Jacob is our refuge. (Ps. 46:4-7)

Additional Readings
2 Chronicles 18:12-22
Sheep without a shepherd

Hebrews 9:23-28
Christ has appeared once for all

Hymn: O God beyond All Praising, ELW 880

Lord of hosts, you enter into our midst in the person of Christ. As Christ offered himself for the sake of forgiveness and life, help us to offer ourselves in grace and forgiveness to others.

Friday, November 22, 2019
Time after Pentecost

1 Peter 1:3-9

An imperishable inheritance

Blessed be the God and Father of our Lord Jesus Christ! By his great mercy he has given us a new birth into a living hope through the resurrection of Jesus Christ from the dead, and into an inheritance that is imperishable, undefiled, and unfading, kept in heaven for you, who are being protected by the power of God through faith for a salvation ready to be revealed in the last time. In this you rejoice, even if now for a little while you have had to suffer various trials, so that the genuineness of your faith—being more precious than gold that, though perishable, is tested by fire—may be found to result in praise and glory and honor when Jesus Christ is revealed. (1 Peter 1:3-7)

Psalm
Psalm 46
The God of Jacob is our stronghold

Additional Reading
Zechariah 11:1-17
Shepherds who desert the flock

Hymn: O Savior, Precious Savior, ELW 820

God, our shepherd and our stronghold, you remain patient even when we are slow to follow you. Lead us through the trials of this life into the glorious inheritance that you have prepared for us.

Saturday, November 23, 2019
Time after Pentecost

Clement, Bishop of Rome, died around 100
Miguel Agustín Pro, martyr, died 1927

Luke 18:15-17

Receiving the kingdom of God

People were bringing even infants to [Jesus] that he might touch them; and when the disciples saw it, they sternly ordered them not to do it. But Jesus called for them and said, "Let the little children come to me, and do not stop them; for it is to such as these that the kingdom of God belongs. Truly I tell you, whoever does not receive the kingdom of God as a little child will never enter it." (Luke 18:15-17)

Psalm

Psalm 46
The God of Jacob is our stronghold

Additional Reading

Jeremiah 22:18-30
The wind shepherds the shepherds

Hymn: Cradling Children in His Arm, ELW 444

Take us into your embrace, loving God, for we are your children. Draw us near to the promise of baptism, by which we are adopted into your family and given the eternal promise of your kingdom.

Sunday, November 24, 2019

Christ the King

Justus Falckner, died 1723; Jehu Jones, died 1852; William Passavant, died 1894; pastors in North America

Luke 23:33-43

Jesus crucified with two thieves

When they came to the place that is called The Skull, they crucified Jesus there with the criminals, one on his right and one on his left. [Then Jesus said, "Father, forgive them; for they do not know what they are doing."] And they cast lots to divide his clothing. And the people stood by, watching; but the leaders scoffed at him, saying, "He saved others; let him save himself if he is the Messiah of God, his chosen one!" The soldiers also mocked him, coming up and offering him sour wine, and saying, "If you are the King of the Jews, save yourself!" (Luke 23:33-37)

Psalm

Psalm 46
The God of Jacob is our stronghold

Additional Readings

Jeremiah 23:1-6
Coming of the shepherd

Colossians 1:11-20
A hymn to Christ, firstborn of all creation

Hymn: Lord, Enthroned in Heavenly Splendor, ELW 475

O God, our true life, to serve you is freedom, and to know you is unending joy. We worship you, we glorify you, we give thanks to you for your great glory. Abide with us, reign in us, and make this world into a fit habitation for your divine majesty, through Jesus Christ, our Savior and Lord, who lives and reigns with you and the Holy Spirit, one God, now and forever.

Monday, November 25, 2019
Time after Pentecost

Isaac Watts, hymnwriter, died 1748

Psalm 24
The King of glory comes

Lift up your heads, O gates!
>   and be lifted up, O ancient doors!
>   that the King of glory may come in.
Who is the King of glory?
>   The Lord, strong and mighty,
>   the Lord, mighty in battle.
Lift up your heads, O gates!
>   and be lifted up, O ancient doors!
>   that the King of glory may come in.
Who is this King of glory?
>   The Lord of hosts,
>   he is the King of glory. (Ps. 24:7-10)

Additional Readings
Jeremiah 46:18-28
God will save Israel

Revelation 21:5-27
God reigns in the holy city

Hymn: Come, Thou Almighty King, ELW 408

King of the nations, you reign forever and you promise us a new kingdom of life. Lift up the faces of those who mourn with your promise of victory over death. Shine upon our paths and bring us into glory.

Tuesday, November 26, 2019
Time after Pentecost

Revelation 22:8-21
Surely, I am coming soon

"See, I am coming soon; my reward is with me, to repay according to everyone's work. I am the Alpha and the Omega, the first and the last, the beginning and the end."

Blessed are those who wash their robes, so that they will have the right to the tree of life and may enter the city by the gates. (Rev. 22:12-14)

Psalm
Psalm 24
The King of glory comes

Additional Reading
Isaiah 33:17-22
Our God rules

Hymn: Love Divine, All Loves Excelling, ELW 631

Show us the beauty of your reign, O God. Give us glimpses of your kingdom among us in deeds of mercy, acts of grace and generosity, and hearts bent toward forgiveness. Remind us of your blessings with each new day.

Wednesday, November 27, 2019
Time after Pentecost

Isaiah 60:8-16

The forsaken become majestic

The descendants of those who oppressed you
 shall come bending low to you,
and all who despised you
 shall bow down at your feet;
they shall call you the City of the LORD,
 the Zion of the Holy One of Israel.
Whereas you have been forsaken and hated,
 with no one passing through,
I will make you majestic forever,
 a joy from age to age.
You shall suck the milk of nations,
 you shall suck the breasts of kings;
and you shall know that I, the LORD, am your Savior
 and your Redeemer, the Mighty One of Jacob. (Isa. 60:14-16)

Psalm
Psalm 24
The King of glory comes

Additional Reading
Luke 1:1-4
That you may know the truth

Hymn: Glorious Things of You Are Spoken, ELW 647

Saving God, you bring vindication to the oppressed. Guide us in the way of truth, that we seek justice for the world and all who live in it. Give us the blessing of your joy from age to age.

Blessing of the Household for Thanksgiving Day

We gather this day to give thanks to God for the gifts of this land and its people, for God has been generous to us. As we ask God's blessing upon this food we share, may we be mindful of the lonely and the hungry.

As we prepare to offer thanks to God, let us listen to the words of scripture:

I give thanks to my God always for you because of the grace of God that has been given you in Christ Jesus, for in every way you have been enriched in him, in speech and knowledge of every kind—just as the testimony of Christ has been strengthened among you—so that you are not lacking in any spiritual gift as you wait for the revealing of our Lord Jesus Christ. He will also strengthen you to the end, so that you may be blameless on the day of our Lord Jesus Christ. (1 Cor. 1:4-8)

Let us pray.
God most provident, we join all creation in offering you praise through Jesus Christ. For generations the people of this land have sung of your bounty. With them, we offer you thanksgiving for the rich harvest we have received at your hands. Bless us and this food that we share with grateful hearts. Continue to make our land fruitful and let our love for you be seen in our pursuit of justice and peace and in our generous response to those in need. We ask this through Christ our Lord. Amen.

May Christ, the living bread, bring us to the feast of eternal life. Amen.

Thursday, November 28, 2019
Time after Pentecost

Day of Thanksgiving (U.S.A.)

Psalm 122
Gladness in God's house

I was glad when they said to me,
> "Let us go to the house of the LORD!"
Our feet are standing
> within your gates, O Jerusalem.

Jerusalem—built as a city
> that is bound firmly together.
To it the tribes go up,
> the tribes of the LORD,
as was decreed for Israel,
> to give thanks to the name of the LORD.
For there the thrones for judgment were set up,
> the thrones of the house of David. (Ps. 122:1-5)

Additional Readings
Daniel 9:15-19
A plea for forgiveness

James 4:1-10
A plea for God's grace and human humility

Hymn: Open Now Thy Gates of Beauty, ELW 533

God, you are our provider and the giver of all grace. With gladness of heart, we give thanks for your gifts and for your presence. Turn our gratitude into deeds of generosity for the sake of your holy name.

Friday, November 29, 2019
Time after Pentecost

Hebrews 11:1-7
Noah acts in faith

By faith Abel offered to God a more acceptable sacrifice than Cain's. Through this he received approval as righteous, God himself giving approval to his gifts; he died, but through his faith he still speaks. By faith Enoch was taken so that he did not experience death; and "he was not found, because God had taken him." For it was attested before he was taken away that "he had pleased God." And without faith it is impossible to please God, for whoever would approach him must believe that he exists and that he rewards those who seek him. By faith Noah, warned by God about events as yet unseen, respected the warning and built an ark to save his household; by this he condemned the world and became an heir to the righteousness that is in accordance with faith. (Heb. 11:4-7)

Psalm
Psalm 122
Gladness in God's house

Additional Reading
Genesis 6:1-10
Humankind's wickedness, Noah's righteousness

Hymn: We Walk by Faith, ELW 635

Bring peace to our homes, to our nations, and to our hearts. Send your reconciling love to all places of war, dissent, or family conflict. Empower leaders, authorities, and advocates to seek the good and the prosperity of all.

Saturday, November 30, 2019
Andrew, Apostle

John 1:35-42
Jesus calls Andrew

One of the two who heard John speak and followed him was Andrew, Simon Peter's brother. He first found his brother Simon and said to him, "We have found the Messiah" (which is translated Anointed). He brought Simon to Jesus, who looked at him and said, "You are Simon son of John. You are to be called Cephas" (which is translated Peter). (John 1:40-42)

Psalm

Psalm 19:1-6
The heavens declare God's glory

Additional Readings

Ezekiel 3:16-21
A sentinel for the house of Israel

Romans 10:10-18
Faith comes from the word of Christ

Hymn: Jesus Calls Us; o'er the Tumult, ELW 696

Almighty God, you gave your apostle Andrew the grace to obey the call of your Son and to bring his brother to Jesus. Give us also, who are called by your holy word, grace to follow Jesus without delay and to bring into his presence those who are near to us, for he lives and reigns with you and the Holy Spirit, one God, now and forever.

Prayer List for December

_____

_____

_____

_____

_____

_____

_____

_____

_____

Advent

In the days of Advent, Christians prepare to celebrate the presence of God's Word among us in our own day. During these four weeks, we pray that the reign of God, which Jesus preached and lived, would come among us. We pray that God's justice would flourish in our land, that the people of the earth would live in peace, that the weak and the sick and the hungry would be strengthened, healed, and fed with God's merciful presence.

During the last days of Advent, Christians welcome Christ with names inspired by the prophets: wisdom, liberator of slaves, mighty power, radiant dawn and sun of justice, the keystone of the arch of humanity, and Emmanuel—God with us.

The Advent Wreath

One of the best-known customs for the season is the Advent wreath. The wreath and winter candle-lighting in the midst of growing darkness strengthen some of the Advent images found in the Bible. The unbroken circle of greens is clearly an image of everlasting life, a victory wreath, the crown of Christ, or the wheel of time itself. Christians use the wreath as a sign that Christ reaches into our time to lead us to the light of everlasting life. The four candles mark the progress of the four weeks of Advent and the growth of light. Sometimes the wreath is embellished with natural dried flowers or fruit. Its evergreen branches lead the household and the congregation to the evergreen Christmas tree. In many homes, the family gathers for prayer around the wreath.

An Evening Service of Light for Advent

This brief order may be used on any evening during the season of Advent. If the household has an Advent wreath (one candle for each of the four weeks of Advent), it may be lighted during this service. Alternatively, one simple candle (perhaps a votive candle) may be lighted instead.

Lighting the Advent Wreath

May this candle/these candles be a sign of the coming light of Christ.

One or more candles may be lighted. Use this blessing when lighting the first candle.

Blessed are you, O Lord our God, ruler of the universe.
You call all nations to walk in your light
and to seek your ways of justice and peace,
for the night is past, and the dawn of your coming is near.
Bless us as we light the first candle of this wreath.
Rouse us from sleep,
that we may be ready to greet our Lord when he comes
and welcome him into our hearts and homes,
for he is our light and our salvation.
Blessed be God forever.
Amen.

Blessings for the second, third, and fourth weeks of Advent are provided on pages 378, 386, and 394, respectively.

Reading

Read one or more of the scripture passages appointed for the day in the dated pages that follow.

Hymn

One of the following, or the hymn suggested for the day, may be sung. The hymn might be accompanied by small finger cymbals.

Light One Candle to Watch for Messiah, ELW 240
People, Look East, ELW 248
Savior of the Nations, Come, ELW 263

During the final seven days of the Advent season (beginning on December 17), the hymn "O Come, O Come, Emmanuel" (ELW 257) is particularly appropriate. The stanzas of that hymn are also referred to as the "O Antiphons." The first stanza of the hymn could be sung each day during the final days before Christmas in addition to the stanza that is specifically appointed for the day.

First stanza
O come, O come, Emmanuel,
and ransom captive Israel,
that mourns in lonely exile here
until the Son of God appear.
Refrain   Rejoice! Rejoice! Emmanuel shall come to you, O Israel.

December 17
O come, O Wisdom from on high,
embracing all things far and nigh:
in strength and beauty come and stay;
teach us your will and guide our way.   *Refrain*

December 18
O come, O come, O Lord of might,
as to your tribes on Sinai's height
in ancient times you gave the law
in cloud, and majesty, and awe.   *Refrain*

December 19
O come, O Branch of Jesse, free
your own from Satan's tyranny;
from depths of hell your people save,
and give them vict'ry o'er the grave.   *Refrain*

December 20

O come, O Key of David, come,
and open wide our heav'nly home;
make safe the way that leads on high,
and close the path to misery.   *Refrain*

December 21

O come, O Dayspring, come and cheer;
O Sun of justice, now draw near.
Disperse the gloomy clouds of night,
and death's dark shadow put to flight.   *Refrain*

December 22

O come, O King of nations, come,
O Cornerstone that binds in one:
refresh the hearts that long for you;
restore the broken, make us new.   *Refrain*

December 23

O come, O come, Emmanuel,
and ransom captive Israel,
that mourns in lonely exile here
until the Son of God appear.   *Refrain*

Text: Psalteriolum Cantionum Catholicarum, Köln, 1710; tr. composite
Text sts. 2, 6, 7 © 1997 Augsburg Fortress

Table Prayer for Advent

For use when a meal follows.

Blessed are you, O Lord our God,
the one who is, who was, and who is to come.
At this table you fill us with good things.
May these gifts strengthen us
to share with the hungry and all those in need,
as we wait and watch for your coming among us
in Jesus Christ our Lord. Amen.

Candles may be extinguished now or after the meal, if one is to follow.

Sunday, December 1, 2019
First Sunday of Advent

Matthew 24:36-44

The sudden coming of salvation

[Jesus said,] "But about that day and hour no one knows, neither the angels of heaven, nor the Son, but only the Father. For as the days of Noah were, so will be the coming of the Son of Man. For as in those days before the flood they were eating and drinking, marrying and giving in marriage, until the day Noah entered the ark, and they knew nothing until the flood came and swept them all away, so too will be the coming of the Son of Man." (Matt. 24:36-39)

Psalm

Psalm 122
Gladness in God's house

Additional Readings

Isaiah 2:1-5
War transformed into peace

Romans 13:11-14
Salvation is near; wake from sleep

Hymn: Wake, Awake, for Night Is Flying, ELW 436

Stir up your power, Lord Christ, and come. By your merciful protection save us from the threatening dangers of our sins, and enlighten our walk in the way of your salvation, for you live and reign with the Father and the Holy Spirit, one God, now and forever.

Monday, December 2, 2019
Week of Advent 1

Psalm 124
We have escaped like a bird

Blessed be the LORD,
>> who has not given us
>> as prey to their teeth.
We have escaped like a bird
>> from the snare of the fowlers;
the snare is broken,
>> and we have escaped.

Our help is in the name of the LORD,
>> who made heaven and earth. (Ps. 124:6-8)

Additional Readings
Romans 6:1-11
Dying and rising with Christ through baptism

Genesis 8:1-19
The flood waters subside

Hymn: Come, Thou Long-Expected Jesus, ELW 254

Mighty God, though your power is infinite, you keep your loving gaze fixed on people at the margins of our sight. Make us your instruments of escape for all who are trapped in systems of oppression and injustice.

Tuesday, December 3, 2019
Week of Advent 1

Francis Xavier, missionary to Asia, died 1552

Genesis 9:1-17
Command to be fruitful; sign of the rainbow

God said [to Noah and to his sons with him], "This is the sign of the covenant that I make between me and you and every living creature that is with you, for all future generations: I have set my bow in the clouds, and it shall be a sign of the covenant between me and the earth. When I bring clouds over the earth and the bow is seen in the clouds, I will remember my covenant that is between me and you and every living creature of all flesh; and the waters shall never again become a flood to destroy all flesh. When the bow is in the clouds, I will see it and remember the everlasting covenant between God and every living creature of all flesh that is on the earth." (Gen. 9:12-16)

Psalm
Psalm 124
We have escaped like a bird

Additional Reading
Hebrews 11:32-40
The heroes of faith

Hymn: Baptized in Water, ELW 456

God of the covenant, you promised peace when you hung up your bow before Noah. Where we are quick to take up arms, help us hang up our own instruments of destruction as signs of your steadfast love toward all creation.

Wednesday, December 4, 2019
Week of Advent 1

John of Damascus, theologian and hymnwriter, died around 749

Isaiah 54:1-10
God will save the people

This is like the days of Noah to me:
>   Just as I swore that the waters of Noah
>   would never again go over the earth,
so I have sworn that I will not be angry with you
>   and will not rebuke you.
For the mountains may depart
>   and the hills be removed,
but my steadfast love shall not depart from you,
>   and my covenant of peace shall not be removed,
>   says the LORD, who has compassion on you. (Isa. 54:9-10)

Psalm
Psalm 124
We have escaped like a bird

Additional Reading
Matthew 24:23-35
The end is coming

Hymn: Praise the Lord! O Heavens, ELW 823

Rock of our salvation, how deep is the foundation we have in you! Wherever our lives are resting dangerously on sinking ground, uproot us and plant us firmly in the strength that comes through faith in you.

Thursday, December 5, 2019
Week of Advent 1

Psalm 72:1-7, 18-19
The righteous shall flourish

Give the king your justice, O God,
>   and your righteousness to a king's son.
May he judge your people with righteousness,
>   and your poor with justice.
May the mountains yield prosperity for the people,
>   and the hills, in righteousness.
May he defend the cause of the poor of the people,
>   give deliverance to the needy,
>   and crush the oppressor. (Ps. 72:1-4)

Additional Readings

Isaiah 4:2-6
God's promised glory for the survivors in Zion

Acts 1:12-17, 21-26
Beginnings of the apostolic ministry

Hymn: Jesus Shall Reign, ELW 434

*Sovereign God, your risen Son rules over all creation with mercy and love.
Place his vision in the eyes of leaders from all nations, that they would strive
for the good of all and govern according to your will.*

Friday, December 6, 2019
Week of Advent 1

Nicholas, Bishop of Myra, died around 342

Isaiah 30:19-26

God's promise to be gracious to Zion

Truly, O people in Zion, inhabitants of Jerusalem, you shall weep no more. He will surely be gracious to you at the sound of your cry; when he hears it, he will answer you. Though the Lord may give you the bread of adversity and the water of affliction, yet your Teacher will not hide himself any more, but your eyes shall see your Teacher. And when you turn to the right or when you turn to the left, your ears shall hear a word behind you, saying, "This is the way; walk in it." (Isa. 30:19-21)

Psalm

Psalm 72:1-7, 18-19
The righteous shall flourish

Additional Reading

Acts 13:16-25
Paul's testimony concerning John the Baptist

Hymn: O Zion, Haste, ELW 668

Ever-present God, your light illumines paths where we see only darkness. Turn us toward you in prayer, in scripture, and in the sacramental life of the church whenever we feel lost and afraid and need guidance.

Saturday, December 7, 2019
Week of Advent 1

Ambrose, Bishop of Milan, died 397

Isaiah 40:1-11

A voice crying in the wilderness

A voice cries out:
"In the wilderness prepare the way of the LORD,
    make straight in the desert a highway for our God.
Every valley shall be lifted up,
    and every mountain and hill be made low;
the uneven ground shall become level,
    and the rough places a plain.
Then the glory of the LORD shall be revealed,
    and all people shall see it together,
    for the mouth of the LORD has spoken." (Isa. 40:3-5)

Psalm

Psalm 72:1-7, 18-19
The righteous shall flourish

Additional Reading

John 1:19-28
John the Baptist concerning his own ministry

Hymn: Savior of the Nations, Come, ELW 263

Holy God, you are the thrill of hope in which this weary world rejoices. In our divided and conflicted world, prepare the way before us by which all people might walk into a shared vision of the future.

Lighting the Advent Wreath

Use this blessing when lighting the first two candles.

Blessed are you, O Lord our God, ruler of the universe.
John the Baptist calls all people to prepare the Lord's way
for the kingdom of heaven is near.
Bless us as we light the candles on this wreath.
Baptize us with the fire of your Spirit,
that we may be a light shining in the darkness
welcoming others as Christ has welcomed us,
for he is our light and our salvation.
Blessed be God forever.
Amen.

Sunday, December 8, 2019

Second Sunday of Advent

Matthew 3:1-12

Prepare the way of the Lord

In those days John the Baptist appeared in the wilderness of Judea, proclaiming, "Repent, for the kingdom of heaven has come near." This is the one of whom the prophet Isaiah spoke when he said,

"The voice of one crying out in the wilderness:
'Prepare the way of the Lord,
    make his paths straight.'" (Matt. 3:1-3)

Psalm

Psalm 72:1-7, 18-19
The righteous shall flourish

Additional Readings

Isaiah 11:1-10
A ruler brings justice and peace

Romans 15:4-13
Living in harmony

Hymn: On Jordan's Bank the Baptist's Cry, ELW 249

Stir up our hearts, Lord God, to prepare the way of your only Son. By his coming nurture our growth as people of repentance and peace; through Jesus Christ, our Savior and Lord, who lives and reigns with you and the Holy Spirit, one God, now and forever.

Monday, December 9, 2019
Week of Advent 2

Psalm 21

God comes with judgment and strength

In your strength the king rejoices, O LORD,
>   and in your help how greatly he exults! . . .
For the king trusts in the LORD,
>   and through the steadfast love of the Most High he shall not be moved.

Your hand will find out all your enemies;
>   your right hand will find out those who hate you. (Ps. 21:1, 7-8)

Additional Readings
Isaiah 24:1-16a
Judgment is coming, but glorify God

1 Thessalonians 4:1-12
Live in holiness and love one another

Hymn: Come Now, O Prince of Peace, ELW 247

God our consolation, you stand by our sides even when those dearest to us fail and hurt us. Grant us reconciliation in broken relationships and strengthen our bonds with those who are hardest to love.

Tuesday, December 10, 2019
Week of Advent 2

Romans 15:14-21

Gentiles are also called to the obedience of faith

I myself feel confident about you, my brothers and sisters, that you yourselves are full of goodness, filled with all knowledge, and able to instruct one another. Nevertheless on some points I have written to you rather boldly by way of reminder, because of the grace given me by God to be a minister of Christ Jesus to the Gentiles in the priestly service of the gospel of God, so that the offering of the Gentiles may be acceptable, sanctified by the Holy Spirit. (Rom. 15:14-16)

Psalm
Psalm 21
God comes with judgment and strength

Additional Reading
Isaiah 41:14-20
God will not forget the poor of Israel

Hymn: O Lord, How Shall I Meet You, ELW 241

Sustaining God, through the Holy Spirit you are always equipping your people for ministry. Make us good stewards of the many and various gifts you have given us for the building up of your kingdom in this world.

Wednesday, December 11, 2019
Week of Advent 2

Genesis 15:1-18
God's covenant with Abram

As the sun was going down, a deep sleep fell upon Abram, and a deep and terrifying darkness descended upon him. Then the LORD said to Abram, "Know this for certain, that your offspring shall be aliens in a land that is not theirs, and shall be slaves there, and they shall be oppressed for four hundred years; but I will bring judgment on the nation that they serve, and afterward they shall come out with great possessions. As for yourself, you shall go to your ancestors in peace; you shall be buried in a good old age. And they shall come back here in the fourth generation; for the iniquity of the Amorites is not yet complete." (Gen. 15:12-16)

Psalm
Psalm 21
God comes with judgment and strength

Additional Reading
Matthew 12:33-37
A good tree bears good fruit

Hymn: Shine, Jesus, Shine, ELW 671

God of our weary years, you sustained the Israelites through centuries of displacement and slavery in Egypt. Provide the love and welcome of your church to all who long for deliverance, especially for immigrants living among us.

Thursday, December 12, 2019
Week of Advent 2

Psalm 146:5-10
God lifts up those bowed down

Happy are those whose help is the God of Jacob,
    whose hope is in the Lord their God,
who made heaven and earth,
    the sea, and all that is in them;
who keeps faith forever;
    who executes justice for the oppressed;
    who gives food to the hungry.

The Lord sets the prisoners free;
    the Lord opens the eyes of the blind.
The Lord lifts up those who are bowed down;
    the Lord loves the righteous.
The Lord watches over the strangers;
    he upholds the orphan and the widow,
    but the way of the wicked he brings to ruin. (Ps. 146:5-9)

Additional Readings
Ruth 1:6-18
Ruth's fidelity toward Naomi and her people

2 Peter 3:1-10
The promise of the Lord's coming

Hymn: Praise the Almighty! ELW 877

Mothering God, your tenderness and care for all people knows no bounds, yet we perpetuate injustices that leave so many feeling abandoned. Use our prayers, our actions, and our advocacy to reveal your care for those who feel unloved.

Friday, December 13, 2019
Week of Advent 2

Lucy, martyr, died 304

2 Peter 3:11-18

Prepare for the Lord's coming

Therefore, beloved, while you are waiting for these things, strive to be found by him at peace, without spot or blemish; and regard the patience of our Lord as salvation. So also our beloved brother Paul wrote to you according to the wisdom given him, speaking of this as he does in all his letters. There are some things in them hard to understand, which the ignorant and unstable twist to their own destruction, as they do the other scriptures. You therefore, beloved, since you are forewarned, beware that you are not carried away with the error of the lawless and lose your own stability. But grow in the grace and knowledge of our Lord and Savior Jesus Christ. To him be the glory both now and to the day of eternity. Amen. (2 Peter 3:14-18)

Psalm
Psalm 146:5-10
God lifts up those bowed down

Additional Reading
Ruth 4:13-17
God's fidelity toward Ruth and her posterity

Hymn: Take, Oh, Take Me As I Am, ELW 814

God of our salvation, in your Son Jesus Christ you have set before our eyes the fullness of your grace. Provide his loving call to quicken our discipleship when other voices beckon us to abandon your way.

Saturday, December 14, 2019
Week of Advent 2

John of the Cross, renewer of the church, died 1591

1 Samuel 2:1-8

Hannah sings in praise of God's fidelity

Hannah prayed and said,
>"My heart exults in the LORD;
>>my strength is exalted in my God.
>
>My mouth derides my enemies,
>>because I rejoice in my victory.
>
>"There is no Holy One like the LORD,
>>no one besides you;
>>
>>there is no Rock like our God....
>
>He raises up the poor from the dust;
>>he lifts the needy from the ash heap,
>
>to make them sit with princes
>>and inherit a seat of honor.
>
>For the pillars of the earth are the LORD's,
>>and on them he has set the world." (1 Sam. 2:1-2, 8)

Psalm
Psalm 146:5-10
God lifts up those bowed down

Additional Reading
Luke 3:1-18
The proclamation of John the Baptist

Hymn: My Soul Now Magnifies the Lord, ELW 573

God our hope, our stories give witness to your uplifting power. Inspire us by Hannah's example to sing your praises at every opportunity so we may grow in gratitude for all you have done for us.

Lighting the Advent Wreath

Use this blessing when lighting three candles.

Blessed are you, O Lord our God, ruler of the universe.
Your prophets spoke of a day when the desert would blossom
and waters would break forth in the wilderness.
Bless us as we light the candles on this wreath.
Strengthen our hearts
as we prepare for the coming of the Lord.
May he give water to all who thirst,
for he is our light and our salvation.
Blessed be God forever.
Amen.

Sunday, December 15, 2019
Third Sunday of Advent

Matthew 11:2-11

The forerunner of Christ

Jesus began to speak to the crowds about John: "What did you go out into the wilderness to look at? A reed shaken by the wind? What then did you go out to see? Someone dressed in soft robes? Look, those who wear soft robes are in royal palaces. What then did you go out to see? A prophet? Yes, I tell you, and more than a prophet. This is the one about whom it is written,

'See, I am sending my messenger ahead of you,

who will prepare your way before you.'

Truly I tell you, among those born of women no one has arisen greater than John the Baptist; yet the least in the kingdom of heaven is greater than he." (Matt. 11:7b-11)

Psalm

Psalm 146:5-10
God lifts up those bowed down

Additional Readings

Isaiah 35:1-10
The desert blooms

James 5:7-10
Patience until the Lord's coming

Hymn: Prepare the Royal Highway, ELW 264

Stir up the wills of all who look to you, Lord God, and strengthen our faith in your coming, that, transformed by grace, we may walk in your way; through Jesus Christ, our Savior and Lord, who lives and reigns with you and the Holy Spirit, one God, now and forever.

Monday, December 16, 2019
Week of Advent 3

Psalm 42

Hope in God

I say to God, my rock,
> "Why have you forgotten me?
Why must I walk about mournfully
> because the enemy oppresses me?"
As with a deadly wound in my body,
> my adversaries taunt me,
while they say to me continually,
> "Where is your God?"

Why are you cast down, O my soul,
> and why are you disquieted within me?
Hope in God; for I shall again praise him,
> my help and my God. (Ps. 42:9-11)

Additional Readings

Isaiah 29:17-24
The infirm will be healed

Acts 5:12-16
Many people healed by the apostles

Hymn: In Deepest Night, ELW 699

God of the darkness, you remain our hope in even our most hopeless moments. When trouble makes the echoes of your saving power grow faint in our ears, place at our sides those whose hearing is stronger than our own.

Tuesday, December 17, 2019
Week of Advent 3

Jude 17-25

Prepare for the Lord's coming

But you, beloved, must remember the predictions of the apostles of our Lord Jesus Christ; for they said to you, "In the last time there will be scoffers, indulging their own ungodly lusts." It is these worldly people, devoid of the Spirit, who are causing divisions. But you, beloved, build yourselves up on your most holy faith; pray in the Holy Spirit; keep yourselves in the love of God; look forward to the mercy of our Lord Jesus Christ that leads to eternal life. (Jude 17-21)

Psalm
Psalm 42
Hope in God

Additional Reading
Ezekiel 47:1-12
The wilderness will flower

Hymn: Shall We Gather at the River, ELW 423

God of the tempest and the whirlwind, in the midst of a raging storm your Son calmed the seas and steadied his disciples' faith. Settle the winds and waves within our hearts when we are overwhelmed with anxiety and fear.

Wednesday, December 18, 2019
Week of Advent 3

Zechariah 8:1-17
God's promise to Zion

For thus says the LORD of hosts: Just as I purposed to bring disaster upon you, when your ancestors provoked me to wrath, and I did not relent, says the LORD of hosts, so again I have purposed in these days to do good to Jerusalem and to the house of Judah; do not be afraid. These are the things that you shall do: Speak the truth to one another, render in your gates judgments that are true and make for peace, do not devise evil in your hearts against one another, and love no false oath; for all these are things that I hate, says the LORD. (Zech. 8:14-17)

Psalm
Psalm 42
Hope in God

Additional Reading
Matthew 8:14-17, 28-34
Jesus heals

Hymn: Lo! He Comes with Clouds Descending, ELW 435

Lord, your gracious word pours forth unceasingly into a world reluctant to hear. Give us courage to speak out with integrity and justice, aligning ourselves with your word, so that the world may be convicted and inspired by your truth.

Thursday, December 19, 2019
Week of Advent 3

Psalm 80:1-7, 17-19

Show the light of your countenance

O Lᴏʀᴅ God of hosts,
>   how long will you be angry with your people's prayers?

You have fed them with the bread of tears,
>   and given them tears to drink in full measure.

You make us the scorn of our neighbors;
>   our enemies laugh among themselves.

Restore us, O God of hosts;
>   let your face shine, that we may be saved. (Ps. 80:4-7)

Additional Readings

2 Samuel 7:1-17
God will build you a house

Galatians 3:23-29
Children of God by Christ's coming

Hymn: Gather Us In, ELW 532

Redeeming God, on the cross your Son brought your grace into the depths of our human suffering. When we approach our own human limits, send your Spirit to assure us of your presence in our pain, frustration, and anger.

Friday, December 20, 2019
Week of Advent 3

Katharina von Bora Luther, renewer of the church, died 1552

2 Samuel 7:18-22

David prays for God's faithfulness toward Israel

Then King David went in and sat before the LORD, and said, "Who am I, O Lord GOD, and what is my house, that you have brought me thus far? And yet this was a small thing in your eyes, O Lord GOD; you have spoken also of your servant's house for a great while to come. May this be instruction for the people, O Lord GOD! And what more can David say to you? For you know your servant, O Lord GOD! Because of your promise, and according to your own heart, you have wrought all this greatness, so that your servant may know it. Therefore you are great, O LORD God; for there is no one like you, and there is no God besides you, according to all that we have heard with our ears." (2 Sam. 7:18-22)

Psalm
Psalm 80:1-7, 17-19
Show the light of your countenance

Additional Reading
Galatians 4:1-7
God's Son, sent in the fullness of time

Hymn: Blessed Be the God of Israel, ELW 250

Lord God, our very lives are pure gift flowing from your creative heart. Flood us with gratitude that overflows into words and actions to serve others. Make us living symbols of your abundance in a world of scarcity.

Saturday, December 21, 2019
Week of Advent 3

John 3:31-36

The one who comes from above

The one who comes from above is above all; the one who is of the earth belongs to the earth and speaks about earthly things. The one who comes from heaven is above all. He testifies to what he has seen and heard, yet no one accepts his testimony. Whoever has accepted his testimony has certified this, that God is true. He whom God has sent speaks the words of God, for he gives the Spirit without measure. The Father loves the Son and has placed all things in his hands. Whoever believes in the Son has eternal life; whoever disobeys the Son will not see life, but must endure God's wrath. (John 3:31-36)

Psalm

Psalm 80:1-7, 17-19
Show the light of your countenance

Additional Reading

2 Samuel 7:23-29
David reminds God of God's promise

Hymn: He Came Down, ELW 253

God of mystery, your ways confound our thoughts and reveal the limits of all our earthly ways of seeing. Move our stuck perceptions beyond the comfortable and controllable and into an open discovery of your immeasurable truth.

Lighting the Advent Wreath

Use this blessing when lighting all four candles.

Blessed are you, O Lord our God, ruler of the universe.
In your Son, Emmanuel,
you have shown us your light
and saved us from the power of sin.
Bless us as we light the candles on this wreath.
Increase our longing for your presence,
that at the celebration of your Son's birth
his Spirit might dwell anew in our midst,
for he is our light and our salvation.
Blessed be God forever.
Amen.

Sunday, December 22, 2019
Fourth Sunday of Advent

Matthew 1:18-25
Our God near at hand

An angel of the Lord appeared to [Joseph] in a dream and said, "Joseph, son of David, do not be afraid to take Mary as your wife, for the child conceived in her is from the Holy Spirit. She will bear a son, and you are to name him Jesus, for he will save his people from their sins." All this took place to fulfill what had been spoken by the Lord through the prophet:

"Look, the virgin shall conceive and bear a son,
and they shall name him Emmanuel,"
which means, "God is with us." (Matt. 1:20b-23)

Psalm
Psalm 80:1-7, 17-19
Show the light of your countenance

Additional Readings
Isaiah 7:10-16
The sign of Immanuel

Romans 1:1-7
Paul's greeting to the church at Rome

Hymn: O Come, O Come, Emmanuel, ELW 257

Stir up your power, Lord Christ, and come. With your abundant grace and might, free us from the sin that hinders our faith, that eagerly we may receive your promises, for you live and reign with the Father and the Holy Spirit, one God, now and forever.

Monday, December 23, 2019
Week of Advent 4

Luke 1:46b-55
My soul gives glory to God

"My soul magnifies the Lord,
    and my spirit rejoices in God my Savior,
for he has looked with favor on the lowliness of his servant.
    Surely, from now on all generations will call me blessed;
for the Mighty One has done great things for me,
    and holy is his name." (Luke 1:46b-49)

Additional Readings
2 Samuel 7:18, 23-29
Your servant will be blessed

Galatians 3:6-14
The promise of the Spirit

Hymn: Canticle of the Turning, ELW 723

Mighty One, you have looked with favor on those from whom we have withheld honor. Cast us down in our pride and make us humble so that the lowly whom you have chosen might see our repentance and forgive us.

Christmas

Over the centuries, various customs have developed which focus the household on welcoming the light of Christ: the daily or weekly lighting of the Advent wreath, the blessing of the lighted Christmas tree, the candle-lit procession of Las Posadas, the flickering lights of the luminaria, the Christ candle at Christmas.

The Christian household not only welcomes the light of Christ at Christmas but celebrates the presence of that light throughout the Twelve Days, from Christmas until the Epiphany, January 6. In the Christmas season, Christians welcome the light of Christ that is already with us through faith. In word and gesture, prayer and song, in the many customs of diverse cultures, Christians celebrate this life-giving Word and ask that it dwell more deeply in the rhythm of daily life.

Table Prayer for the Twelve Days of Christmas

With joy and gladness we feast upon your love, O God.
You have come among us in Jesus, your Son,
and your presence now graces this table.
May Christ dwell in us that we might bear his love to all the world,
for he is Lord forever and ever. Amen.

Lighting the Christmas Tree

Use this prayer when you first illumine the tree or when you gather at the tree.

Holy God,
we praise you as we light this tree.
It gives light to this place
as you shine light into darkness through Jesus,
the light of the world.

God of all,
we thank you for your love,
the love that has come to us in Jesus.
Be with us now as we remember that gift of love
and help us to share that love with a yearning world.

Creator God,
you made the stars in the heavens.
Thank you for the light that shines on us in Jesus,
the bright morning star.
Amen.

Blessing of the Nativity Scene

This blessing may be used when figures are added to the nativity scene and throughout the days of Christmas.

Bless us, O God, as we remember a humble birth. With each angel and shepherd we place here before you, show us the wonder found in a stable. In song and prayer, silence and awe, we adore your gift of love, Christ Jesus our Savior.
Amen.

Tuesday, December 24, 2019
Nativity of Our Lord
Christmas Eve

Luke 2:1-14 [15-20]
God with us

But the angel said to [the shepherds], "Do not be afraid; for see—I am bringing you good news of great joy for all the people: to you is born this day in the city of David a Savior, who is the Messiah, the Lord. This will be a sign for you: you will find a child wrapped in bands of cloth and lying in a manger." And suddenly there was with the angel a multitude of the heavenly host, praising God and saying,

"Glory to God in the highest heaven,
    and on earth peace among those whom he favors!"
(Luke 2:10-14)

Psalm
Psalm 96
Let the earth be glad

Additional Readings
Isaiah 9:2-7
A child is born for us

Titus 2:11-14
The grace of God has appeared

Hymn: Love Has Come, ELW 292

Almighty God, you made this holy night shine with the brightness of the true Light. Grant that here on earth we may walk in the light of Jesus' presence and in the last day wake to the brightness of his glory; through your Son, Jesus Christ our Lord, who lives and reigns with you and the Holy Spirit, one God, now and forever.

Wednesday, December 25, 2019
Nativity of Our Lord
Christmas Day

John 1:1-14
The Word became flesh

In the beginning was the Word, and the Word was with God, and the Word was God. He was in the beginning with God. All things came into being through him, and without him not one thing came into being. What has come into being in him was life, and the life was the light of all people. The light shines in the darkness, and the darkness did not overcome it.

And the Word became flesh and lived among us, and we have seen his glory, the glory as of a father's only son, full of grace and truth. (John 1:1-5, 14)

Psalm
Psalm 98
The victory of our God

Additional Readings
Isaiah 52:7-10
Heralds announce God's salvation

Hebrews 1:1-4 [5-12]
God has spoken by a son

Hymn: Of the Father's Love Begotten, ELW 295

Almighty God, you gave us your only Son to take on our human nature and to illumine the world with your light. By your grace adopt us as your children and enlighten us with your Spirit, through Jesus Christ, our Redeemer and Lord, who lives and reigns with you and the Holy Spirit, one God, now and forever.

Thursday, December 26, 2019
Stephen, Deacon and Martyr

Matthew 23:34-39

Jesus laments that Jerusalem kills her prophets

[Jesus said,] "Therefore I send you prophets, sages, and scribes, some of whom you will kill and crucify, and some you will flog in your synagogues and pursue from town to town, so that upon you may come all the righteous blood shed on earth, from the blood of righteous Abel to the blood of Zechariah son of Barachiah, whom you murdered between the sanctuary and the altar. Truly I tell you, all this will come upon this generation.

"Jerusalem, Jerusalem, the city that kills the prophets and stones those who are sent to it! How often have I desired to gather your children together as a hen gathers her brood under her wings, and you were not willing! See, your house is left to you, desolate. For I tell you, you will not see me again until you say, 'Blessed is the one who comes in the name of the Lord.'" (Matt. 23:34-39)

Psalm

Psalm 17:1-9, 15
I call upon you, O God

Additional Readings

2 Chronicles 24:17-22
Zechariah is stoned to death

Acts 6:8—7:2a, 51-60
Stephen is stoned to death

Hymn: What Child Is This, ELW 296

We give you thanks, O Lord of glory, for the example of Stephen the first martyr, who looked to heaven and prayed for his persecutors. Grant that we also may pray for our enemies and seek forgiveness for those who hurt us, through Jesus Christ, our Savior and Lord, who lives and reigns with you and the Holy Spirit, one God, now and forever.

Friday, December 27, 2019
John, Apostle and Evangelist

John 21:20-25
The beloved disciple remains with Jesus

Peter turned and saw the disciple whom Jesus loved following them; he was the one who had reclined next to Jesus at the supper and had said, "Lord, who is it that is going to betray you?" When Peter saw him, he said to Jesus, "Lord, what about him?" Jesus said to him, "If it is my will that he remain until I come, what is that to you? Follow me!" So the rumor spread in the community that this disciple would not die. Yet Jesus did not say to him that he would not die, but, "If it is my will that he remain until I come, what is that to you?"

This is the disciple who is testifying to these things and has written them, and we know that his testimony is true. But there are also many other things that Jesus did; if every one of them were written down, I suppose that the world itself could not contain the books that would be written. (John 21:20-25)

Psalm
Psalm 116:12-19
The death of faithful servants

Additional Readings
Genesis 1:1-5, 26-31
Humankind is created by God

1 John 1:1—2:2
Jesus, the word of life

Hymn: Let Our Gladness Have No End, ELW 291

Merciful God, through John the apostle and evangelist you have revealed the mysteries of your Word made flesh. Let the brightness of your light shine on your church, so that all your people, instructed in the holy gospel, may walk in the light of your truth and attain eternal life, through Jesus Christ, our Savior and Lord, who lives and reigns with you and the Holy Spirit, one God, now and forever.

Saturday, December 28, 2019
The Holy Innocents, Martyrs

1 Peter 4:12-19
Continue to do good while suffering

Beloved, do not be surprised at the fiery ordeal that is taking place among you to test you, as though something strange were happening to you. But rejoice insofar as you are sharing Christ's sufferings, so that you may also be glad and shout for joy when his glory is revealed. If you are reviled for the name of Christ, you are blessed, because the spirit of glory, which is the Spirit of God, is resting on you. (1 Peter 4:12-14)

Psalm
Psalm 124
We have escaped like a bird

Additional Readings
Jeremiah 31:15-17
Rachel weeps for her children

Matthew 2:13-18
Herod kills innocent children

Hymn: Lo, How a Rose E'er Blooming, ELW 272

We remember today, O God, the slaughter of the innocent children of Bethlehem by order of King Herod. Receive into the arms of your mercy all innocent victims. By your great might frustrate the designs of evil tyrants and establish your rule of justice, love, and peace, through Jesus Christ, our Savior and Lord, who lives and reigns with you and the Holy Spirit, one God, now and forever.

Sunday, December 29, 2019
First Sunday of Christmas

Matthew 2:13-23

The slaughter of innocent children

When Herod saw that he had been tricked by the wise men, he was infuriated, and he sent and killed all the children in and around Bethlehem who were two years old or under, according to the time that he had learned from the wise men. Then was fulfilled what had been spoken through the prophet Jeremiah:

"A voice was heard in Ramah,

wailing and loud lamentation,

Rachel weeping for her children;

she refused to be consoled, because they are no more."

(Matt. 2:16-18)

Psalm

Psalm 148
God's splendor is over earth and heaven

Additional Readings

Isaiah 63:7-9
Israel saved by God's own presence

Hebrews 2:10-18
Christ frees humankind

Hymn: Let All Together Praise Our God, ELW 287

O Lord God, you know that we cannot place our trust in our own powers. As you protected the infant Jesus, so defend us and all the needy from harm and adversity, through Jesus Christ, our Savior and Lord, who lives and reigns with you and the Holy Spirit, one God, now and forever.

Monday, December 30, 2019
Week of Christmas 1

Psalm 20

Answer us when we call

The LORD answer you in the day of trouble!
   The name of the God of Jacob protect you!
May he send you help from the sanctuary,
   and give you support from Zion.
May he remember all your offerings,
   and regard with favor your burnt sacrifices. (Ps. 20:1-3)

Additional Readings

Isaiah 26:1-9
Trust in God forever

2 Corinthians 4:16-18
The temporary and the eternal

Hymn: Good Christian Friends, Rejoice, ELW 288

God of abundance, all the earth is yours and everything in it. Give us cheerful hearts to offer all that you have given us to aid those who cry out for your help in their day of trouble.

Tuesday, December 31, 2019
Week of Christmas 1

1 Kings 3:5-14
God grants a discerning mind

At Gibeon the LORD appeared to Solomon in a dream by night; and God said, "Ask what I should give you." And Solomon said, "You have shown great and steadfast love to your servant my father David, because he walked before you in faithfulness, in righteousness, and in uprightness of heart toward you; and you have kept for him this great and steadfast love, and have given him a son to sit on his throne today. And now, O LORD my God, you have made your servant king in place of my father David, although I am only a little child; I do not know how to go out or come in. And your servant is in the midst of the people whom you have chosen, a great people, so numerous they cannot be numbered or counted. Give your servant therefore an understanding mind to govern your people, able to discern between good and evil; for who can govern this your great people?" (1 Kings 3:5-9)

Psalm
Psalm 20
Answer us when we call

Additional Reading
John 8:12-19
I am the light

Hymn: Peace Came to Earth, ELW 285

Wonderful Counselor, through our various callings you give each of us responsibilities and opportunities. As we use your gifts to face the challenges before us, turn us to you for wisdom and discernment that we may serve others faithfully.

Lesser Festivals and Commemorations

Interested in enriching your prayer life further and in learning more about the people included among the festivals and commemorations? See Gail Ramshaw's *More Days for Praise: Festivals and Commemorations in Evangelical Lutheran Worship.* Each day's entry includes a brief chronology of the person's life; a summary of why the person is remembered by the church; an image of, or related to, the commemoration; a quote from the person, where possible; and devotional hymn and prayer suggestions for the day (Augsburg Fortress, 2016; 320 pages; ISBN 9781451496215).

January 1—Name of Jesus Every Jewish boy was circumcised and formally named on the eighth day of his life. Already in his infancy, Jesus bore the mark of a covenant that he made new through the shedding of his blood on the cross.

January 2—Johann Konrad Wilhelm Loehe Wilhelm Loehe was a pastor in nineteenth-century Germany. From the small town of Neuendettelsau he sent pastors to North America, Australia, New Guinea, Brazil, and the Ukraine.

January 15—Martin Luther King Jr. Martin Luther King Jr. is remembered as an American prophet of justice among races and nations. Many churches hold commemorations near Dr. King's birth date of January 15, in conjunction with the American civil holiday honoring him.

January 17—Antony of Egypt Antony was one of the earliest Egyptian desert fathers. He became the head of a group of monks who lived in a cluster of huts and devoted themselves to communal prayer, worship, and manual labor.

January 17—Pachomius Another of the desert fathers, Pachomius was born in Egypt about 290. He organized hermits into a religious community in which the members prayed together and held their goods in common.

January 18—Confession of Peter; *Week of Prayer for Christian Unity begins* The Week of Prayer for Christian Unity is framed by two commemorations, the Confession of Peter and the Conversion of Paul. On this day the church remembers that Peter was led by God's grace to acknowledge Jesus as "the Christ, the Son of the living God" (Matt. 16:16).

January 19—Henry When Erik, king of Sweden, determined to invade Finland for the purpose of converting the people there to Christianity, Henry went with him. Henry is recognized as the patron saint of Finland.

January 21—Agnes Agnes was a girl of about thirteen living in Rome, who had chosen a life of service to Christ as a virgin, despite the Roman emperor Diocletian's ruling that had outlawed all Christian activity. She gave witness to her faith and was put to death as a result.

January 25—Conversion of Paul; *Week of Prayer for Christian Unity ends* As the Week of Prayer for Christian Unity comes to an end, the church remembers how a man of Tarsus named Saul, a former persecutor of the early Christian church, was led to become one of its chief preachers.

January 26—Timothy, Titus, Silas On the two days following the celebration of the Conversion of Paul, his companions are remembered. Timothy, Titus, and Silas were missionary coworkers with Paul.

January 27—Lydia, Dorcas, Phoebe On this day the church remembers three women who were companions in Paul's ministry.

January 28—Thomas Aquinas Thomas Aquinas was a brilliant and creative theologian who immersed himself in the thought of Aristotle and worked to explain Christian beliefs in the philosophical culture of the day.

February 2—Presentation of Our Lord Forty days after the birth of Christ, the church marks the day Mary and Joseph presented him in the temple in accordance with Jewish law. Simeon greeted Mary and Joseph, responding with the canticle that begins "Now, Lord, you let your servant go in peace."

February 3—Ansgar Ansgar was a monk who led a mission to Denmark and later to Sweden. His work ran into difficulties with the rulers of the day, and he was forced to withdraw into Germany, where he served as a bishop in Hamburg.

February 5—The Martyrs of Japan In the sixteenth century, Jesuit missionaries, followed by Franciscans, introduced the Christian faith in Japan. By 1630, Christianity was driven underground. This day commemorates the first martyrs of Japan, twenty-six missionaries and converts, who were killed by crucifixion.

February 14—Cyril, Methodius These brothers from a noble family in Thessalonika in northeastern Greece were priests who are regarded as the founders of Slavic literature. Their work in preaching and worshiping in the language of the people is honored by Christians in both East and West.

February 18—Martin Luther On this day Luther died at the age of sixty-two. For a time, he was an Augustinian monk, but it is primarily for his work as a biblical scholar, translator of the Bible, reformer of the liturgy, theologian, educator, and father of German vernacular literature that he is remembered.

February 23—Polycarp Polycarp was bishop of Smyrna and a link between the apostolic age and the church at the end of the second century. At the age of eighty-six he was martyred for his faith.

February 25—Elizabeth Fedde Fedde was born in Norway and trained as a deaconess. Among her notable achievements is the establishment of the Deaconess House in Brooklyn and the Deaconess House and Hospital of the Lutheran Free Church in Minneapolis.

March 1—George Herbert Herbert was ordained a priest in 1630 and served the little parish of St. Andrew Bremerton until

his death. He is best remembered, however, as a writer of poems and hymns, such as "Come, My Way, My Truth, My Life" and "The King of Love My Shepherd Is."

March 2—John Wesley, Charles Wesley The Wesleys were leaders of a revival in the Church of England. Their spiritual methods of frequent communion, fasting, and advocacy for the poor earned them the name "Methodists."

March 7—Perpetua, Felicity In the year 202 the emperor Septimius Severus forbade conversions to Christianity. Perpetua, a noblewoman; Felicity, a slave; and other companions were all catechumens at Carthage in North Africa, where they were imprisoned and sentenced to death.

March 10—Harriet Tubman, Sojourner Truth Harriet Tubman helped about three hundred slaves to escape via the Underground Railroad until slavery was abolished in the United States. After slavery was abolished in New York in 1827, Sojourner Truth became deeply involved in Christianity, and in later life she was a popular speaker against slavery and for women's rights.

March 12—Gregory the Great Gregory held political office and at another time lived as a monk, all before he was elected to the papacy. He also established a school to train church musicians; thus Gregorian chant is named in his honor.

March 17—Patrick Patrick went to Ireland from Britain to serve as a bishop and missionary. He made his base in the north of Ireland and from there made many missionary journeys, with much success.

March 19—Joseph The Gospel of Luke shows Joseph acting in accordance with both civil and religious law by returning to Bethlehem for the census and by presenting the child Jesus in the temple on the fortieth day after his birth.

March 21—Thomas Cranmer Cranmer's lasting achievement is contributing to and overseeing the creation of the Book of Common Prayer, which remains (in revised form) the worship book of the Anglican Communion. He was burned at the stake under Queen Mary for his support of the Protestant Reformation.

March 22—Jonathan Edwards Edwards was a minister in Connecticut and has been described as the greatest of the New England Puritan preachers. Edwards carried out mission work among the Housatonic

Indians of Massachusetts and became president of the College of New Jersey, later to be known as Princeton University.

March 24—Oscar Arnulfo Romero Romero is remembered for his advocacy on behalf of the poor in El Salvador, though it was not a characteristic of his early priesthood. After several years of threats to his life, Romero was assassinated while presiding at the eucharist.

March 25—Annunciation of Our Lord Nine months before Christmas, the church celebrates the annunciation. In Luke the angel Gabriel announces to Mary that she will give birth to the Son of God, and she responds, "Here am I, the servant of the Lord."

March 29—Hans Nielsen Hauge Hans Nielsen Hauge was a layperson who began preaching in Norway and Denmark after a mystical experience that he believed called him to share the assurance of salvation with others. At the time, itinerant preaching and religious gatherings held without the supervision of a pastor were illegal, and Hauge was arrested several times.

March 31—John Donne This priest of the Church of England is commemorated for his poetry and spiritual writing. Most of his poetry was written before his ordination and is sacred and secular, intellectual and sensuous.

April 4—Benedict the African Although Benedict was illiterate, his fame as a confessor brought many visitors to him, and he was eventually named superior of a Franciscan community. A patron saint of African Americans, Benedict is remembered for his patience and understanding when confronted with racial prejudice and taunts.

April 6—Albrecht Dürer, Matthias Grünewald, Lucas Cranach These great artists revealed through their work the mystery of salvation and the wonder of creation. Though Dürer remained a Roman Catholic, at his death Martin Luther wrote to a friend, "Affection bids us mourn for one who was the best." Several religious works are included in Grünewald's small surviving corpus, the most famous being the Isenheim Altarpiece. Lucas Cranach was widely known for his woodcuts, some of which illustrated the first German printing of the New Testament.

April 9—Dietrich Bonhoeffer In 1933, and with Hitler's rise to power, Bonhoeffer became a leading spokesman for the Confessing Church, a resistance movement against the Nazis. After leading a worship service on April 8, 1945, at Schönberg prison, he was taken away to be hanged the next day.

April 10—Mikael Agricola Agricola began a reform of the Finnish church along Lutheran lines. He translated the New Testament, the prayer book, hymns, and the mass into Finnish and through this work set the rules of orthography that are the basis of modern Finnish spelling.

April 19—Olavus Petri, Laurentius Petri These two brothers are commemorated for their introduction of the Lutheran movement to the Church of Sweden after studying at the University of Wittenberg. Together the brothers published a complete Bible in Swedish and a revised liturgy in 1541.

April 21—Anselm This eleventh-century Benedictine monk stands out as one of the greatest theologians between Augustine and Thomas Aquinas. He is perhaps best known for his "satisfaction" theory of atonement, in which God takes on human nature in Jesus Christ in order to make the perfect payment for sin.

April 23—Toyohiko Kagawa Toyohiko Kagawa's vocation to help the poor led him to live among them. He was arrested for his efforts to reconcile Japan and China after the Japanese attack of 1940.

April 25—Mark Though Mark himself was not an apostle, it is likely that he was a member of one of the early Christian communities. The gospel attributed to him is brief and direct and is considered by many to be the earliest gospel.

April 29—Catherine of Siena Catherine of Siena was a member of the Order of Preachers (Dominicans), and among Roman Catholics she was the first woman to receive the title Doctor of the Church. She also advised popes and any uncertain persons who told her their problems.

May 1—Philip, James Philip and James are commemorated together because the remains of these two saints were placed in the Church of the Apostles in Rome on this day in 561.

May 2—Athanasius At the Council of Nicea in 325 and when he himself served as bishop of Alexandria, Athanasius defended the full divinity of Christ against the Arian position held by emperors, magistrates, and theologians.

May 4—Monica Almost everything known about Monica comes from Augustine's *Confessions*, his autobiography. Her dying wish was that her son remember her at the altar of the Lord, wherever he was.

May 8—Julian of Norwich Julian was most likely a Benedictine nun living in an isolated cell attached to the Carrow Priory in Norwich, England. When she was about thirty years old, she reported visions that she later compiled into a book, *Sixteen Revelations of Divine Love*, which is a classic of medieval mysticism.

May 9—Nicolaus Ludwig von Zinzendorf Drawn from an overly intellectual Lutheran faith to Pietism, at the age of twenty-two Count Zinzendorf permitted a group of Moravians to live on his lands. Zinzendorf participated in worldwide missions emanating from this community and is also remembered for writing hymns characteristic of his Pietistic faith.

May 14—Matthias After Christ's ascension, the apostles met in Jerusalem to choose a replacement for Judas. Though little is known about him, Matthias had traveled among the disciples from the time of Jesus' baptism until his ascension.

May 18—Erik Erik, long considered the patron saint of Sweden, ruled there from 1150 to 1160. He is honored for efforts to bring peace to the nearby pagan kingdoms and for his crusades to spread the Christian faith in Scandinavia.

May 21—Helena Helena was the mother of Constantine, a man who later became the Roman emperor. Helena is remembered for traveling through Palestine and building churches on the sites she believed to be where Jesus was born, where he was buried, and from which he ascended.

May 24—Nicolaus Copernicus, Leonhard Euler Copernicus formally studied astronomy, mathematics, Greek, Plato, law, medicine, and canon law and is chiefly remembered for his work as an astronomer and his idea that the sun, not the earth, is the center of the solar system. Euler is regarded as one of the founders of the science of pure mathematics and made important contributions to mechanics, hydrodynamics, astronomy, optics, and acoustics.

May 27—John Calvin Having embraced the views of the Reformation by his mid-twenties, John Calvin was a preacher in Geneva, was banished once, and later returned to reform the city with a rigid, theocratic discipline. Calvin is considered the father of the Reformed churches.

May 29—Jiří Tranovský Jiří Tranovský is considered the "Luther of the Slavs" and the father of Slovak hymnody. He produced a translation of the Augsburg Confession and published his hymn collection *Cithara Sanctorum* (Lyre of the Saints), also known as the Tranoscius, which is the foundation of Slovak Lutheran hymnody.

May 31—Visit of Mary to Elizabeth Sometime after the annunciation, Mary visited her cousin Elizabeth, who greeted Mary with the words, "Blessed are you among women," and Mary responded with her famous song, the Magnificat.

June 1—Justin Justin was a teacher of philosophy and engaged in debates about the truth of Christian faith. Having been arrested and jailed for practicing an unauthorized religion, he refused to renounce his faith, and he and six of his students were beheaded.

June 3—The Martyrs of Uganda King Mwanga of Uganda was angered by Christian members of the court whose first allegiance was not to him but to Christ. On this date in 1886, thirty-two young men were burned to death for refusing to renounce Christianity. Their persecution led to a much stronger Christian presence in the country.

June 3—John XXIII Despite the expectation upon his election that the seventy-seven-year-old John XXIII would be a transitional pope, he had great energy and spirit. He convened the Second Vatican Council in order to open the windows of the church. The council brought about great changes in Roman Catholic worship and ecumenical relationships.

June 5—Boniface Boniface led large numbers of Benedictine monks and nuns in establishing churches, schools, and seminaries. Boniface was preparing a group for confirmation on the eve of Pentecost when he and others were killed by a band of pagans.

June 7—Seattle The city of Seattle was named after Noah Seattle against his wishes. After Chief Seattle became a Roman Catholic, he began the practice of morning and evening prayer in the tribe, a practice that continued after his death.

June 9—Columba, Aidan, Bede These three monks from the British Isles were pillars among those who kept alive the light of learning and devotion during the Middle

Ages. Columba founded three monasteries, including one on the island of Iona, off the coast of Scotland. Aidan, who helped bring Christianity to the Northumbria area of England, was known for his pastoral style and ability to stir people to charity and good works. Bede was a Bible translator and scripture scholar who wrote a history of the English church and was the first historian to date events anno Domini (AD), the "year of our Lord."

June 11—Barnabas Though he was not among the Twelve mentioned in the gospels, the book of Acts gives Barnabas the title of apostle. When Paul came to Jerusalem after his conversion, Barnabas took him in over the fears of the other apostles who doubted Paul's discipleship.

June 14—Basil the Great, Gregory of Nyssa, Gregory of Nazianzus, Macrina The three men in this group are known as the Cappadocian fathers; all three explored the mystery of the Holy Trinity. Basil's Longer Rule and Shorter Rule for monastic life are the basis for Eastern monasticism to this day, and express a preference for communal monastic life over that of hermits. Gregory of Nazianzus defended Orthodox trinitarian and christological doctrine, and his preaching won over the city of Constantinople. Gregory of Nyssa is remembered as a writer on spiritual life and the contemplation of God in worship and sacraments. Macrina was the older sister of Basil and Gregory of Nyssa, and her teaching was influential within the early church.

June 21—Onesimos Nesib Onesimos, an Ethiopian, was captured by slave traders and taken from his homeland to Eritrea, where he was bought, freed, and educated by Swedish missionaries. He translated the Bible into Oromo and returned to his homeland to preach the gospel there.

June 24—John the Baptist The birth of John the Baptist is celebrated exactly six months before Christmas Eve. For Christians in the Northern Hemisphere, these two dates are deeply symbolic, since John said that he must decrease as Jesus increased. John was born as the days are longest and then steadily decrease, while Jesus was born as the days are shortest and then steadily increase.

June 25—Presentation of the Augsburg Confession On this day in 1530 the German and Latin editions of the Augsburg Confession were presented to Emperor Charles of the Holy Roman Empire. The Augsburg Confession was written by Philipp Melanchthon and endorsed by Martin Luther and consists of a brief summary of points in which the reformers saw their teaching as either agreeing with or differing from that of the Roman Catholic Church of the time.

June 25—Philipp Melanchthon Though he died on April 19, Philipp Melanchthon is commemorated today because of his connection with the Augsburg Confession. Colleague and co-reformer with Martin Luther, Melanchthon was a brilliant scholar, known as "the teacher of Germany."

June 27—Cyril Remembered as an outstanding theologian, Cyril defended the Orthodox teachings about the person of Christ against Nestorius, who was at that time bishop of Constantinople. Eventually it was decided that Cyril's interpretation, that Christ's person included both divine and human natures, was correct.

June 28—Irenaeus Irenaeus believed that only Matthew, Mark, Luke, and John were trustworthy gospels. As a result of his battles with the Gnostics, he was one of the first to speak of the church as "catholic," meaning that congregations did not exist by themselves but were linked to one another throughout the whole church.

June 29—Peter, Paul One of the things that unites Peter and Paul is the tradition that says they were martyred together on this date in AD 67 or 68. What unites them even more closely is their common confession of Jesus Christ.

July 1—Catherine Winkworth, John Mason Neale Many of the most beloved hymns in the English language are the work of these gifted poets. Catherine Winkworth devoted herself to the translation of German hymns into English, while John Mason Neale specialized in translating many ancient Latin and Greek hymns.

July 3—Thomas Alongside the doubt for which Thomas is famous, the Gospel according to John shows Thomas moving from doubt to deep faith. Thomas makes one of the strongest confessions of faith in the New Testament, "My Lord and my God!" (John 20:28).

July 6—Jan Hus Jan Hus was a Bohemian priest who spoke against abuses in the church of his day in many of the same ways Luther would a century later. The followers of Jan Hus became known as the Czech Brethren and later became the Moravian Church.

July 11—Benedict of Nursia Benedict is known as the father of Western monasticism. Benedict encouraged a generous spirit of hospitality. Visitors to Benedictine communities are to be welcomed as Christ himself.

July 12—Nathan Söderblom In 1930 this Swedish theologian, ecumenist, and social activist received the Nobel Prize for peace. Söderblom organized the Universal Christian Council on Life and Work, which was one of the organizations that in 1948 came together to form the World Council of Churches.

July 17—Bartolomé de Las Casas Bartolomé de Las Casas was a Spanish priest and a missionary in the Western Hemisphere. Throughout the Caribbean and Central America, he worked to stop the enslavement of native people, to halt the brutal treatment of women by military forces, and to promote laws that humanized the process of colonization.

July 22—Mary Magdalene The gospels report Mary Magdalene was one of the women of Galilee who followed Jesus. As the first person to whom the risen Lord appeared, she returned to the disciples with the news and has been called "the apostle to the apostles" for her proclamation of the resurrection.

July 23—Birgitta of Sweden Birgitta's devotional commitments led her to give to the poor and needy all that she owned while she began to live a more ascetic life. She founded an order of monks and nuns, the Order of the Holy Savior (Birgittines), whose superior was a woman.

July 25—James James was one of the sons of Zebedee and is counted as one of the twelve disciples. James was the first of the Twelve to suffer martyrdom and is the only apostle whose martyrdom is recorded in scripture.

July 28—Johann Sebastian Bach, Heinrich Schütz, George Frederick Handel These three composers did much to enrich the worship life of the church. Johann Sebastian Bach drew on the Lutheran tradition of hymnody and wrote about two hundred cantatas, including at least two for each Sunday and festival day in the Lutheran calendar of his day. George Frederick Handel was not primarily a church musician, but his great work *Messiah* is a musical proclamation of the scriptures. Heinrich Schütz wrote choral settings of biblical texts and paid special attention to ways his composition would underscore the meaning of the words.

July 29—Mary, Martha, Lazarus of Bethany Mary and Martha are remembered for the hospitality and refreshment they offered Jesus in their home. Following the characterization drawn by Luke, Martha represents the active life, and Mary, the contemplative.

July 29—Olaf Olaf is considered the patron saint of Norway. While at war in the Baltic and in Normandy, he became a Christian; then he returned to Norway and declared himself king, and from then on Christianity was the dominant religion of the realm.

August 8—Dominic Dominic believed that a stumbling block to restoring heretics to the church was the wealth of clergy, so he formed an itinerant religious order, the Order of Preachers (Dominicans), who lived in poverty, studied philosophy and theology, and preached against heresy.

August 10—Lawrence Lawrence was one of seven deacons of the congregation at Rome and, like the deacons appointed in Acts, was responsible for financial matters in the church and for the care of the poor.

August 11—Clare At age eighteen, Clare of Assisi heard Francis preach a sermon. With Francis's help she and a growing number of companions established a women's Franciscan community called the Order of Poor Ladies, or Poor Clares.

August 13—Florence Nightingale, Clara Maass Nightingale led a group of thirty-eight nurses to serve in the Crimean War, where they worked in appalling conditions. She returned to London as a hero and there resumed her work for hospital reform. Clara Maass was born in New Jersey and served as a nurse in the Spanish-American War, where she encountered the horrors of yellow fever. Later responding to a call for subjects in research on yellow fever, Maass contracted the disease and died.

August 14—Maximilian Kolbe, Kaj Munk Confined in Auschwitz, Father Kolbe was a Franciscan priest who gave generously of his meager resources and finally volunteered to be starved to death in place of another man who was a husband and father. Kaj Munk, a Danish Lutheran pastor and playwright, was an outspoken critic of the Nazis. His plays frequently highlighted the eventual victory of the Christian faith despite the church's weak and ineffective witness.

August 15—Mary, Mother of Our Lord The honor paid to Mary as mother of our Lord goes back to biblical times, when Mary herself sang, "From now on all generations will call me blessed" (Luke 1:48). Mary's song speaks of reversals in the reign of God: the mighty are cast down, the lowly are lifted up, the hungry are fed, and the rich are sent away empty-handed.

August 20—Bernard of Clairvaux Bernard was a Cistercian monk who became an abbot of great spiritual depth. Through translation his several devotional writings and hymns are still read and sung today.

August 24—Bartholomew Bartholomew is mentioned as one of Jesus' disciples in Matthew, Mark, and Luke. Except for his name on these lists of the Twelve, little is known.

August 28—Augustine As an adult, Augustine came to see Christianity as a religion appropriate for a philosopher. Augustine was baptized by Ambrose at the Easter Vigil in 387, was made bishop of Hippo in 396, and was one of the greatest theologians of the Western church.

August 28—Moses the Black A man of great strength and rough character, Moses the Black was converted to Christian faith toward the close of the fourth century. The change in his heart and life had a profound impact on his native Ethiopia.

September 2—Nikolai Frederik Severin Grundtvig Grundtvig was a prominent Danish theologian of the nineteenth century. From his university days, he was convinced that poetry spoke to the human spirit better than prose, and he wrote more than a thousand hymns.

September 9—Peter Claver Peter Claver was born into Spanish nobility and was persuaded to become a Jesuit missionary. He served in Cartagena (in what is now Colombia) by teaching and caring for the slaves.

September 13—John Chrysostom John was a priest in Antioch and an outstanding preacher. His eloquence earned him the nickname Chrysostom ("golden mouth"), but he also preached against corruption among the royal court, whereupon the empress sent him into exile.

September 14—Holy Cross Day The celebration of Holy Cross Day commemorates the dedication of the Church of the Resurrection in 335 on the location believed to have been where Christ was buried.

September 16—Cyprian During Cyprian's time as bishop, many people had denied the faith under duress. In contrast to some who held the belief that the church should not receive these people back, Cyprian believed they ought to be welcomed into full communion after a period of penance.

September 17—Hildegard, Abbess of Bingen Hildegard lived virtually her entire life in convents yet was widely influential. She advised and reproved kings and popes, wrote poems and hymns, and produced treatises in medicine, theology, and natural history.

September 18—Dag Hammarskjöld Dag Hammarskjöld was a Swedish diplomat and humanitarian who served as secretary general of the United Nations. The depth of Hammarskjöld's Christian faith was unknown until his private journal, *Markings*, was published following his death.

September 21—Matthew Matthew was a tax collector, an occupation that was distrusted, since tax collectors were frequently dishonest and worked as agents for the Roman occupying government; yet it was these outcasts to whom Jesus showed his love. Since the second century, tradition has attributed the first gospel to him.

September 29—Michael and All Angels The scriptures speak of angels who worship God in heaven, and in both testaments angels are God's messengers on earth. Michael is an angel whose name appears in Daniel as the heavenly being who leads the faithful dead to God's throne on the day of resurrection, while in the book of Revelation, Michael fights in a cosmic battle against Satan.

September 30—Jerome Jerome translated the scriptures into the Latin that was spoken and written by the majority of people in his day. His translation is known as the Vulgate, which comes from the Latin word for "common."

October 4—Francis of Assisi Francis renounced wealth and future inheritance and devoted himself to serving the poor. Since Francis had a spirit of gratitude for all of God's creation, this commemoration has been a traditional time to bless pets and animals, creatures Francis called his brothers and sisters.

October 4—Theodor Fliedner Fliedner's work was instrumental in the revival of the ministry of deaconesses among Lutherans. Fliedner's deaconess motherhouse in Kaiserswerth, Germany, inspired Lutherans all over the world to commission deaconesses to serve in parishes, schools, prisons, and hospitals.

October 6—William Tyndale Tyndale's plan to translate the scriptures into English met opposition from Henry VIII. Though Tyndale completed work on the New Testament in 1525 and worked on a portion of the Old Testament, he was tried for heresy and burned at the stake.

October 7—Henry Melchior Muhlenberg Muhlenberg was prominent in setting the course for Lutheranism in the United States by helping Lutheran churches make the transition from the state churches of Europe to independent churches of America. Among other things, he established the first Lutheran synod in America and developed an American Lutheran liturgy.

October 15—Teresa of Avila Teresa of Avila (also known as Teresa de Jesús) chose the life of a Carmelite nun after reading the letters of Jerome. Teresa's writings on devotional life are widely read by members of various denominations.

October 17—Ignatius Ignatius was the second bishop of Antioch in Syria. When his own martyrdom approached, he wrote in one of his letters, "I prefer death in Christ Jesus to power over the farthest limits of the earth.... Do not stand in the way of my birth to real life."

October 18—Luke Luke, as author of both Luke and Acts, was careful to place the events of Jesus' life in both their social and religious contexts. Some of the most loved parables and canticles are found only in this gospel.

October 23—James of Jerusalem James is described in the New Testament as the brother of Jesus, and the secular historian Josephus called James, the brother of Jesus, "the so-called Christ." Little is known about James, but Josephus reported that the Pharisees respected James for his piety and observance of the law.

October 26—Philipp Nicolai, Johann Heermann, Paul Gerhardt These three outstanding hymnwriters all worked in Germany in the seventeenth century during times of war and plague. Philipp Nicolai's hymns "Wake, Awake, for Night Is Flying" and "O Morning Star, How Fair and Bright!" were included in a series of meditations he wrote to comfort his parishioners during the plague. The style of Johann Heermann's hymns (including "Ah, Holy Jesus") moved away from the more objective style of Reformation hymnody toward expressing the emotions of faith. Paul Gerhardt, whom some have called the greatest of Lutheran hymnwriters, lost a preaching position at St. Nicholas's Church in Berlin because he refused to sign a document stating he would not make theological arguments in his sermons.

October 28—Simon, Jude Little is known about Simon and Jude. In New Testament lists of the apostles, Simon the "zealot" or Cananaean is mentioned, but he is never mentioned apart from these lists. Jude, sometimes called Thaddaeus, is also mentioned in lists of the Twelve.

October 31—Reformation Day By the end of the seventeenth century, many Lutheran churches celebrated a festival commemorating Martin Luther's posting of the 95 Theses, a summary of abuses in the church of his time. At the heart of the reform movement was the gospel, the good news that it is by grace through faith that we are justified and set free.

November 1—All Saints Day The custom of commemorating all of the saints of the church on a single day goes back at least to the third century. All Saints Day celebrates the baptized people of God, living and dead, who make up the body of Christ.

November 3—Martín de Porres Martín was a lay brother in the Order of Preachers (Dominicans) and engaged in many charitable works. He is recognized as an advocate for Christian charity and interracial justice.

November 7—John Christian Frederick Heyer, Bartholomaeus Ziegenbalg, Ludwig Nommensen Heyer was the first missionary sent out by American Lutherans, and he became a missionary in the Andhra region of India. Ziegenbalg was a missionary to the Tamils of Tranquebar on the southeast coast of India. Nommensen worked among the Batak people, who had previously not seen Christian missionaries.

November 11—Martin of Tours In 371 Martin was elected bishop of Tours. As bishop he developed a reputation for intervening on behalf of prisoners and heretics who had been sentenced to death.

November 11—Søren Aabye Kierkegaard Kierkegaard, a nineteenth-century Danish theologian whose writings reflect his Lutheran heritage, was the founder of modern existentialism. Kierkegaard's work attacked the established church of his day—its complacency, its tendency to intellectualize faith, and its desire to be accepted by polite society.

November 17—Elizabeth of Hungary This Hungarian princess gave away large sums of money, including her dowry, for relief of the poor and sick. She founded hospitals, cared for 392 orphans, and used the royal food supplies to feed the hungry.

November 23—Clement Clement is best remembered for a letter he wrote to the Corinthian congregation still having difficulty with divisions in spite of Paul's canonical letters. Clement's letter is also a witness to early understandings of church government and the way each office in the church works for the good of the whole.

November 23—Miguel Agustín Pro Miguel Agustín Pro grew up among oppression in Mexico and worked on behalf of the poor and homeless. Miguel and his two brothers were arrested, falsely accused of throwing a bomb at the car of a government official, and executed by a firing squad.

November 24—Justus Falckner, Jehu Jones, William Passavant Not only was Falckner the first Lutheran pastor to be ordained in North America, but he published a catechism that was the first Lutheran book published on the continent. Jones was the Lutheran Church's first African American pastor and carried out missionary work in Philadelphia, which led to the formation there of the first African American Lutheran congregation (St. Paul's). William Passavant helped to establish hospitals and orphanages in a number of cities and was the first to introduce deaconesses to the work of hospitals in the United States.

November 25—Isaac Watts Watts wrote about six hundred hymns, many of them in a two-year period beginning when he was twenty years old. When criticized for writing hymns not taken from scripture, he responded that if we can pray prayers that are not from scripture but written by us, then surely we can sing hymns that we have made up ourselves.

November 30—Andrew Andrew was the first of the Twelve. As a part of his calling, he brought other people, including Simon Peter, to meet Jesus.

December 3—Francis Xavier Francis Xavier became a missionary to India, Southeast Asia, Japan, and the Philippines. Together with Ignatius Loyola and five others, Francis formed the Society of Jesus (Jesuits).

December 4—John of Damascus John left a career in finance and government to become a monk in an abbey near Jerusalem. He wrote many hymns as well as theological works, including *The Fount of Wisdom,* a work that touches on philosophy, heresy, and the orthodox faith.

December 6—Nicholas Nicholas was a bishop in what is now Turkey. Legends that surround Nicholas tell of his love for God and neighbor, especially the poor.

December 7—Ambrose Ambrose was baptized, ordained, and consecrated a bishop all on the same day. While bishop he gave away his wealth and lived in simplicity.

December 13—Lucy Lucy was a young Christian of Sicily who was martyred during the persecutions under Emperor Diocletian. Her celebration became particularly important in Sweden and Norway, perhaps because the feast of Lucia (whose name means "light") originally fell on the shortest day of the year.

December 14—John of the Cross John was a monk of the Carmelite religious order who met Teresa of Avila when she was working to reform the Carmelite Order and return it to a stricter observance of its rules. His writings, like Teresa's, reflect a deep interest in mystical thought and meditation.

December 20—Katharina von Bora Luther Katharina took vows as a nun, but around age twenty-four she and several other nuns who were influenced by the writings of Martin Luther left the convent. When she later became Luther's wife, she proved herself a gifted household manager and became a trusted partner.

December 26—Stephen Stephen, a deacon and the first martyr of the church, was one of those seven upon whom the apostles laid hands after they had been chosen to serve widows and others in need. Later, Stephen's preaching angered the temple authorities, and they ordered him to be put to death by stoning.

December 27—John John, the son of Zebedee, was a fisherman and one of the Twelve. Tradition has attributed authorship of the gospel and the three epistles bearing his name to the apostle John.

December 28—The Holy Innocents The infant martyrs commemorated on this day were the children of Bethlehem, two years old and younger, who were killed by Herod, who worried that his reign was threatened by the birth of a new king named Jesus.

Anniversary of Baptism (abbreviated)

This order is intended for use in the home. It may be adapted for use in another context, such as a Christian education setting. When used in the home, a parent or sponsor may be the leader. A more expanded version of this order appears in *Evangelical Lutheran Worship Pastoral Care* (pp. 128-135).

A bowl of water may be placed in the midst of those who are present.

Gathering

A baptismal hymn or acclamation (see Evangelical Lutheran Worship #209-217, 442-459) may be sung.

The sign of the cross may be made by all in remembrance of their baptism as the leader begins.

In the name of the Father, and of the + Son, and of the Holy Spirit.
Amen.

The candle received at baptism or another candle may be used. As it is lighted, the leader may say:

Jesus said, I am the light of the world.
Whoever follows me will have the light of life.

Reading

One or more scripture readings follow. Those present may share in reading.

A reading from Mark: People were bringing little children to Jesus in order that he might touch them; and the disciples spoke sternly to them. But when Jesus saw this, he was indignant and said, "Let the little children come to me; do not stop them; for it is to such as these that the kingdom of God belongs." And he took them up in his arms, laid his hands on them, and blessed them. *(Mark 10:13-14, 16)*

A reading from Second Corinthians: If anyone is in Christ, there is a new creation: everything old has passed away; see, everything has become new! *(2 Corinthians 5:17)*

A reading from First John: Beloved, let us love one another, because love is from God; everyone who loves is born of God and knows God. *(1 John 4:7)*

Those present may share experiences related to baptism and their lives as baptized children of God. A portion of the Small Catechism (Evangelical Lutheran Worship, pp. 1160–1167) may be read as part of this conversation.

A baptismal hymn or acclamation may be sung.

Baptismal Remembrance

A parent or sponsor may trace a cross on the forehead of the person celebrating a baptismal anniversary. Water from a bowl placed in the midst of those present may be used. These or similar words may be said.

Name, when you were baptized, you were marked with the cross of Christ forever.
Remember your baptism with thanksgiving and joy.

Prayers

Prayers may include the following or other appropriate prayers. Others who are present may place a hand on the head or shoulder of the one who is celebrating the anniversary.

Let us pray.
Gracious God, we thank you for the new life you give us through holy baptism. Especially, we ask you to bless *name* on the anniversary of *her/his* baptism. Continue to strengthen *name* with the Holy Spirit, and increase in *her/him* your gifts of grace: the spirit of wisdom and understanding, the spirit of counsel and might, the spirit of knowledge and the fear of the Lord, the spirit of joy in your presence; through Jesus Christ, our Savior and Lord.
Amen.

Other prayers may be added. Those present may offer petitions and thanksgivings.

The prayers may conclude with the Lord's Prayer.

Our Father in heaven,
    hallowed be your name, your kingdom come,
    your will be done, on earth as in heaven.
Give us today our daily bread.
Forgive us our sins
    as we forgive those who sin against us.
Save us from the time of trial and deliver us from evil.
For the kingdom, the power, and the glory are yours,
    now and forever. Amen.

Blessing

The order may conclude with this or another suitable blessing.

Almighty God, who gives us a new birth by water and the Holy Spirit
and forgives us all our sins, strengthen us in all goodness and by the
power of the Holy Spirit keep us in eternal life through Jesus Christ our
Lord.
Amen.

The greeting of peace may be shared by all.

Other suggested readings for this service:
John 3:1-8: *Born again from above*
Romans 6:3-11: *Raised with Christ in baptism*
Galatians 3:26-28: *All are one in Christ*
Ephesians 4:1-6: *There is one body and one Spirit*
Colossians 1:11-13: *Claimed by Christ, heirs of light*
1 Peter 2:2-3: *Long for spiritual food*
1 Peter 2:9: *Chosen in baptism to tell about God*
Revelation 22:1-2: *The river of the water of life*

Prayers for Various Situations

A prayer to begin the work day

May the graciousness of the Lord our God be upon us;
prosper the work of our hands. (Ps. 90:17, *ELW*)
Generous God, you call us to lives of service.
In my words and actions this day, move me to serve in Christ's name.
When I lack energy, inspire me. When I lack courage, strengthen me.
When I lack compassion, be merciful to me.
You may make the sign of the cross.

In all things, O God, you are our way, our truth and our life. Reveal through me
your life-giving work, that I love my neighbors as myself. I ask this in Jesus'
name. Amen.

A prayer to begin the school day

Show me your ways, O LORD, and teach me your paths. (Ps. 25:4, *ELW*)
Christ be with me: in you I am never alone.
Christ within me: your Spirit is at work in me.
Christ behind me: reassure me when I struggle.
Christ before me: lead me when I am uncertain.
Christ beneath me: support me when I am weak.
Christ above me: encourage me to do my best.
Christ in quiet: I listen for the sound of your voice.
Christ in danger: I will not fear, for you are with me.
You may make the sign of the cross.

In all things, O God, you are our way, our truth, and our life.
Teach me to love you and my neighbors as myself.
I ask this in Jesus' name. Amen.
(Based on the Prayer of St. Patrick)

Time of conflict, crisis, disaster

O God, where hearts are fearful and constricted, grant courage and hope.
Where anxiety is infectious and widening, grant peace and reassurance.

Where impossibilities close every door and window, grant imagination and resistance. Where distrust twists our thinking, grant healing and illumination. Where spirits are daunted and weakened, grant soaring wings and strengthened dreams. All these things we ask in the name of Jesus Christ, our Savior and Lord. Amen.

The care of children

Almighty God, with a mother's love and a father's care you have blessed us with the joy and responsibility of children. As we bring them up, give us gracious love, calm strength, and patient wisdom, that we may teach them to love whatever is just and true and good, following the example of Jesus Christ, our Savior. Amen.

Health of body and soul

By your power, great God, our Lord Jesus healed the sick and gave new hope to the hopeless. Though we cannot command or possess your power, we pray for those who want to be healed. Mend their wounds, soothe fevered brows, and make broken people whole again. Help us to welcome every healing as a sign that, though death is against us, you are for us, and have promised renewed and risen life in Jesus Christ the Lord. Amen.

Those in affliction

Lord Christ, you came into the world as one of us, and suffered as we do. As we go through the trials of life, help us to realize that you are with us at all times and in all things; that we have no secrets from you; and that your loving grace enfolds us for eternity. In the security of your embrace we pray. Amen.

Those in emotional distress

Merciful God, you give us the grace that helps in time of need. Surround *name* with your steadfast love and lighten *her/his* burden. By the power of your Spirit, free *her/him* from distress and give *her/him* a new mind and heart made whole in the name of the risen Christ. Amen.

Those who suffer abuse and violence

Holy One, you do not distance yourself from the pain of your people, but in Jesus you bear that pain with all who suffer at others' hands. With your cleansing love bring healing and strength to *name*; and by your justice, lift *her/him* up, that in body, mind, and spirit, *she/he* may again rejoice. In Jesus' name we pray. Amen.

Those in trouble or bereavement

Almighty God, your love never fails, and you can turn the shadow of death into daybreak. Help us to receive your word with believing hearts, so that, confident in your promises, we may have hope and be lifted out of sorrow into the joy and peace of your presence; through Jesus Christ our Savior and Lord. Amen.

Those suffering from addiction

O blessed Jesus, you ministered to all who came to you. Look with compassion upon all who through addiction have lost their health and freedom. Restore to them the assurance of your unfailing mercy; remove the fears that attack them; strengthen those who are engaged in the work of recovery; and to those who care for them, give honesty, understanding, and persevering love; for your mercy's sake. Amen.

The chronically ill and those who support them

Loving God, your heart overflows with compassion for your whole creation. Pour out your Spirit on all people living with illness for which there is no cure, as well as their families and loved ones. Help them to know that you claim them as your own and deliver them from fear and pain; for the sake of Jesus Christ, our healer and Lord. Amen.

Caregivers and others who support the sick

God, our refuge and strength, our present help in time of trouble, care for those who tend the needs of *name*. Strengthen them in body and spirit. Refresh them when weary; console them when anxious; comfort them in grief; and hearten them in discouragement. Be with us all, and give us peace at all times and in every way; through Christ our peace. Amen.

Recovery from sickness

Almighty and merciful God, you are the only source of health and healing; you alone can bring calmness and peace. Grant to us, your children, an awareness of your presence and a strong confidence in you. In our pain, our weariness, and our anxiety, surround us with your care, protect us by your loving might, and permit us once more to enjoy health and strength and peace; through Jesus Christ, our Savior and Lord. Amen.

A prayer attributed to Francis of Assisi

Lord, make us instruments of your peace. Where there is hatred, let us sow love; where there is injury, pardon; where there is discord, union; where there is doubt, faith; where there is despair, hope; where there is darkness, light; where there is sadness, joy. Grant that we may not so much seek to be consoled as to console; to be understood as to understand; to be loved as to love. For it is in giving that we receive; it is in pardoning that we are pardoned; and it is in dying that we are born to eternal life. Amen.

A prayer of Catherine of Siena

Power of the eternal Father, help me. Wisdom of the Son, enlighten the eye of my understanding. Tender mercy of the Holy Spirit, unite my heart to yourself. Eternal God, restore health to the sick and life to the dead. Give us a voice, your own voice, to cry out to you for mercy for the world. You, light, give us light. You, wisdom, give us wisdom. You, supreme strength, strengthen us. Amen.

A prayer of Julian of Norwich

In you, Father all-mighty, we have our preservation and our bliss. In you, Christ, we have our restoring and our saving. You are our mother, brother, and savior. In you, our Lord the Holy Spirit, is marvelous and plenteous grace. You are our clothing; for love you wrap us and embrace us. You are our maker, our lover, our keeper. Teach us to believe that by your grace all shall be well, and all shall be well, and all manner of things shall be well. Amen.

A prayer of Martin Luther

Behold, Lord, an empty vessel that needs to be filled. My Lord, fill it. I am weak in the faith; strengthen me. I am cold in love; warm me and make me fervent, that my love may go out to my neighbor. I do not have a strong and firm faith; at times I doubt and am unable to trust you altogether. O Lord, help me. Strengthen my faith and trust in you. In you I have sealed the treasure of all I have. I am poor; you are rich and came to be merciful to the poor. I am a sinner; you are upright. With me, there is an abundance of sin; in you is the fullness of righteousness. Therefore I will remain with you, of whom I can receive, but to whom I may not give. Amen.

Prayers on pages 419–422 from *Evangelical Lutheran Worship*.

Morning Blessing

You may make the sign of the cross.

I am a beloved child of God, marked with the cross of Christ forever.

Your mercies are new every morning. *(Based on Lam. 3:23)*

Thank you, gracious God, for the gift of this new day.
Awaken me to your abiding presence;
open my eyes to your creation;
open my ears to your promises;
open my heart to the needs of others.
Fill me with your Spirit and guide me this day
in works of kindness, justice, and mercy.
I ask this in the name of Jesus, the light and life of the world.
Amen.

A Simplified Form for Morning Prayer

Opening

O Lord, open my lips,
and my mouth shall proclaim your praise.
Glory to the Father, and to the Son,
and to the Holy Spirit:
as it was in the beginning, is now,
and will be forever. Amen.

The alleluia is omitted during Lent.

[Alleluia.]

Psalmody

The psalmody may begin with Psalm 63, Psalm 67, Psalm 95, Psalm 100, or another
psalm appropriate for morning. Psalms provided in this book for each week may be used
instead of or in addition to the psalms mentioned.

A time of silence follows.

A hymn may follow (see the suggested hymn for each day).

Readings

One or more readings for each day may be selected from those provided in this book.
The reading of scripture may be followed by silence for reflection.

The reflection may conclude with these or similar words.

Long ago God spoke to our ancestors
in many and various ways by the prophets,
but in these last days God has spoken to us by the Son.

Gospel Canticle

The song of Zechariah may be sung or said.

Blessed are you, Lord, the God of Israel,
you have come to your people and set them free.
You have raised up for us a mighty Savior,
born of the house of your servant David.
Through your holy prophets, you promised of old
to save us from our enemies,
from the hands of all who hate us,
to show mercy to our forebears,
and to remember your holy covenant.
This was the oath you swore to our father Abraham:
to set us free from the hands of our enemies,
free to worship you without fear,
holy and righteous before you, all the days of our life.
And you, child, shall be called the prophet of the Most High,
for you will go before the Lord to prepare the way,
to give God's people knowledge of salvation
by the forgiveness of their sins.
In the tender compassion of our God
the dawn from on high shall break upon us,
to shine on those who dwell in darkness and the shadow of death,
and to guide our feet into the way of peace.

Prayers

*Various intercessions may be spoken at this time. The prayer provided in this book for
each day may also be used.*

The following prayer is especially appropriate for morning.

Almighty and everlasting God,
you have brought us in safety to this new day.
Preserve us with your mighty power,
that we may not fall into sin
nor be overcome in adversity.

In all we do, direct us to the fulfilling of your purpose;
through Jesus Christ our Lord.
Amen.

The Lord's Prayer

Our Father in heaven,
hallowed be your name,
your kingdom come,
your will be done, on earth as in heaven.
Give us today our daily bread.
Forgive us our sins
as we forgive those who sin against us.
Save us from the time of trial
and deliver us from evil.
For the kingdom, the power, and the glory are yours,
now and forever. Amen.

Blessing

Let us bless the Lord.
Thanks be to God.

Almighty God,
the Father, + the Son, and the Holy Spirit,
bless and preserve us.
Amen.

Additional materials for daily prayer are available in Evangelical Lutheran Worship
(pp. 295–331) and may supplement this simple order.

A Simplified Form for Evening Prayer

Opening

Jesus Christ is the light of the world,
the light no darkness can overcome.
Stay with us, Lord, for it is evening,
and the day is almost over.
Let your light scatter the darkness
and illumine your church.

Psalmody

The psalmody may begin with Psalm 141, Psalm 121, or another psalm appropriate for evening. Psalms provided in this book for each week may be used instead of or in addition to the psalms mentioned.

A time of silence follows.

A hymn may follow (see the suggested hymn for each day).

Readings

One or more readings for each day may be selected from those provided in this book. The reading of scripture may be followed by silence for reflection.

The reflection may conclude with these or similar words.

Jesus said, I am the light of the world.
Whoever follows me will never walk in darkness.

Gospel Canticle

The song of Mary may be sung or said.

My soul proclaims the greatness of the Lord,
my spirit rejoices in God my Savior,
for you, Lord, have looked with favor on your lowly servant.
From this day all generations will call me blessed:
you, the Almighty, have done great things for me,
and holy is your name.
You have mercy on those who fear you,
from generation to generation.
You have shown strength with your arm
and scattered the proud in their conceit,
casting down the mighty from their thrones
and lifting up the lowly.
You have filled the hungry with good things
and sent the rich away empty.
You have come to the aid of your servant Israel,
to remember the promise of mercy,
the promise made to our forebears,
to Abraham and his children forever.

Prayers

Various intercessions may be spoken at this time. The prayer provided in this book for each day may also be used.

The following prayer is especially appropriate for evening.

We give thanks to you, heavenly Father,
through Jesus Christ your dear Son,
that you have graciously protected us today.
We ask you to forgive us all our sins, where we have done wrong,
and graciously to protect us tonight.

For into your hands we commend ourselves:
our bodies, our souls, and all that is ours.
Let your holy angels be with us,
so that the wicked foe may have no power over us.
Amen.

The Lord's Prayer

Our Father in heaven,
   hallowed be your name,
   your kingdom come,
   your will be done, on earth as in heaven.
Give us today our daily bread.
Forgive us our sins
   as we forgive those who sin against us.
Save us from the time of trial
   and deliver us from evil.
For the kingdom, the power, and the glory are yours,
   now and forever. Amen.

Blessing

Let us bless the Lord.
Thanks be to God.

The peace of God,
which surpasses all understanding,
keep our hearts and our minds in Christ Jesus.
Amen.

Additional materials for daily prayer are available in Evangelical Lutheran Worship
(pp. 295–331) and may supplement this simple order.

Evening Blessing

You may make the sign of the cross.

I am a beloved child of God, marked with the cross of Christ forever.
Come to me, all you that are weary . . . and I will give you rest.
(Matt. 11:28).

Thank you, gracious God, for the gift of this coming night.
Restore me with your right spirit. Calm my mind. Quiet my heart.
Enfold me with your bountiful mercy.
Protect me from all harm,
that I sleep assured of the peace found in you alone.
I ask this in the name of Jesus, who gives us rest. Amen.

Night Prayers with Children

Dear Jesus, as a hen covers her chicks with her wings to keep them safe,
protect us this night under your golden wings; for your mercy's sake.
Amen.

We bless you, God, for the day just spent,
for laughter, tears, and all you've sent.
Grant us, Good Shepherd, through this night,
a peaceful sleep till morning light.

A parent or caregiver may trace the cross on the child's forehead or heart and say one of these blessings:

God the Father, Son, and Holy Spirit watch over you.
May God protect you through the night.
May the Lord Jesus keep you in his love.

Suggestions for Daily Reflection

God's word for me this day is:

God's word will shape my day by:

I will share God's word with others through:

My prayers today will include:

- The church universal, its ministry, and the mission of the gospel

- The well-being of creation

- Peace and justice in the world, the nations and those in authority, the community

- The poor, oppressed, sick, bereaved, lonely

- All who suffer in body, mind, or spirit

- Special concerns